Drummond Welburn, Drummond Welburn

The American Epic. A Concise Scenic History of the United States and Other Selected Poems

Vol. 2

Drummond Welburn, Drummond Welburn

The American Epic. A Concise Scenic History of the United States and Other Selected Poems
Vol. 2

ISBN/EAN: 9783337477813

Printed in Europe, USA, Canada, Australia, Japan

Cover: Foto ©Thomas Meinert / pixelio.de

More available books at **www.hansebooks.com**

THE AMERICAN EPIC:

A CONCISE SCENIC

HISTORY OF THE UNITED STATES,

AND OTHER

SELECTED POEMS,

WITH REFERENCES TO

THE EPICS OF THE AGES
AND BRIEF BIOGRAPHIES OF THEIR AUTHORS.

BY DRUMMOND WELBURN,
Of Nashville, Tenn.

PRINTED FOR THE AUTHOR.
PUBLISHING HOUSE OF THE METHODIST EPISCOPAL CHURCH, SOUTH.
BARBEE & SMITH, AGENTS, NASHVILLE, TENN.
1894.

CONTENTS.

BOOK FIRST.—1764–1766.

Britain from Julius Cæsar to George III.—William Pitt—Grenville—The Stamp Act—America a Greater Britain—Jamestown the Nursery of American Piety and Civilization—New England's Enterprise—Virginia's Burgesses the First American Legislature—All the Colonies Aroused ... 5

BOOK SECOND.—1766–1773.

Satan's Soliloquy—Pitt Prime Minister—Gets Sick—The Boston Massacre—Royal Piety—Death of Whitefield.... 21

BOOK THIRD.—1773–1776.

Chatham is "Junius"—Boston's Tea Party—The Boston Port Bill—Virginia Fasts—The South Feeds Boston—Gage Inclosed by a Human Wall—Dunmore Driven Out of Virginia—Battle of Lexington—Battle of Bunker Hill—British Driven from Boston—Declaration of Independence—French Offers of Arms, Ammunition, Money...... 44

BOOK FOURTH.—1776–1783.

Revolutionary Battles from Long Island to Yorktown—Sufferings at Valley Forge—Plots Against Washington—Arnold's Treason—French Co-operate at Savannah—At Yorktown—Peace—Washington Resigns His Command.. 69

BOOK FIFTH.—1787–1811.

Constitutional Convention—No Power to Coerce States—Virginia Convention Disturbed by a Storm While Henry Speaks—A Tribunate of States Desirable—The Bargain between New England, Georgia, and the Carolinas—Washington Inaugurated—Satan's Scheme for War Between the States—Jay's Treaty—Adams President—War with France—Alien and Sedition Laws—Jefferson President—Louisiana Purchased—The Embargo—John Henry and New England—Madison President............... 90

BOOK SIXTH.—1811–1829.

War—Battles from Tippecanoe to New Orleans—Hartford Convention—Peace—An International Court to Prevent War—Monroe President—Missouri Compromise—Florida Purchased—Texas Given Away—J. Q. Adams President—A High Tariff—Lafayette's Visit—Tariff Higher....... 115

(3)

BOOK SEVENTH.—1829-1860.

Jackson President—A Gradual Reduction of the Tariff—Van Buren's Ascendency—Battle of San Jacinto—Van Buren President—Slade's Petitions against Slavery—Satan's Boast—Harrison President—Tyler President—Texas to Be Annexed—The Magnetic Telegraph—Polk President—Mexico Makes War—Is Conquered—Much of It Annexed—A Tariff for Revenue—Gold Discovered—Taylor President—Fillmore President — Clay's Compromise—Pierce President—Satan's Cyclone —Buchanan President—The Dred Scott Decision—John Brown at Harper's Ferry—Historic Discussion of Slavery 134

BOOK EIGHTH.—1860-1862.

South Carolina Secedes—Argument on the Folly of Secession—On the Right to Secede—No Troops to Coerce States—A Nation's Immorality—Argument on the Nature of the Union—Lincoln President—Battles from Fort Sumter to Fredericksburg—Criticisms on Generals.............. 158

BOOK NINTH.—1862-1864.

Battles from Fredericksburg to Nashville—Death of Stonewall Jackson—The North Goes to the Bosom of John Brown—Onward and Skyward at Lookout—John H. Morgan—Georgians Banished from Their Homes as Cherokees Were—Argument against Arson—Naval Conflicts... 181

BOOK TENTH.—1864-1868.

Bachman Ill-treated by Sherman's Hell-hounds—Richmond Keeping the Sabbath—Ford's Theater—Johnson President—Davis a Vicarious Sufferer—Right or Wrong of Slavery—The Guilty—Retribution—Cruel Treatment of President Davis—Johnson Impeached—Alaska Acquired—Fire in Chicago—Boston—The North-west—Retribution—Black Friday—Tweed—Credit Mobilier—Grant President. 206

BOOK ELEVENTH.—1876-1885.

Centennial Exhibition—Pittsburg Railroad Riots—Argument on Arson—On Labor and Capital—Taxation—Finance, etc.—Hayes President—Garfield President—Death of Garfield—Arthur President—Burial of Emerson—Theological Arguments 231

BOOK TWELFTH.—1885-1890.

Cleveland President—Reform in Civil Service—Discoveries and Inventions—Burial of Grant—Harrison President—Michael's Sublime Visions of America's Future—Satan's Threats and Predictions—Politics—Enrich the Poor Without Impoverishing the Rich...................... 253

WESTMINSTER ABBEY.

THE AMERICAN EPIC

BOOK FIRST.

Scene: *Westminster Abbey. Time, early morning, March 11, 1764.*
MICHAEL *and* GABRIEL *approach each other.*

Gabriel. Hail, faithful leader of the heavenly hosts!
My loving comrade since creation's dawn!
At thy approach bright days of early years
Come tripping lightly from the silent shades,
Flitting with airy tread o'er memory's paths.
In their light footsteps comes the grand array,
The princely pomp, the brief magnificence
Of hoary nations that then claimed our care.
They rose, they flourished, fell, and are but dust.

Michael. These are the tombs of kings and famous men;
Fortune's most flattered fav'rites molder here.
This is ambition's goal. Here ends the race
For wealth, for power, for fame's green laurel-wreath.
Here human greatness shows its littleness,
And earthly glory ends in sordid dust.

Gabriel. Yes, Michael; guilty greatness has no dreams
Of heav'nly joy to cheer the sleep of death.
Hope holds no vigils where the wicked rest.
They will not wake to everlasting bliss,
Nor stand approved before the Judge of all.

Michael. To men this place is ancient. In its gloom
The ghosts of solemn centuries seem near.
To us 'twas but last week or yesterday
That Julius Cæsar first to Britain came,
With conq'ring legions to subdue its tribes
And to great Rome's vast empire add their home.

Gabriel. True, Michael; but since then Teutonic hordes,
Danes, Scandinavians, and Scots, and Picts,
And cruel Norman conquerors, have slain
Unnumbered thousands here, and fertilized
Their fruitful fields with blood. Yes, blood has flowed
In copious streams through dreary centuries
Of fratricidal strife. War's iron hoof,
Trampling on civil law, has crushed in dust
All sacred human rights; with impious tread
Profaned all holy places. Peace perished.
Religion hid in humble cottage homes,
Where heavenly light still glimmered mid the gloom.
Justice was outraged—fled beyond the seas,
And bleeding freedom followed in her train.
The hand of industry was paralyzed,
The wheels of progress clogged. Art languished,
While star-eyed science, shudd'ring and dismayed,
Took refuge in far-distant Moslem lands.

Michael. But now how changed! These happy islanders
Shed no fraternal blood. Justice protects
All classes: the prince, the peer, the peasant.
Law, liberty, and love enthrone themselves
In hearts that thrill with joyous gratitude.
Religion kindles pure celestial fires
In princely palaces, in humble homes,
In gorgeous temples, and in darksome mines.
Her hymns of praise ring grandly through the land,
And float toward heaven on every breeze that blows.
Britannia's wat'ry walls, by hearts of oak
Well guarded, give calm security to
Peaceful homes against all foreign nations.
A native king sits on her royal throne,
And hurls defiance at her every foe.
He wields his scepter over distant lands
In all earth's continents. Fair, fertile isles
Of all the sunny seas obey his laws.
In widening streams wealth from the Indies flows
To fill his coffers and extend his sway.
This busy London, central mart of trade,
Most active ant-hill of the human race,

WESTMINSTER ABBEY.

Outgrows all cities earth has ever seen.
In days to come so great will be its growth
That Paris, Pekin, Nankin, Jeddo, Rome,
Might all be piled in splendor on its plains,
Lost in the pomp of its magnificence.
How wonderful this little island world!

Gabriel. Michael, thy wisely spoken, truthful words
Befit the tongue of one who long has watched
The rise and fall of empires. But yesterday
Blind folly aimed a blow at human rights,
That soon shall echo loudly round the world.
If I forecast aright, 'twill break the ties
That bind Americans to England's throne,
And lay in rightful, honest principles
The firm foundations of a government
Better than earth has ever known before.
Its peaceful flag shall float triumphantly
O'er sea and land through all the hemisphere
Columbus found by sailing westwardly.
This mighty nation, now in embryo,
Shall be a "Greater Britain," which in time,
By the attraction of its excellence,
Shall draw admiring millions to its shores,
And neighb'ring nations to its kind embrace,
Till myriads of enlightened freemen join
To honor law and banish tyranny.

Michael. Gabriel, why should not Britain still hold sway,
Guiding America with gentle hand
Through peaceful paths to glory and renown?
Why should they not munificently march
Together, scattering blessings round the world?

Gabriel. Michael, they should, but selfishness forbids;
A few self-centered fosterlings of hell
May yet involve two continents in war,
And rend the grandest empire under heaven.
This nation had for its Prime Minister
Wise William Pitt. His statesmanship
Made no mistakes. 'Twas such as we beheld

In saintly Daniel at the Persian court.
He found his country fleeing from her foes,
To be the prey of harpies in her home;
Corruption's vermin in her ulcers fed;
No hand was raised to help her in distress.
He to her rescue rushed to bring relief,

ALFRED THE GREAT.

And heal the fest'ring wounds from which she bled.
The venal factions fled before his frown,
The cringing courtiers from his shadow shrunk.
His patriot voice called heroes, and they came,
To marshal armies and command his fleets,
Giving him victories on land and sea.

He brought the nation to the highest pitch
Of unexampled grandeur and renown,
And would have held the vantage he had gained
Had not the youthful king, by Satan moved,
Dismissed the minister whose mighty mind
O'ershadowed royalty and with strong hand
Heroically saved country and king
From self-inflicted ruin and distress.
Then came the pressing need of untold wealth
To settle debts, and meet the urgent claims
Of bold, insatiate, fawning favorites.
Commerce with open hand would have paid Pitt
All needed revenues, trusting his plans
To pay her back again a thousand-fold,
By fost'ring trade in ev'ry distant mart;
But blund'ring imbeciles are in his place.
Grenville proposes awkward robbery,
And through the Parliament asserts a right
To tax the colonists without consent,
Not merely once a year, but ev'ry hour
Of ev'ry busy day; the Stamp act taunts,
And aggravates the honest man it robs.
'Twill hound him through the avenues of trade,
Track him to legal courts with steady step,
Intrude upon his happy nuptial hours,
Pursue him to his solemn death-bed scene,
Nor let him will his fortune to his heirs,
Without this sad humiliating sign
Of his own degradation in the act.
Let us away to climes beyond the waves
And watch the storms that rend this mighty State.

Michael. Gabriel, not now. I go at duty's call
To distant Asia, where Britannia's flag
Floats o'er the sunny shores of Hindostan.
It now protects the selfish sons of trade,
But in the happier days of years to come
One-third of Asia's children shall with joy
Serve the Lord Jesus under its broad folds.
A year from now that western hemisphere
Shall claim attention through its vast extent.

I will examine it from pole to pole,
And from the centers of surrounding seas,
On what day shall we meet? and at what place?

   Gabriel. Let us meet May the first, and at the place
Where the first British settlement began.
Till then, farewell. But who are these we see
Moving so orderly at early dawn?

   Michael. 'Tis the two Wesleys and their followers,
Going to worship God at break of day.
These are the servants of the Lord. Farewell.

Scene: *Jamestown, Va., May 1, 1765, at sunrise.* GABRIEL *and* MICHAEL *approach.*

   Gabriel. Hail, Michael, of created princes chief!
Please tell thy thoughts of this grand continent,
And the great nation that shall flourish here.

   Michael. Gabriel, since last we met, this hemisphere
Has been my constant study. I have seen
Its boundless oceans, fertile isles, vast lakes,
Broad bays, safe harbors, long peninsulas;
Its lofty mountains; rich, productive vales;
Its wide savannas, decked in Eden's bloom;
Its tow'ring forests, lifting giant arms
To prop the clouds and draw their moisture down
On fruitful plains, where plenty ever smiles.
Here bounteous nature gathers ample stores
To feast her ev'ry tribe that treads the ground,
Or cleaves the ambient air on buoyant wing,
Or glides in glory through the sparkling waves.
With steadfast gaze I've watched where rippling rills
On lofty mountains in the frozen north
Make pathways for themselves through frowning rocks,
To seek the company of limpid streams,
That hasten to unite with rivulets,
That gently moving claim companionship
With grand, majestic rivers on their march
T'assuage the burning thirst of sunny climes.
Intensely interested, I have traced
The mountain ranges that direct the course

Of healthful currents of the atmosphere.
I've seen the arctic icebergs moving down,
To meet the genial warmth of tropic streams,
And lave these favored shores with waves of health.
The earth, the air, the waters teem with food;
Exhaustless mines of ore lift up the hills,
Inviting industry to gather wealth.
Internal commerce may be limitless,
And claim with ease the commerce of the world.
Earth's grandest seat of empire here is found.
Tell me, dear Gabriel, of the men who claim
This happy land and its encircling seas.

Gabriel. Michael, the swarthy tribes Columbus found,
Self-doomed, seem swiftly journeying to death.
The white man's vices, added to their own,
Hurry them downward into gaping graves,
Yet a small remnant may be saved by grace.
Pitt, in his day of power, subdued the French.
Spain, trembling, saw her colonies submit,
And must have yielded all, if England's king
Had not dismissed his mighty minister.
But Spain decays, and England's sons hold sway.
Here is the spot where English piety
First claimed this hemisphere for the most high.
Here liberty and law came hand in hand
To plant an Eden in the wilderness.
Here holy faith and hope and love and truth
And lofty honor firm foundations laid
For a great nation; noblest, grandest, best
Known to the world through all its centuries.
Religion here lit her first altar fires,
Built her first temple on this continent,
Where English hearts might worship the Great God.
Here Western savages bowed suppliant knees,
And meekly claimed the Saviour as their own.
From this bright spot went forth with joyous smiles
All human excellences, leading on
All Christian graces to exalt mankind.
In their fair footsteps rose on every hand
Such habitations as the angels love,

Having for inmates earth's most noble men,
And women loveliest of all the race.
From these have sprung the principles and men
That are to govern this delightful land.
What think you of our nascent nation now?

Michael. Gabriel, I am most hopeful of its growth
In all that God approves and men admire,
But lead me now where I myself may see
The rock on which the Plymouth pilgrims stood
When they first landed in America.
Was it not there that English liberty
First found a home upon this continent,
And English Protestants first worshiped God?

Gabriel. Michael, 'tis so reported, but not so.
That far-famed rock defies the howling storms
That beat in fury on New England's coast,
Five hundred miles away, far to the north.
I knew that earth and hell had long proclaimed
That Plymouth Rock was freedom's natal home,
And pure religion's earliest cradle-bed,
But marvel much if Heav'n has been deceived!
'Twas not in heaven that you were so informed?
I knew it could not be. Such history
May have been taught at Harvard or at Yale.
Those grand old schools, where wise men of the East
Proclaim New England's glory and renown,
May have taught this so long, so heartily
That they believe it in their inmost souls;
But long before the Pilgrim Fathers left
The muddy shore of Holland, Robert Hunt
And his co-laborers had worshiped God
And planted churches in this colony,
Where prayer and praise and God's most holy word
Drew forth the inmates of a thousand homes
Whene'er a Sabbath brought relief from toil.
Such happy homes earth never saw before.
In them Religion wore no scowling frown,
But sweetly told of love and hope and joy,
While smiles of God lit with celestial rays

The glowing face of Hospitality,
Who stood with open door and beck'ning hand,
While Plenty welcomed every joyful guest.
These pioneers of English liberty,
These missionaries of the faith of Christ,
Had founded Churches, opened courts of law;
By vote had chosen representatives
To the first Legislature of the West,
Established civil liberty, and won
Their Indian neighbors for the Lord before
The famous Mayflower sailed across the deep.

Michael. Then it was not on famous Plymouth Rock
Religion, liberty, and civil law
Began their grand career in Western wilds?

Gabriel. No, Michael; but permit me now to say;
All honor to the men of Plymouth Rock!
New England has no need of stolen fame.
Ten thousand glories sparkle on her brow,
Fame's greenest laurels bend above her head.
Her restless industry, inventive skill,
And boundless enterprise have made a world
Pay tribute at her gates. Her busy hand
Planted a fair and fruitful paradise,
Where barren rocks and thirsty, sterile sands
Frowned on a stormy coast. In distant seas
She sought and found rich floating mines of wealth;
Transferred the yellow treasure to her ships,
And bore it safely to her busy ports.
All coming generations of her sons
Shall sing her well-earned praises through the world.
But in this sisterhood of colonies
Are others high in honor and renown.
Fair Georgia, youngest of the family,
Was nurtured in the lap of piety,
Is heir of Oglethorpe's heroic zeal,
Of Whitefield's eloquence, and Wesley's prayers.
The Carolinas, wise, polite, and brave,
Blend Huguenot and Scotch and English blood.
New Jersey, Delaware, and Maryland,

In all the Christian virtues panoplied,
Repose in loveliness by their broad bays.
Great Pennsylvania grows rich and strong
With German industry and Quaker thrift.
New York can boast the brave and valiant blood
That drove the Spaniards from the Netherlands.
These embryonic States draw vital force,
Hereditary virtues, and the strength
Of Christian principles from num'rous lines
Of grand old ancestors. Here meet and join
The Norman, Saxon, Celt, the Cavalier,
The Covenanter, Roundhead, and the Welsh;
French Huguenots, brave Irishmen and Swedes,
Heroic Poles, Swiss, Germans, Hollanders—
All sons of liberty in union joined.

  ABDIEL *approaches and addresses* MICHAEL *and* GABRIEL.

 Abdiel. Hail, holy princes of the hosts of God!
To meet you here gives unexpected joy:
Your presence fills all places with delight.
At your approach all anxious cares depart,
Gay smiles irradiate the cheeks of time,
And make them glow with dimpled, youthful charms,
While gleeful gladness sports with playful hours.
But now your presence is most opportune:
I need instruction and enlightenment
On great events transpiring in this land.
Portentous gloom seems gathering around,
As if preceding mighty earthquake throes.
Alarming rumblings break upon the ear,
And startling tremors shake the solid ground.
Throughout the north, excitement rules the hour.
The Stamp act rouses men to mutiny.
Here order reigns. These people live at ease;
In quiet dignity they dwell at home.
They have no grievances to madden them,
Hereditary hatreds they have not.
They are the favored subjects of their king,
His "Old Dominion" is their lovely land.
If they demand, the Stamp act perishes,
And mild conciliation rules around.

Happy, unselfish, prosperous, polite,
They have not hastily provoked the king;
And on a simple question of finance
Would freely grant him more than he would ask;
But on a point of honor or of right
Their indignation flashes into wrath.
They know their rights, and, brave in their defense,
Would meet defiantly a world in arms;
Or, moved by sympathy for other men,
Their gushing blood may flow in plenteous streams.
This day Virginia's House of Burgesses
Convenes at Williamsburg in high debate.
Ithuriel went thither yesterday
To witness the proceedings of the day.

Gabriel. Let us go now to see what they will do,
And listen to the matchless orators.

Scene: *A street in Williamsburg. Afternoon of May 1, 1765.* ITHU-
RIEL *meeting* MICHAEL, GABRIEL, *and* ABDIEL.

Ithuriel. Comrades, I greet you with intense delight.
The legislators of this colony
Have filled us with astonishment to-day.
Your wisdom may inform my ignorance
On the great themes discussed by statesmen here.
The House of Burgesses denies the right
Of Parliament to tax the colonies.
They boldly and defiantly demand
That the most odious Stamp act be repealed.
One of their orators made such a speech
As shook the ground beneath King George's throne,
And startled nations by its mighty force.
Men shuddered as they heard the brave man say
"Cæsar his Brutus had, and Charles the First
His Cromwell, and George the Third"—then treason
Rang out loudly on the air. Defiant
Stood the orator to say: "George the Third
May profit by their fate." Then scornfully:
"If that be treason, make the most of it."
In former times such fearless words as these

Took off the heads of those who uttered them;
But now they bring the hope of better days.
You are too late to hear their great men speak,
But see, they come this way. What men they are!
Rome never had in her heroic times
A Senate such as this. Britannia's lords
Are dwarfed by these great statesmen of the West.
There is George Wythe, and Richard Henry Lee,
George Nicholas, and Edmund Pendleton,
John Randolph, Peyton Randolph, Colonel Bland,
And Carter Braxton; and there the hero
Of the present hour, bold Patrick Henry,
Orator unequaled, whose thunder tones
Shake kingdoms and arouse a wond'ring world.
And there George Washington, grandest of men.
Behold that tall, slim youth, thoughtful and grave:
Too young to be a burgess at this time.
That's Thomas Jefferson, whose honored name
Shall echo through the ages as the friend
Of equal rights against all tyranny.
And there are others worthy of all praise.
Ye sapient leaders of angelic hosts,
Tell us what mean these movements of mankind?
Will God forsake and turn against King George?
Will Britain fall like Babylon or Rome?
Will God raise up a nation on these shores?

Michael. God will not utterly forsake the king
And the great country over which he rules,
But they will lose these prosp'rous colonies—
Just retribution for their many sins
Against their brethren of this Western world.
God will raise up a nation on these shores,
And give to it the half of this round world.
The western hemisphere shall be its home,
But all mankind shall gladden in its smile.
Humiliation is proud Albion's doom,
But God has wondrous work for her to do.
She and these daughters she so rashly spurns
Shall long stand side by side in truth's defense,
And bless the world with Christian principles.

Gabriel. Comrades, what has been witnessed here to-day
Begins a union of these colonies.
The cities have been ringing muffled bells,
Mourning for liberty by Britain slain.
The Congress at New York with potent voice
Shall call her back to life, and bid mankind
Rejoicing gather to enjoy her smile.
Till then we part to go where duty calls.

Scene: *Trinity Church-yard, Broadway, New York, by moonlight, December 31–January 1, 1766.* GABRIEL, ITHURIEL, ABDIEL, UZZIEL. *A clock strikes twelve.*

Gabriel. Another year has passed. Its hasty steps
Have left deep foot-prints upon Time's rough road;
Its busy hands have forged enduring links
For destiny's bright chain, binding with gold
In loving union these rich colonies.
Its voice has roused the sons of liberty
From Southern Georgia to the coasts of Maine.

Ithuriel. Brave Patrick Henry, in Virginia's name,
First hurled defiance at the robber hosts
Of venal lords and commons and their king.
Millions, responding to his thunder tones,
Caused quailing minions of despotic greed,
Though backed by Britain's might and majesty,
To throw up their commissions, and with haste
Forsake the hateful ways of infamy.

Uzziel. Here in New York the craven officer
Gave to the city council his vile stamps.
Thus do the people triumph o'er the king.

Abdiel. Gabriel, what next? Shall war with cruel hand
Spread desolation o'er this Western world?

Gabriel. Abdiel, not yet; this law will be repealed,
And but for stubborn pride and selfish greed
A happy reconcilement might take place.
King George means to be better than he is.
If he could be a private citizen,
He would appear to be a model saint,
A Christian gentleman to be admired.

He frowns on vice, is honest, truthful, chaste,
Hates war, aims not at conquests, loves England;
But he thinks a king must rule: a king must
Be obeyed, must overawe his subjects.
With this in view, he browbeats wiser men,
And those he cannot frighten tries to buy.
He thinks men have their price and are for sale,
From basest menials up through ev'ry rank.
'Tis even whispered he will try to buy,
With a poor, paltry earldom and kind words,
Great William Pitt, the grandest of mankind.
The king spends thirty millions annually
Buying white free-born native Englishmen.
That he may have more money to buy men,
Inflicts the slave trade on his colonies,
Tramples on law and right and common sense
By taxing those he has no right to tax.
The venal Parliament, like cringing slaves,
Wait on his royal will for smiles, for wealth,
For titles, honors, and for offices.
The vilest of them all have English pride;
With fancied self-sufficiency look down
On all who were not born on English ground.
The wealthy nobles may not sell themselves
For filthy lucre, payable in coin;
But if a farthing added to their tax
Would save from ruin a whole continent,
They would resist it to the last extreme,
Nor pay a copper till the law compelled.
The laborer may toil in agony,
Till bloody sweat breaks forth from every pore;
Taxes may kill him if they may escape.
What if the Hindoos starve, the negroes sink
Beneath old ocean's waves, in frontier homes
Fair women lose their scalps, so Britain's wealth,
Her glory and renown, be the result?

Abdiel. Gabriel, there must be better men than these,
Or Sodom's fate would overwhelm the land.

Gabriel. Yes, Abdiel, there are thousands who believe
In God, in Christ, in Christian principles;

But most of these so idolize their king,
Their Parliament, and their own native land,
That all who dare resist them are despised.
The few true friends the colonies can claim,
They count upon the fingers of a man.
Pitt, Shelburne, Conway, Barre, and Oglethorpe,
With Burke and Camden faintly following,
Comprise the names that dare to sympathize.
Unthinking millions live and toil and die,
Leaving their offspring following in their steps.
Such is the best of human governments.
Is it not time a better should arise?

Abdiel. Yes, Gabriel, this broad wilderness shall bloom,
And this shall be the grandest of all lands.
God sifted Europe for the best of seed,
To plant a nation he will own and bless.
All human excellences here shall meet
Under divinest blessings from on high.
Earth shall behold with wonder and delight
And holy angels guard its happy homes.
Let us depart each to his proper work,
But see the patriots Jay and Livingston!
They've watched the old year out, the new year in.

BOOK SECOND.

Scene: *Gamble's Hill, Richmond, Va., March 1, 1766.* SATAN'S
Soliloquy.

Satan. Remorse! remorse! remorse! Fierce, horrible,
Insatiate harpy preying upon guilt.
But why should I repine? My pride forbids
The useless whispering of vain regrets.
If penitence could plead, 'twould plead in vain.
Ruined! doomed! damned! Despairing agony
Drives hence all thoughts of possible relief.
Even forgetfulness flies far away
On swiftest wing, from writhing wretchedness;
Pours no Lethean drop into the cup
Of sinful anguish. She strews no restful
Down o'er sleepless beds of sin's sad victims.
Helpless! Undone forever! Bound in the
Galling chains of ever black'ning darkness.
Unceasing torment is my dreadful doom,
And fearful looking for of fiery wrath.
Just retribution! I was first to sin.

. . . .

Such scenes as this, earth's fairest, brightest, best,
Most comforting, give no surcease of pain.
These wooded heights and this majestic stream
Remind me of my days of innocence
And heavenly landscapes I shall see no more.
These dear, delightful homes, the blest abodes
Of Adam's noblest offspring, recall to
Fond and mournful memory, the blissful
Joys that waited on God's angel children
When first they woke to life, to light, to love
On the bright morning of their natal day.
Peace walks the earth in smiling loveliness;
And plenty, tripping lightly in her steps,
Thrills human hearts with rapturous delight.

Religion, science, industry combine
To elevate the families of men,
That they may gladden in the smile of God,
While on my vitals pent-up furies prey.
Britannia sways her scepter o'er the seas,
And steps from land to land in majesty,
Triumphant over all her ancient foes.
They seek her friendship as they dread her might.
All Europe sits admiring at her feet.
Old Asia rests supinely with her sons,
Amid the hoary ruins of all time,
In meek submission taking on the yoke
Of these her latest, noblest conquerors;
While helpless Africa with outstretched arms
Sees from her dusky bosom her dark brood
Snatched by the ruthless hand of cruelty,
That Britain and New England may grow rich
By trading rum for servile sons of Ham.
'Tis true the slave trade flourishes,
And feasts the hungry sharks on filthy flesh
Of dead and dying negroes.   But ages
Of most hopeless degradation have doomed
The race to end in cruel deaths, lives of
Despairing agony.   No chance or change
Makes their condition worse than that of their
Long line of barb'rous ancestors.   Indeed,
These kindly, careful, Christian mistresses
Have so emparadised their happy slaves
That I must seek new marts in Orient lands
For this nefarious human merchandise,
Or my malicious schemes to eternize
The woes of Africans will counteract
My own most wily plans.   The savage tribes
That tread the Western wilds live peaceably.
There's not a wigwam home or warlike chief
But owns the potent spell of England's name.
These peaceful times hang heavily upon
My restless energies.   The trifling sins
By which the common herd of men insult
Their God and wrong their fellow-men require
No care of mine.   I must have war.   With war

Comes all that God forbids, all man can do
To injure and degrade the human race.

Enter BAAL, AZAZEL, *and* MAMMON.

All hail! my trusted, wise compeers; all hail!
What of your conflicts with the hateful race
Whose misery so long has been our sport?
Speak, Baal, tell us of your worthy deeds.

Baal. I have been ranging through the courts of kings
And other rulers of the Orient.
The tycoon still permits no intercourse
Between Japan and hated foreigners.
Old China, with a third of all the race,
Excludes outside barbarians from her shores.
Their presence would, she thinks, pollute the soil
Of her celestial, central, flowery land.
But rulers and their subjects all are ours.
Japan and China wear our weighty chains:
No voice disputes our long-established sway.
The Shah of Persia sees his realms decay,
Submits to destiny without a sigh.
So of the Turkish sultan and the sons
Of Saracenic chiefs in Hindostan.
The thrones of Moslem rulers tottering,
And gilded scepters dropping from weak hands,
Foretoken revolutions soon to come.
Clive and his English merchants with strong hands
Lay helpless India bleeding at their feet;
But all are ours, the conq'rors and their slaves.

Satan. Now, Azazel, let us hear your report.

Azazel. I have been watching Europe. Cossack hordes
Only await lascivious Cath'rine's word
To arm by millions as she sends them forth
To devastate and conquer neighb'ring lands.
This huge despotic empire, like some vast
Avalanche, throws its cold shadow over
Two continents, threat'ning to fall upon
And crush the shudd'ring nations all around.
Great Frederick baffles all of Prussia's foes.

Defeats have shown him paths to victory.
He triumphs over kings and emperors.
Fair Italy, still fettered, languishes
In Austria's baleful shadow. The pontiff,
Triple crowned and doubly throned on seven hills,
Sits like an incubus on half the world.
The Kings of Spain and France degenerate.
No thoughts of statesmanship stir their dull brains.
These worthless sons of Henry of Navarre
Live only for their lusts and appetites.
The Portuguese, the petty German States,
Swiss, Belgians, Hollanders, Poles, Danes, and Swedes,
Require no comments here. But Choiseul
At St. Cloud watches the English closely,
Hoping to see their colonies detached
And lost forever to the British crown.
To you, O leader of our busy hosts,
I must report the writings of Rousseau,
Voltaire, and other authors less conspicuous.
These work a silent revolution in
The minds of readers, tending to o'erthrow
All confidence in God, in priest, in kings,
And human government. Unbridled lusts
Cast off all decency, all fear of God
In those who follow these admirèd men.
They sugar-coat or gild their mental pills
With science, art, and literary taste,
And schemes for elevating all mankind.
Their inspiration must have come from you,
Our sapient chief, or they could not have been
So wondrous shrewd in helping our designs.
I leave their books to you. Let Mammon speak.

Satan. But suffer me to say that subjects, kings,
And literati all belong to us.
Yes, Mammon, I committed to your care
Your clients of New England and their king,
With questions of taxation and finance.
You have for ages had your sovereign will
Without constraint from me. I trust you still.
Proceed with your report. We wait to hear.

Mammon. Two years have passed since Grenvillle
  moved the king
And Parliament to tax Americans
By what is called the Stamp act. Discontent
Mutters and growls in every colony,
As if 'twould bite the hand stretched out to seize
Its treasured hoards. Lawyers and merchants prate
Of rights and robberies, and utter threats
Of stern resistance to tyrannic power.
They say the stamps shall not be introduced,
Nor even offered to indignant men.
A wordy warfare everywhere prevails:
All men expectant wait for bloody deeds.

Satan. Mammon, enough of words. I want not words,
But manly forms writhing in agony:
I must have war to rouse my intellect
And gratify malignant, fiendish hate.
But how? The nations dread Britannia's pow'r.
They fear to strike the mistress of the sea.
King George and all his cabinet love peace.
They have the strength to conquer half a world,
But live at ease and most ingloriously
Turn from the priceless prizes they could grasp.
They will not even strike these colonists,
Whose upstart boldness calls for chastisement,
But prate of England's glory, her renown,
Her king's prerogatives, her Parliament,
Its right to tax, and how, and when, and whom.
Meanwhile, by their neglect the world grows rich,
The nations prosper, while earth's myriad homes
Gather about them all that gladdens life.
I must have war to revel in its sins,
To gloat upon the miseries of men.
I'll have it. These colonists are cautious:
For them we wait in vain. They shed no blood.
Comrades, we cross the ocean. In London
Meet me two weeks from to-day. Be promptly
In the House of Commons then, to make them
Execute our wrathful plans of carnage.
Lord Botetourt, Virginia's Governor,
Is drawing near, taking his daily walk.

Scene: *Interior of the House of Commons. March 18, 1766. Enter*
SATAN, BAAL, AZAZEL, MAMMON, BELIAL.

    Satan. Welcome, my worthy friends! What news have you
From his most stubborn Majesty, King George?
Or from his Majesty's subservient tools,
The Cabinet, the Commons, and the Lords?
What of the Stamp act? Will it be repealed?
Or will resistless armies subjugate
Defiant and rebellious colonists?

    Baal. Pacific measures suit the monarch's whim.
He now proposes to repeal the Act,
While Pitt, ennobled and made Earl of Chatham,
Becomes Prime Minister and rules in peace.

    Satan. This must not be. 'Twould thwart our crafty plans,
And crown the king with loving gratitude
More glorious far than royal diadem
Or glitt'ring gems in an imperial crown.
'Twould span the ocean with a bow of hope,
Bright'ning with beauty two broad continents.
Pitt must not dominate the Cabinet.
His august presence and imperious will
Would awe the king, control the ministry,
Restrain the Parliament, and paralyze
All the mischievous factions of the realm.
His potent voice would hush the raging storms
That shake the firm foundations of the throne,
Threat'ning to crush both law and liberty.

    Azazel. The colonists would hail him as their friend,
And help him to save England from herself.

    Mammon. He at the helm would steer the ship of state
To peaceful ports, and gather boundless wealth
From ev'ry clime beneath the shining sun.

    Satan. 'Tis this I would prevent. Please tell me how.

    Belial. His tender toes shall feel a cruel twinge
Of agonizing gout. He shall not sleep.

I'll shatter all his nerves, disturb his brain,
And lay him on his bed in helplessness.
Then his subordinates, to please the king,
May tax the colonists till discontent
Shall ripen to rebellion and to war.
Meanwhile, to keep Americans enraged,
The venal Parliament shall claim the right
To tax them as it wills in any case,
And in all cases, whatsoever, rule.
So hatred shall burn on with bright'ning blaze.

Satan. I thank you, Belial; your plan shall be mine.
Let us depart. To Mammon we will leave
The wordy worthies of the Parliament.
He knows the current price of each in gold,
In empty honors, or in offices.
King George, with thirty millions, year by year,
Still trades in men, in high-born Englishmen:
All slaves to Mammon, under his control.
There enters Townshend, and there William Pitt.
After to-night, Pitt in the House of Lords
Stoops to an earldom and a servant's place.
Come, trusty comrades, let us now retire.

Scene: *Windsor Castle, June 29, 1767.* SATAN, BAAL, AZAZEL, MAMMON, BELUS.

Satan. Companions of my grandeur and my toils,
Heirs of dominions broad and limitless,
Immortal monarchs of immensity,
All empires, kingdoms, principalities
Fade into insignificance before
Th' expanding grandeur and magnificence
Of our unequaled, glorious domains.
Here is the palace of an earthly king,
Clothed in the robes of human royalty,
Enthroned and sceptered, ruling over men
Of four great continents with sovereign sway.
Among the sons of men his pow'r is great,
But compared with ours less than a glow-worm's
To the noonday sun's refulgent splendor.

WINDSOR CASTLE.

Belus. He owns more land, but is not half so great
As my old Babylonian worshipers,
Nor are his palaces so grand as theirs.

Satan. Baal, you need not boast of Syria's kings,
But tell me how your crafty plans succeed.

Baal. When Chatham was again Prime Minister,
I feared the very worst that could occur
To counteract our bold, malignant schemes.
I counterworked, with wonderful success,
His efforts to secure some potent friends
And allies in the north. Choiseul, of France,
Outwitted the great man, which made him sick.
His king distrusted him, and only wished
To use him to humiliate the lords.
The people loved the simple name of Pitt.
When the great commoner became an earl,
I taught them to be very much displeased;
But when the odious Stamp act was repealed,
The colonists gave honors to his name.
Charleston set up his statue, and the king
Shared in great Chatham's popularity.
New York set up his image, made of lead,
But the soft metal can be turned to shot,
For firing at his Majesty's dragoons.
The cabinet, with Chatham to direct,
Would have conciliated colonists,
But the great earl went groaning to his couch,
With shattered nerves and restless, aching head.
George then, indeed, was ev'ry inch a king;
King of his lords, commons, and colonists;
And of his meek, subservient ministers.
The lion-hearted earl might from his lair
Growl, or roar loudly in impotent rage;
The meaner beasts despised his helplessness.
The royal kennel holds no yelping cur,
No snapping mastiff to disturb the king:
All fawn upon their master. At his will
They go or come, and his broad collar wear.
The unregretted absence of their chief

Leaves domineering Townshend to hold sway.
Camden and Shelburne, Conway, Rockingham,
And even pious Dartmouth yield to him.
Impulsive, bold, quick, eloquent, and proud,
I've used him for my fiendish purposes,
So as to tax tea, paper, paints, and glass.

Satan. Aha! aha! King George shall quickly find
Thorns in the bed of roses where he rests.
Taxation soon shall change the gleeful tunes
Now sung by grateful colonists to threats
Of fearful vengeance against tyranny.
The smallest tax will rouse indignant men
To stern resistance and to bloody deeds.
Speak, Mammon, let us hear what you have done.

Mammon. I have stirred up the colonists to strife
About the right of Parliament to bind
Them and their children through all time to come.
The greedy courtiers, and the lords of trade,
And all the vulgar herd who toil for wealth,
I have so worked upon that to their eyes
The dazzling brightness of a golden coin
Outshines the noonday radiance of the sun.
They'll sell their souls and heav'nly hopes for gold.

Satan. Azazel, what report have you to make?

Azazel. I have inflated with such pride the king
That to himself he's higher than the heavens
And mightiest of all created ones.
His wisdom's infinite, his right supreme,
His smile can gladden earth and gild the sky.
He's prouder far than all the Eastern kings,
Craving your pardon: "Proud as Lucifer."
The old nobility I've so puffed up
That vain, hereditary honors seem
Superior to all inherent worth,
All excellences that belong to man.
Their smallest ancient privilege o'errides
The most important rights of other men.
For them and theirs they judge the world was made.

Old England's *literati* I have moved
To dip in gall the keenest of their pens.
T' asperse the colonists with bitter words.
From old Sam Johnson to young Hannah More,
They all agree to hate Americans.
When some explosive spark shall kindle war,
All classes here will blaze with wrathful flames.

Satan. Comrades, our schemes work well. If Chatham lives
And is restored to health, he will not stoop
To bandy idle words with such colleagues,
Nor condescend to serve a king whose smile
Approves bold Townshend's base, unfaithful act,
By which his gifted premier was betrayed.
This hateful Tax bill soon must separate
The statesman from both king and cabinet.
When the insulted great man shall withdraw,
Grenville and Townshend's mercenary plans
Will banish peace and send forth horrid war
To walk the earth with murder in his train.
King George, Queen Charlotte, and their royal babes
Come this way, walking toward their place of prayer.
Let us depart, and cross old ocean's waves.

Scene: *Boston, near Faneuil Hall, October 1, 1768.* SATAN, MARS, MAMMON, BELIAL. *Martial music, soldiers marching.*

Mars. Hark! hark! That music falls upon my ear
Like martial sounds from ancient centuries.
It wakes within me the mysterious joy
With which I led old Nimrod from the chase
Of fierce, wild beasts to that of fiercer men.
I hear the measured tread of the well-drilled,
Whose glorious trade is sanguinary war.
Yes, here they march. That steady tramp recalls
The grand achievements of the mighty men
To whom I gave the conquering millions
Of earth's early times. In memory's view
Their gorgeous standards float above the heads
Of empire builders going forth to war.

Satan, what enemies has Britain here
Demanding such a warlike armament?

Satan. This will make foes of peaceful citizens:
All signs are ominous of bloody war.
Ours is the task to hurry on the fight.
I shall exult to see the storm come down
With lightning flashes from bright bayonets,
And deep-toned thunder from the cannon's mouth;
To see red torrents of warm, flowing blood,
And hear war's music in the groans of men.
To me, 'twas worth ten thousand years in hell
To witness one such battle as Blenheim.
War's flashes gild with transitory beams
The ever deep'ning darkness of my chains.
Mammon, what news have you about the tax,
The troops, the discontent, the threats of war?

Mammon. The people will not bear taxation now;
They will not use an article that's taxed.
They all make common cause against the right
Of Parliament to tax Americans.
They use as emblems of their unity,
Sacred and true, the strength of banded sticks.
Soldiers at New York, in a time of peace,
Asked for support from those they came to enslave.
This was refused. The right to legislate
Was then withdrawn from the defiant men.
From north to south the country was incensed.
Indignant people talked of human rights
Existing ere a human law was made;
Of sacred rights, God-given; and above
Thrones, Legislatures, and judicial courts
Bold Samuel Adams even dared to speak
Of independence as the people's right.
The tools of tyranny became alarmed;
They asked for soldiers to protect themselves
Against the unarmed friends of liberty.

Belial. Dalrymple came with two full regiments.
Next month two more will come to join them here.

Each soldier that we see has sixteen rounds
Of deadly ammunition to discharge.
In bold bravado they march proudly here
With glitt'ring bayonets, as if to probe
The heart of Boston with their shining steel.
Dalrymple, in his red coat, comes this way,
Followed by Samuel Adams, freedom's friend.

Satan. The people are insulted by demands
For quarters and provisions for the troops
That come to undermine their liberty.
'Twill not be long till folly yields its fruit
In mad rebellion and in bloody war.
Let us depart and wait expectantly.

Scene: *Boston Common, by moonlight, March 4, 1770. Enter* SATAN, BAAL, MOLOCH, MAMMON, BELIAL, SERAPIS, MARS.

Satan. Princes, potentates, powers! trusted, true!
I seek your counsel as in league with me
Against the hateful millions of mankind.
The nations still are tranquil. Earth pours forth
Her plenteous harvest in the lap of peace,
And joyful myriads walk in flow'ry paths.
Ingloriously we sit; while envy, hate,
And malice prey upon us. Kings, courtiers,
Statesmen, I in vain have tried; and wasted
Upon worthless demagogues wise counsels.
Now let your wisdom charm my list'ning ear,
And teach me how to banish peace from men.
Speak, Baal, let us hear what you propose.

Baal. I still tempt men to war against the Lord,
And bring his righteous judgments on themselves.
Their suff'rings then fill me with great delight.

Satan. Moloch, my friend, say, what do you advise?

Moloch. With horrid superstitions is my work,
My myriad victims perish day by day
Along the banks of Congo, Niger, Nile,
The Indus, Ganges, and the Hoang Ho;

But Europe treats my counsels with disdain.
No emperor, nor sultan, nor the king
Of France or Spain or Naples listens now
With satisfaction to the cries of pain
And shrieks of anguish wrung from tortured men
By superstition racked. Even the pope
Seems to be wearied with the human groans
That tell how worse than useless is the task
That cruelly constrains all men to say
That they will think, speak, and believe alike.
Mammon, report; say, what do you advise?

Mammon. I tempt the covetous: king, cabinet,
Lords, commons, and old England's populace
Combine to madden and provoke to war
The colonists, who all are covetous.
By persevering efforts in this line
'Twill not be long until they fight like dogs.

Satan. You once were active, ancient Serapis,
Worshiped by millions on the banks of Nile.

Serapis. Nor am I idle now, my worthy chief.
The mighty Mississippi owned my sway,
When a vile Spanish tyrant, moved by me,
Slaughtered in cold blood the republicans
Who tried self-government at New Orleans.
I'll watch the lowlands. Spaniards led by me
Became oppressors of the Netherlands.

Satan. Mars, what have you to say? What have you done?

Mars. I've seen Lord Chatham, full of lofty pride,
Resign his place in the king's cabinet;
Witnessed the death of Townshend; seen Lord North
Become Prime Minister to please the king.
In England stupid weaklings now bear rule,
While in the colonies the wisest guide.
I saw Virginia's House of Burgesses,
With dignity and unanimity,
By formal resolutions take the lead,

Declaring that they never would be taxed
But by their own expressed authority.
Nor should their fellow-citizens be tried
But by a jury of the vicinage,
Nor should a tyrant's troops be quartered there.
The other colonies fall into line,
Hoping to crown union with liberty.
I have done nothing but await events.

 Satan. I have grown weary waiting for events.
The king sends ammunition, soldiers, ships;
Talks threat'ningly, but hangs no traitor chief.
The colonists resolve, defy, make threats;
Talk bravely, but carefully do nothing.
Belial, 'tis yours to strike the spark that soon
Shall kindle blazing flames of horrid war.
These troops are not all quiet, peaceful saints,
Nor all these people meek as Moses was.
In spite of learning, pride, and piety,
Boston still breeds among her citizens
Certain lewd fellows of the baser sort,
True sons of Belial, ready to your hand.
Can you not artfully stir up your sons
To silly actions and provoking words,
By which t' enrage the rash, impatient troops
Till British lead stains Boston's streets with blood
Drawn from the veins of yankee patriots?
Then will King George be called a murderer;
And those who fall, martyrs of liberty.
What say you, Belial? Can the work be done?

 Belial. Yes, mighty chief, it can. To-morrow night
Shall see bright moonbeams playing on earth's robes
Of snow-white purity, stained red with streams
Of flowing human gore. Will that suffice?

 Satan. Yes, Belial, let the work of death begin.
'Twill fill all hearts with hatred and revenge,
Providing for long years of bloody war.
My trusty friends, let us be here to see,
And duly honor Belial for success.

Scene: *Boston sidewalk near the court-house, March 5, 1770. Five bleeding bodies are in sight. Cries of agony are heard from unseen wounded men being carried away.* RAPHAEL, ZEPHON, ZOPHIEL, ARIEL.

Ariel. Why all this flowing blood? The virgin snow
Is red with crimson blushes. On the air
Comes agonizing cries, startling and sad,
Filling the night with horror, promising
A gloomy morning full of sighs and tears.
Who killed these men? And why? Say, Raphael
What dreadful crime caused this grave tragedy?

Raphael. The guilt of these rash murders, Ariel,
Rests first on Satan, author of all sin.
He stirs the hatreds that provoke fierce wars:
His restless malice has been working here.
Next, on the king and his Prime Minister.
'Tis shared in part by selfish governors,
Whose cowardice led them to ask for troops;
In part by Capt. Preston and his men;
In part, by sons of Belial on the street.
The thoughtful people feared such scenes as this,
And longed to see the regiments removed.
To-night the rabble, with insulting words,
Pressed on a sentinel; he called for help.
His comrades were defied, insulted, struck.
Sticks, stones, snow, rubbish flying thick and fast,
Provoked the soldiery to desp'rate deeds.
One fell, another had his gun knocked up;
They heard themselves called lobsters, cowards, knaves,
Rogues, villains, dastards, slaves who did not dare
To use their weapons in their own defense.
Then came the fatal order. At the flash,
Guilty and innocent together fell.
The dead and dying and the soldiery
Who fired the fatal shots that laid them low
Were quite too ignorant to understand
Or know the cause of their most cruel strife.
Untaught in ethics, law, or statesmanship,
These slaves of blind resentment shoot, or fall;
Yet this dark deed may sever all the ties

That bind these States to England and her king,
May make of the best people in the world
Most bitter enemies, though now they're friends.
But there are Warren, Otis, and a crowd
Of most indignant, irate citizens.
They understand the questions in dispute.
They say a freeman taxed without consent
Is but a milder name for robbery.
They will pay taxes levied by themselves
Or their own chosen representatives.
No act of Parliament shall confiscate
The property that they have earned and saved.
It was no act of Parliament that sent
Their brave forefathers to this distant land.
The settlers came as freemen. Protected
By the common law of England and all
The muniments of British liberty,
They claimed their birthright as inherited.
True to old England, loyal to their king,
They took up arms and freely shed their blood
For Britain's glory and her king's domains;
With their own money fed and clothed themselves,
So long as Britons found a foe to fight.
Their sons will freely fight for Britain still,
But not be driv'n as mercenary slaves.
They say to quarter soldiers in this town
In time of peace is cruel tyranny,
An insult and an outrage and a farce,
Ending to-night in bloody tragedy.

Zophiel. How unexpected this has been to me!
'Tis but a few short years since with delight
I gazed admiringly on Britain's king
And on his dutiful and pious queen.
The old abuses and disgraceful sins,
Brought o'er the sea from Hanover, had ceased;
No more was heard the drunken revelry,
The oaths profane, the vulgar, ribald jests,
Nor seen th' outrageous, brazen harlotry
That long disgraced the royal palaces.
The king and queen bowed to the King of kings,

Most humbly and devoutly worshiping;
While multitudes, by their example led,
Paid meek devotion to the Lord most high.
The royal children, early taught to pray,
Won ev'ry heart that saw their loveliness.
All holy angels loved to linger near,
And wait upon the blissful heirs of life.
From the home circle of chaste royalty
Virtue and decency walked forth to bless
Millions with holy, conjugal delights,
In the pure homes of people of all ranks.

Zephon. I saw the fine arts yield to royalty
Their grateful homage and obedience,
And imitate the chaste and decent court.
Handel and Haydn sent sublimest strains
Of heav'nly music ringing round the world.
Obscenity and folly fled away
From halls of music, pure and undefiled.
Reynolds and West to glowing canvas gave,
In fairest features and most perfect forms,
The grandest charms of manhood's majesty,
And beauty's blooming loveliness unveiled,
Yet brought no burning blush to virtue's cheek.
From heathen haunts and pagan practices,
The muse of poetry turned quite away,
With chaste and lofty thoughts and ringing words
T' inspire Johnson and Goldsmith, Beattie,
Gray, and Cowper. To good Charles Wesley gave
Songs fit for seraphs near th' eternal throne,
That charm the ear, that thrill and melt the heart,
Inspire devotion, till the classic muse
Goes singing like a modest Methodist,
To win for Christ the millions of mankind.
Great Chatham was the king's Prime Minister,
Who drove domestic discord from the land,
And gave his monarch thrones in loyal hearts.
Prosperity and loyalty and love,
With gleeful gladness, hand in hand rejoiced.
All foreign foes were vanquished and in peace.
The savage Indians of the western wilds

Most gladly owned King George's sovereignty.
"They buried tomahawks and scalping-knives,
And planted over them the tree of peace."
Th' uncounted millions of old Asia's sons
Began to seek protection 'neath his flag.
Far distant lands and isles of ev'ry sea
Waited for England's colonies and laws;
But now disorder reigns. Red-handed war,
With gory banners, frights the trembling land.
Please tell me, Raphael, why this mournful change?

Raphael. Zephon, this melancholy change has sprung
From stubborn pride and greedy selfishness.
When Pitt had laid the world at Britain's feet,
The cost of such great triumphs must be paid.
The question was, by whom? Wise statesmanship
Could see broad streams of richest revenues
Deep'ning their channels toward the treasury;
But Pitt no longer ruled the prosp'rous land.
Unlawful taxes laid on colonists,
Instead of lawful taxes on themselves,
Was what the king and cabinet proposed.
This roused the colonists. From bad to worse
The government has gone. To-night we see
Most bloody fruits of selfish arrogance.
The full, red harvest ripens rapidly,
And fearful retribution marches on
To punish Britain's pride and selfishness.

Scene: *Front of John Street Church, New York, with Trinity Church in view by moonlight, October 5, 1770.* RAPHAEL, ARIEL, UZZIEL, ZEPHON.

Raphael. The snowy robes of Boston stained with blood
Of slaughtered citizens in peaceful times
Drew forth our sympathies when last we met.
Since then, where have you ministered? what seen?

Ariel. The dwellings of the saints have been my care.
I have seen many Eastern colonists,
Have watched their struggles, helped them in distress,

And poured celestial comforts into hearts
That throbbing sunk in hopeless agony.
My latest most delightful work has been
By Whitefield's death-bed, and with his freed soul,
His escort to the paradise of God.
With work well done he rested from his toils,
And like a weary child he fell asleep,
Not taking time to talk of works or faith.
Friends watched his latest hours, and gently laid
His mortal body near the sacred desk
From which he loved to tell of saving grace.
Two continents seem orphaned by his death;
Their wailing lamentations now are heard.
Please tell me of your labors and your cares.

Raphael. The Southern sea-coasts I have visited,
From far Savannah to the Chesapeake
Thousands whose burning brows have felt my touch
Drive off the fever fiend, and heal the wounds
His fiery feet had made, rejoice to-day;
And thousands more, cast down by many cares,
Now lift their heads in Christian cheerfulness.
Zephon, report what you have seen and done.

Zephon. Along the deep, broad rivers of the West,
I've sought the hunters of the wilderness
And carried comfort to their rude, rough homes;
But I beheld in Western Maryland
A sight so grand 'tis worth reporting here.
'Twas in a frontier cabin. Death approached
And called its brave defender to depart.
The husband, father, neighbor said farewell
To weeping loved ones whom he soon must leave;
Then, with a shout of triumph over death,
Set his firm foot upon the tyrant's neck,
And with ecstatic rapture passed away
To endless life, forever with the Lord.
Three days of solemn, joyful mourning passed,
And holy men took up their comrade's corpse.
No bell was counting out his years below;
But through the grand old woods rung out such sounds

As none but Christ's most holy ones could raise.
Such thrilling tones, pathetic and sublime,
So full of gracious fervor, could not spring
From voices that had not been tuned by grace.
Slowly, with measured, reverential steps,
The train moved onward to the Christian's grave,
Still bravely singing in heroic lays
The song triumphant of victorious faith:
  "Rejoice for a brother deceased;
     Our loss is his infinite gain;
   A soul out of prison released,
     And freed from his bodily chain:
   With songs let us follow his flight,
     And mount with his spirit above,
   Escaped to the mansions of light,
     And lodged in the Eden of love."

  Ariel. Please tell us more about those singing saints
Who thus defy the keenest darts of death,
And raise glad shouts of vict'ry o'er the grave.

  Uzziel. Ten years ago, there came to Maryland
An Irishman, of lowly, humble birth.
But being "born again"—born from above—
Though poor in purse, was very rich in faith.
This child of God—heir of immensity—
Has called mankind to share his heritage.
Heeding his invitation with delight,
His humble neighbors sought like precious faith,
Are children of their God in very deed,
Crowned with divinest honor, wealth, and power.
Death owns his conquerors in such as these.
When Robert Strawbridge, called of God to preach,
Asked for a license under Wesley's hand,
'Twas not believed that such a man could lay
The broad foundations of the greatest Church
Known to this Western world for centuries
To come. But so it was. In the same year,
Two other families of the same faith
Came from the same green isle and landed here.
Six years of modest diffidence passed by,

While secret prayers ascended from their hearts.
Then others came to join the holy band.
Brave Barbara Heck moved Philip Embury
To preach the gospel to these emigrants.
At first a few, then crowds came out to hear.
Soon Captain Webb came down from Albany,
True soldier of the cross, with sword in hand,
In his red regimentals gayly clad,

ROBERT STRAWBRIDGE.

Entered the pulpit, laid at Jesus' feet
The glittering steel, and with a giant's strength
Wielded the Holy Spirit's two-edged sword.
This lowly, humble temple is the place
Where these religious people meet to-night.
And yet another, worthy of all praise,
Has come to join them in their loving work.

He goes to wave the blazing torch of truth
Where it first flashed upon this continent,
Held in the hands of Hunt and Whitaker,
Assisted by the greatest of John Smiths.
'Tis Robert Williams. He's Virginia's own.
See at his side young Francis Asbury,
Destined to lead the hosts of Methodism;

CAPTAIN WEBB.

And there is Embury, here Barbara Heck,
The noblest of them all. There Captain Webb,
Who lost an eye while fighting gallantly
When Wolfe fell, crowned with vict'ry, at Quebec.
Let us go in and worship with them here.

BOOK THIRD.

Scene: *Heights of Richmond, April 2, 1773.* MICHAEL, GABRIEL, ITHURIEL.

 Gabriel. Hail, prince of our angelic brotherhood,
Guardian of empires and great statesmen's guide,
This day Virginia's burgesses have crowned,
With unexampled glory and renown,
This noblest of all noble commonwealths;
With reverential love and lofty pride
They led their young majestic mother forth,
Blooming and fair, in beauteous gracefulness,
To hold her bright, impenetrable shield
Between her trembling sisters and their foe.
This must be " freedom's home or glory's grave."
No room is found for craven dastards here.

 Michael. Gabriel, your admiration is deserved;
I share it with you. But a selfish world
Oft takes advantage of the generous.
The time may come when those she now defends
Will, quite forgetful of all gratitude,
Trample upon the compact made by States,
And gather millions from the teeming North
To subjugate this little, lovely town,
Or sweep creation for a hireling host,
To lay Virginia's beauty in the dust.

 Ithuriel. In such a case her stalwart sons would fight
As men in armies never fought before.
Her fairest fields they'd fertilize with blood,
And send swift retribution on her foes.
But I forbear to scan futurity.
Foreknowledge does not now belong to us:
'Tis with the present that we have to do.

This latest action taken here to-day
Will unify and organize defense.
The colonists in constant intercourse
Will act in concert to resist all wrongs,
Or, possibly, for independence strike.
The busy printing-press gives active aid
To those defending civil liberty.
The "Farmer's Letters" by John Dickinson,
Pour floods of light upon the public mind,
And teach great truths in a most winning way.

Abdiel. The pen of Junius, "keen and dipped in gall,"
Punctures abuses most relentlessly.
But why does he conceal his skillful hand?
Who is he? What is his own proper name?

Gabriel. Abdiel, opinions differ as to that.
I only give you mine for what it's worth.
One man alone can use such forceful words:
But one in reputation's rich enough
To be so prodigal of fame as not
To claim the honor of such authorship.
But one knew all the secrets he reveals,
While mercilessly lashing ministers
And even his most gracious Majesty.
One man, and only one, could feel—could make
His burning words express—such lofty pride,
Such grand, imperious, disdainful scorn
Of high-born littleness in seats of power.
That man is Chatham. "Junius" did not write
Till after Chatham left the cabinet.
The sick man's comforts, his domestic joys,
His social rank were chains of gratitude
He could not break, though duty sternly called
For patriot toils to save a sinking State.
Even the great man's title then proclaimed
His deep indebtedness to George the Third.
The unknown "Junius" gave the unfettered strength
Of Pitt's unequaled genius to mankind
To save them from the follies of the times.
The more completely to conceal his hand

He praised himself. So, of necessity,
"Junius" must rest in Chatham's honored grave.

Michael. Among these gifted backwoods burgesses
Are men whose honored names shall soon outshine
Illustrious Chatham's on the list of fame;

WILLIAM PITT, EARL OF CHATHAM.

And one, the peerless name of Washington,
Shall stand confessed the highest of mankind.
Behold! The noblest of the human race!

Scene: *Boston, in front of the old South Church, at night, December 15, 1773.* SATAN, BELIAL, AZAZEL.

Satan to Belial. My trusty friend, I need your services.
This question of taxation, simplified,
Turns now on tea alone. The Parliament

And king bid the obedient merchants send
Cheap tea to tempt weak colonists to buy.
Charleston, New York, and Philadelphia
Have kept the tempting leaves from cheerful homes;
But Hutchinson, to enrich his selfish sons,
Would gladly give Bostonians all they want.
Mammon delights to help the covetous.
He would not have a single leaf destroyed.
To you I therefore come. What can you do?

Belial. To-morrow night the citizens meet here
To talk of grievances and remedies.
I will bring fifty of my chosen sons,
Arrayed as Indians, to destroy the tea.
The crowd shall follow us to Griffin's Wharf;
We'll seize the tea and throw it in the dock.
This great "tea party" long shall be renowned.
The king, intoxicated with its fumes,
Shall loose his dogs of war against this town,
And wreak his vengeance on its citizens.

Azazel. Will that bring on the war so much desired,
Or Boston be the only sufferer?

Satan. We can but try it. Here to-morrow night
We come to witness Belial's great success.

Scene: *Boston, in front of the old South Church, at night, December 16, 1773.* SATAN *and* AZAZEL *approach.*

Satan. Ho! Belial, where are now your fifty men?
Belial. Satan, they restless sit amid the crowd,
Waiting our signal to begin their work.
Satan. Belial, give them the expected signal now.
Belial. Satan, that's all arranged and understood:
There's one within who will attend to that.
Come with me now to Griffin's Wharf before
The crowd comes rushing and the fray begins.

Scene: *Griffin's Wharf.*

Belial to Satan and Azazel. Step with me on this elevated spot,
Whence we can see destructive work go on.

The war-whoop sounds and hundreds rush this way.
The work begins; the tea is seized; the chests
Are emptied in the foaming waves and sink.
Now, Satan, can you praise my handiwork?

Satan. Belial, I can. But we must cross the sea.
Our work is incomplete until the king
Grows furious and begins to strike his foes.

Scene: *Front of the palace, January 11, 1774.* SATAN, AZAZEL,
BELIAL, MAMMON.

Satan. The privy council met the king to-day
To talk of letters that have passed between
Hillsboro and the royal governor.
Petitions from the colonists have come
Demanding the removal of their foes—
For such they count their governor, their judge;
And by those letters prove that enmity
Reigns in the hearts of those high officers.
The king and his advisers do not deign
To notice such petitions for relief.
The ministers were troubled, and would learn
Who 'twas that told state secrets out of school.
Each charged another with the grave offense,
And duels might have shed their noble blood
If nobler Franklin had not helped his foes
By telling them 'twas he that sent the news.
The cabinet became enraged at him
And said he must appear before King George.
Belial, your matchless talents I require.
These high-born dignitaries of the realm
Furnish lewd fellows of the baser sort,
Lower in vulgar vices than the scum
Fermenting in the slums of wretchedness.
One, Wedderburne, belongs to this vile class.
On this he-harpy try your utmost skill.
Let fangs and talons rend old Franklin's heart;
Bid weaker vultures share the hateful feast
Until King George shall sicken at the sight.
Meanwhile, Azazel, go stir up the king
Until his rage exceeds all decent bounds;
Then meet me here again in eighteen days.

Scene: *Front of the palace, by moonlight, January 29, 1774.* SATAN, BELIAL, AZAZEL.

Belial. My honored chief, your deep-laid plot works well.
Franklin was present by the king's command;
Base Wedderburne in rudest wrathfulness
Hurled at him accusations, insults, threats,
And every wordy weapon he could find
In the whole armory of human speech.
Dignified and brave, unmoved by malice,
Unsubdued by fear, unawed by all the
Frowns of royalty or threats of power,
The hero told them most unwelcome truths.
The laughing lordlings and ungracious king
Were dwarfed before this wise man of the West.

Satan. Azazel, what have you to tell to-night?
Was royalty submissive to your will?

Azazel. More than submissive to all fiendish schemes
For crushing the rebellious colonists.
Alas! poor king, he is insanely mad
Against all persons who resist his will.

Satan. This but promotes our hellish purposes,
And promises a long, long, cruel strife.
To-night peace spreads her snow-white wings for flight,
While howling hatred calls for bloody war.

Belial. Say, Satan, is my latest work approved?

Satan. It is. I give you my most hearty thanks.
But there remains another work for you:
Gage is in London. He must see the king
And fill him with vain hopes of victory.
To you I trust him: work him to your will
By hast'ning on the conflicts that must come.
These men deceive each other and themselves;
We understand them and are not deceived.
How despicable is all human pride!
How inconsistent man's most lauded acts!

Not twenty months ago these islanders
Boasted most loudly of the liberty
Conferred by Mansfield on one negro slave
A Massachusetts man had landed here.
Cheap charity, without expense, could free
Another's slave and glory in the deed,
Singing loud songs about philanthropy,
Boasting of freedom and of English air
Inhaled by slaves to give them liberty.
We laugh to scorn such bold, pretentious boasts,
While Parliament and king for paltry gold
Encourage merchants still to trade in slaves.
Yes, judges, legislators, and the king
Turn a deaf ear to accents of distress
In which Virginia begs to be relieved
From the accursed slave trade and its woes.
The horrid traffic, with its burning shame,
Still brings bright blushes to her glowing cheeks,
As such vile merchandise pollutes her shores.
Mansfield approaches. North is by his side.

Scene: *House of Lords after adjournment, March 18, 1774.* SATAN, BAAL, MARS, AZAZEL, BELIAL.

Satan. My great compeers, we've triumphed here to-day.
The Boston Port bill passed and is approved.
An empire wreaks its vengeance on a town;
Blockades its ports, removes its government,
Fills it with soldiers, starves its citizens:
(Those of them that it does not choose to hang)
To this king, lords, and commons have agreed.

Baal. Satan, this must be quite an easy task
Imposed upon themselves: an hour's pastime.
How many people are there in the town?

Satan. When full, not more than sixteen thousand souls;
But now, with numbers frightened and away,
Soldiers outnumber quiet citizens.

Belial. Then why not go to hanging instantly,
And end the troubles of the trembling town?

Azazel. That is a game attended by great risks.
More than two millions threaten to take part
In such proceedings, if they once begin.

Satan. Ha! Comrade Mars, great gallant god of war!
I see the smile that lights your countenance.
Make ready for the strife: there's work for you.
To Massachusetts let us wend our way.

Scene: *Market Street Wharf, Philadelphia, June 1, 1774. Flags on shipping at half-mast; crape on closed houses; muffled bells tolling.*
ABDIEL, ITHURIEL, ZEPHON, UZZIEL, RAPHAEL.

Zephon. What mean these signs of mourning, those sad sounds
That echo like the dirge of some lost soul?
Has death struck down the monarch on his throne?
Do continents lament their loss to-day?

Abdiel. Death in a palace brings no gloom like this;
'Tis liberty has died, and millions mourn.
These half-mast flags, these melancholy bells,
Those crape-clad dwellings, and those solemn throngs,
Proclaim the indignation and distress
That patient Pennsylvania feels to-day
Because the Boston Port bill is enforced.

Ithuriel. Virginia fasts, and lifts her solemn prayers
For help from God against the enemies
Of human freedom and the rights of man.
She summons a convention of her sons
To choose a delegation that shall meet
A Continental Congress in this place.
She calls back liberty to life again,
Ready to arm brave sons in her defense,
Making one nation of these colonies.

Abdiel. Comrades, Virginia lives in quietness.
So do the other Southern colonies;
Their ports are not blockaded, nor their towns
Beleaguered by a hostile soldiery.
With lords of trade they have no rivalries,
No ships of theirs the rich slave trade divide
With merchants of old England. Salem, Boston,

And New York provoke the jealousy of
Liverpool and Bristol for its profits.
Savannah, Charleston, Norfolk, Baltimore
Send out no ships for captured Africans.
Those Southerners are favorites of the king.
He does not ask the heads of their great men,
Nor would he have them sent across the sea.
Why, then, does Boston rouse their sympathies
So that they risk their all in her defense?

Uzziel. Thus all the colonies make common cause
Against the right of king and Parliament
To tax them all without their own consent;
To rule them in all cases; quarter troops
On them in time of peace; to transport men
Across the sea for trial. If Boston
Suffers now without redress, why may not
Charleston, Norfolk, Baltimore, whenever
Whims of tyrants may demand? Their innate,
Home-bred love of liberty, law, justice,
Impels them to contend for human rights.

Raphael. That doubtless is the truth; but gratitude,
Stronger than bands of steel, must ever bind
New England to the people of the South.
Their interests she will guard as if her own;
Wrongs done to them she'll hasten to redress;
Insults to them must be insults to her,
Her loving-kindness their rich heritage.

Abdiel. After the coming Congress shall convene,
Let us meet here again at duty's call.
But see, there comes this way John Dickinson:
The "Farmer's Letters" flowed from his keen pen.

Scene: *In front of Carpenter's Hall, Philadelphia, October 25, 1774.*
  ABDIEL, ITHURIEL, RAPHAEL, ZOPHIEL, ZEPHON.

Abdiel. The Congress has completed its great work:
Will soon adjourn to meet again in May.
Such wisdom, prudence, boldness, bravery
Earth never saw before in any land.

They buried bigotry. Opposing sects
Built on his grave the altar of our God.
They banished selfishness, and in his place,
Enthroned triumphant, love-crowned unity.
They came to speak of grievances endured
By persecuted, struggling colonies;
They go, the representatives and chiefs
Of millions that refuse to be oppressed.

JOHN WYCKLIFFE.

Uzziel. Comrades, if that be so, why do they not
Cast off the British yoke and rule themselves?

Ithuriel. Their gen'rous hearts retain a ling'ring love
Of Britain, as the happy home of their
Revered forefathers. They share her glory,
Her renown inherit. Her mighty arm
Subdues all foreign foes, and is a sure
Defense for all on whom she deigns to smile.

They love her ancient laws, and dare to hope
For the repeal of those tyrannic acts
That now oppress them. Some are not ready
For the final step to independence.
Self-government will come. They wisely wait
For full consent and unanimity.
To freedom's friends this comes with quick'ning speed.
The wrongs that suff'ring Boston now endures
Awaken indignation in all hearts.
Some, praying, call aloud for heav'nly help;
Others, with wrath, hurl fierce anathemas
At the hard-hearted king and ministers.

Zephon. But who provides for Boston's families,
And drives the wolf of famine from their homes?

Raphael. The harvests of a continent are theirs,
Laid at their feet by patriotic hands.
Gadsden, of Carolina, was the first
Whose gen'rous heart responded to their wants.
His crop of rice was liberty's first-fruits,
By union brought to freedom's sacred shrine;
Then followed the rich products of broad fields
From Alleghanian heights to ocean's shore.
Boston most gratefully records these gifts,
Sent in her hour of need from Southern soil.
All time shall witness with approving smiles
The tokens of her loving gratitude.
Gadsden and Charleston shall be household words,
Honored and loved beyond all other names.

Zophiel. 'Tis less than half a year since General Gage,
With colors flying and with booming guns,
Sailed into Boston Harbor with eclat;
Then through the perfumed air of flow'ry May,
Escorted by cadets that Hancock led,
He marched in triumph to the state-house square;
In Fanueil Hall dined with the patriots,
Assured them that " the troubles of the times
Were only lovers' quarrels," and would end
In halycon days of loving happiness.

While thus dissembling, he was pledged to send
Their leading men as pris'ners o'er the sea
To meet the vengeance of their irate king.

Uzziel. Does his pretense of friendship still deceive?
Or has he dropped the mask that hid his hate?

Abdiel. His gleesome gala days are ended now.
Prison bounds restrain his wonted freedom.
His troops to narrow limits are confined:
A living, human wall forbids escape.
Broad as New England now he sees it rise,
And firmer than her frowning granite hills.
His civic honors, his vice-regal powers,
And all the glory of supreme command
Hide not the horrors of his dismal fate.
Escape by sea would lead to dire disgrace;
He dare not venture upon hostile acts.
In vain he fortifies against his foes:
His piteous cries for help in his great need
Burden the west winds and disturb the king.
It is not "Boston's rabble" he now fears;
"Substantial citizens" arise in arms.
He asks that peaceful counsels may prevail;
Demands more troops—English or Scotch, Irish
Or mercenary Germans, negro slaves,
Canadian French or Indian savages—
To save him in this dread extremity.
Without more troops to fight the colonists,
Ingloriously idle he remains.
Shut up in Boston with his well-drilled men,
Sees brave Virginians boldly take up arms,
Drive hostile Indians from their heritage,
And firmly hold their own with steel-clad hands
Against King George and Frenchmen of Quebec.
The boundless acres of the wid'ning West
As to their fathers giv'n are still their own.

Zephon. Did the mad king give Canada those lands?

Abdiel. He did. His hatred of the colonies
Was stronger than his bitter bigotry,

Prompting vain efforts to convey the lands
Of true Virginia English Protestants
To Roman Catholics of French Quebec,
Trying to check the Old Dominion's growth
By this mad folly of an insane king.
Even Dunmore, the Tory governor,
Saw with delight Virginians driving back
King George's Indians and Canadians.
But see, the Congress now hast just adjourned.
There's Washington, Lee, Henry, Jefferson,
John Adams, Livingston, Gadsden, and Jay,
And Samuel Adams, who was first to see
The sun of independence in the east.
Undying fame leads them to lofty heights
Of high renown and immortality.

Scene: *Front of St. John's Church, Richmond, Va., April 2, 1775.*
MICHAEL, GABRIEL, ITHURIEL, ABDIEL.

Michael. Guardians of nations, comrades tried and true,
The dawn of independence now appears
From the St. Lawrence down to Florida.
The eastern skies are glowing with its light,
While frontier settlers in the distant West
With exultation hail the bright'ning beams.
Chatham and Burke have eloquently plead
With lords and commons for colonial rights;
But their appeals have both been made in vain.
Franklin returns to tell his countrymen
That Britain spurns their representative.
The royal governors retire in haste,
Or give their king's commissions to the flames.

Ithuriel. Michael, the breezes from the distant North
Come burdened with reports of horrid war.
'Tis said that thirty thousand freemen armed
Toward Boston now are marching rapidly;
That Gage cannot escape but by the sea;
That his drilled troops, whipped by provincial boys,
Seek safety in intrenchments and in forts.

Abdiel. This colony to-day resolves to arm
Her stalwart sons to fight for liberty.

Lee, Washington, Henry, and Jefferson
Are to devise the military plan
By which Virginia's troops shall take the field.
Lord Dunmore threatens to burn up her towns,
Arm slaves, and bid them desolate her homes;
Give to the gallows leading citizens,
To scalping-knives the tresses that adorn
The loveliness of youth and innocence.
He thinks that with three thousand stand of arms,

SIR ISAAC NEWTON.

Four pieces of artillery at hand,
Three thousand saucy, well-fed negro slaves,
His brave marines and Indian savages,
He can subdue these freemen. What say you?

Gabriel. I say these patriots despise his threats.

Ithuriel. Five thousand men, the bravest of the brave,
Are ready now to drive him to his ships.

Michael. The Congress meets in May. Let us remain
And meet at Alexandria on the road.
Thence we can travel with the delegates
To witness the proceedings and debates.

Scene: *Alexandria, Va., May 1, 1775.* MICHAEL, GABRIEL, AB-
DIEL, ITHURIEL.

Michael. Comrades, I hail you happy on your way
To the fair city where the Congress meets.
Georgia, with but three thousand fighting men,
Sees on her soil ten thousand Indian braves,
Ready, for British gold, to slay her sons;
Yet does not hesitate in freedom's cause
To seize five hundred pounds of gunpowder
That had been stored in the king's magazine;
And further, to defy his Majesty,
Sends to rebellious Boston rice and gold.

Abdiel. South Carolina by heroic deeds
Defies Great Britain and her hireling hosts;
Lays hold upon eight hundred stand of arms,
With ammunition and rich army stores,
Ready for independence or for war.
North Carolina is in arms to-day:
Her governor, a fugitive, makes haste
To leave the land that spurns his tyranny.

Gabriel. List to the martial music on the air!
Virginia's Congressmen are coming now,
Escorted to the border of their State
By the brave men who drove Lord Dunmore out.
The journey of these statesmen toward the North
Has now become a grand triumphal march.
Applauding thousands hail the conquerors,
Victorious over boasting tyranny.
They drove the British regulars in fight,
And did not lose a single combatant,
While the red-coated officers were slain
Till English blood had fertilized the soil.
They forced the braggart governor to pay

For their State's powder which he basely stole;
Then drove the terror-stricken wretch to seek
With hasty steps a refuge on his ships.
The fiendish vandal, filled with hellish hate,
Gave Norfolk to the flames as he passed by.
'Twas well with fire to purify the spot
Where his foul foot last touched the sacred soil.
His and his master's last official act
In this, the purest of all commonwealths,
Forced its protesting citizens to bear,
For England's glory and emolument,
The vile, polluting horrors that belonged
To the dark slave trade which their souls abhorred.
But royalty and loyalty depart
And false philanthropy is following
To keep the trio out; Randolph and Bland
Have just sold forty slaves, that they may buy
Powder to drive the slave-ships of King George
Far from their honest, flourishing young State
And free New England from his galling yoke.

Scene: *Lexington, Mass., before day, April 19, 1775.* SATAN, BAAL, MOLOCH, MARS.

Satan. Hail! princes of my more than royal court,
Bold leaders of my brave embattled hosts!
The conflict we have waited for begins.
There's Paul Revere. He's riding in hot haste
To warn the watchful sons of liberty.
December saw him rousing Sullivan,
Who captured Cochrane and a royal fort
And carried off its powder and its arms.
This action of the bold New Hampshire men
Has led King George to order General Gage
To seize all arms and powder to be found
Among his rash rebellious colonists.
Obedient to this order of the king,
Gage sent out Major Pitcairn and some troops
Upon a midnight search to capture stores.
But Paul Revere outrides the royalists,
And fighting men are gath'ring at his call.
Wives arm their husbands, mothers their young sons.

They come through by paths, lanes, and fields and woods
To battle for the loved ones of their homes
Against the hireling hosts of tyranny.

 Baal. See! There is Pitcairn with his well-armed men,
Confronting these defiant, rustic youths.
He gives the order that begins the war;
He calls them rebels, tells them to disperse.
Behold those flashes! hear the sharp reports!
The rustics fall: seven have ceased to breathe,
Nine others from red wounds pour out their lives.
Hark! hark! Death flies upon the morning breeze!
The red-coats fall! The boasting Britons flee
In wild disorder from their untrained foes.
Vengeance awaits them whereso'er they turn.
They rally, they stand firm, and standing die.

 Mars. Ha-ha! Ha-ha! This, this, indeed, is war.
I revel in delight amid such scenes.

 Satan. I join you in your reveling. Hell howls
Responsively to jubilations loud.
With us it joins to gloat on human woe.

 Moloch. Pitcairn and Smith and their brave followers
Took ammunition from their enemies,
But it came through the muzzles of their guns
And kept them from arresting patriots.
So Samuel Adams cannot now be hanged,
Nor must John Hancock die for his good deeds.

Scene: *Chestnut Street, Philadelphia, June 15, 1775.* MICHAEL and GABRIEL.

 Michael. What think you, Gabriel, of this Congress now?

 Gabriel. Michael, its wisdom is most wonderful.
So patient, yet so firm against all wrong.
It was a master-stroke of policy
That placed proscribed John Hancock in the chair.
Virginia, through the lips of Harrison,
Thus told King George with hearty emphasis:

"Your royal fury cannot strike this man
Till our strong arms are laid in patriots' graves."
To-day John Adams named George Washington
To be the chief commander of all troops
Raised by the colonies for their defense.
Already thirty thousand rush to arms
To claim New England for her stalwart sons,
The Congress calls for twenty thousand more;
But independence is the only path
Which leads to freedom on this continent.
Here comes the modest hero who commands
The armies that defend America.
See how the holy angels guide his steps
And shield him from the dangers that surround!

Scene: *Bunker Hill, Mass., June 18, 1775.* SATAN, MARS, MOLOCH, MAMMON.

Satan. Companions of my life, partners in toil,
The triumphs of these times are justly yours.
I hail you victors on this field of fame,
And add my plaudits to the well-earned praise
Hell's countless legions thunder in your ears.
The bloody battle fought on yesterday
Involves mankind in years of bitter strife.
'Twas your contrivance that laid low in dust
More than fourscore of Britain's officers;
The flow'r and pride of England's chivalry,
By rustic hands unskilled in arts of war,
That gave to death three British regulars
For each provincial that in battle fell.
Humiliation, such as England bears,
Will drive to desperation those who rule.
A cry for vengeance will ring through the realm
Ruled by the baffled, disappointed king—
Vengeance and rage that will not count the cost
In cash, or tears, or blood, or agony.
Moloch, you shall see blood in torrents flow,
While fearful shrieks and groans shall charm your ears.
Brave Mars, embattled hosts in many a field
To you rich harvests of delight shall yield.

Ho! Mammon, why are you so thoughtful grown?
Why melancholy, mid our revelry?

 Mammon. 'Tis not that men are hated less by me,
Not that I less delight in human woe;
But the destruction of their treasured hoards
Consumes the bait with which I fish for souls.
I saw them die in agony, and laughed;
But when the flames licked up and turned to dust
Charlestown's four hundred dwellings and their wealth,
'Twas a sad sight to see such willful waste
Of what I could have used to ruin souls.
War hurries men to death in tender youth,
Untutored in the worst of villainies;
Wealth schools in vice and graduates in crime,
While hearts grow harder than the hoarded gold.
Wealth leads to war that's worthy of the name,
And peoples hell with its worst denizens.
Give me the time to make these rustics rich,
Then they will glut war's strongest appetite.
You well remember how old Nineveh,
Tyre, Babylon, Damascus, mighty Rome,
Had wealth worth fighting for, and fearful crimes:
Were rich, ripe, rotten, filled with wasting spoils.
When cow-boy armies plunder villages,
What honor has great Mars, the god of war?
When Alexander reaped old Asia's fields,
Harvests of glory round his footsteps fell.

 Mars. Mammon, to work out ruin for your friends,
You can improve uncounted centuries;
But war is now the order of the day,
And hast'ning thousands swiftly rush to arms.
One man like Warren, upon Bunker Hill,
Outweighs the worth of countless stores of gold.
Even his ashes centuries to come
Shall still inspire the bravest, noblest deeds.
Know ye that when Ticonderoga fell
The king lost what had cost his treasury
Eight millions sterling and vast army stores,
With sixscore pieces of artillery?

Crown Point surrendered two days afterward.
If Ethan Allen, leading fourscore men,
Wrought such destruction in a few brief hours,
Uncounted millions must most freely blaze
As fiery-footed war walks through the land.

Satan. Comrades, your disputation profits not.
Since men destroy each other, we exult.
Be ours the task to keep their hate inflamed,
And urge them on to deeds of violence.
Conquer who may, ours is the victory.

Mars. There's Prescott, who commanded on that hill;
There Gridley, his accomplished engineer,
And Israel Putnam, brave as man can be.

Scene: *American encampment, near Boston, July 10, 1775.* SATAN and MARS.

Mars. What mean the acclamations that we hear?
They sound like joyous shouts of men in arms.
Has a detachment gained a victory,
Or does the royal army leave the place?

Satan. Not so. The chosen chief of thirteen States
Reviews the troops placed under his command.
The patriot army hears, for the first time,
The wise and weighty words of the great man
Who leads them forth to vict'ry or defeat.
To-day they all seem jubilant and proud,
Defying Britain's king and Parliament
And all the forces they may have to meet.
Let them crow on. These game birds soon shall set
Their sharp, strong spurs to drawing kindred blood.

Scene: *Independence Square, Philadelphia, July 3, 1776.* MICHAEL, GABRIEL, ABDIEL, ITHURIEL, ZEPHON, RAPHAEL, ARIEL.

Michael. Hail! honored comrades, offspring of our God!
Behold a nation struggling into life!
The noblest, greatest, grandest of all time.
Gabriel, the nations long have claimed your care:
These rising States you've watched with partial eye.
Say, are they ripe for independence now?

Gabriel. Michael, they are. It is their own by right.
I joy to see them claim their heritage,
And crown themselves with wise self-government.

Michael. Zophiel, we turn to you inquiringly.
The English and their king to you are dear.
Have they not forfeited their claims to rule
This generous people and their lovely land?

Zophiel. Yes, England blooms in beauty and in grace.
Her youthful king seems crowned with piety;
Her people full of wisdom from on high.
Alas! poor king! Insanity's at fault
For half his folly and for all his crime.
But these fair States ought now to be set free
From king and nobles and all foreign sway;
Owning allegiance to the King of kings,
And living in obedience to his laws.
More than a year England has stood appalled.
Lord North would gladly have resigned his place
And called an abler man to save the state.
Wesley besought the king to shed no blood.
London demanded peace, while statesmen wept.
But the crazed king hearkened to no appeal:
His own rash hand plucked from his diadem
The brightest jewel that was glitt'ring there.

Michael. What think you, Abdiel? Is the rich, ripe fruit
Of independence in the reach of these
Brave sons of liberty? If not, say why.

Abdiel. Yes. Independence now is theirs of right.
Virginia long ago demanded it.
The pen of Jefferson, the eloquence
Of Henry and of Lee, the solid sense
Of Washington and Wythe convince all minds
That independence is the people's right.
When last November a French agent came
To offer ammunition, money, arms,
This seemed to give assurance of success
In spite of all the armies of King George.

Michael. Ithuriel, we wait your true report
Of the position of the sunny South.

Ithuriel. Michael, 'twas more than fourteen months ago
That independence freely was proclaimed
By Carolinians at Mecklenburg.
A few days since eight hours of bombardment
Stranded three British ships near Moultrie's fort,
Wounded the Admiral and drove his fleet
To seek for shelter with his loyal friends
In some safe harbor near to Halifax;
Killed brave Lord Campbell, last of governors
To rule by royal right or royal wrong.
From the Potomac down to Florida
Immediate independence is the cry.

Michael. Zephon, what news have you from Canada?
Does the St. Lawrence own our union's sway?

Zephon. September saw Montgomery's brave men
March northward, take Fort Chambly and St. Johns,
Seize Montreal and move to strong Quebec.
Success attended them upon their march.
When stern December hurled her fearful blasts,
Chilling their vitals on the battle-field,
They bravely faced the storms and fought their foes,
Until their leader fell with glory crowned.
Then, turning from the conflict with sad hearts,
They mourned the loss their country had sustained;
While tears of grief froze on their manly cheeks,
And gnawing hunger fed upon their strength.
'Twas sad to know Montgomery was dead;
Far more than sad to know that his shed blood
Had failed to waken in Canadian hearts
Longings for liberty and civil rights.
Staining the frozen snow with bleeding feet,
Southward their melancholy march began.
Perhaps 'tis well the expedition failed.
Untrained in freedom's Anglo-Saxon school,
Canadians have not learned the patriots' lore;
Their undrilled, slow-paced feet could not keep step
With freedom's rapid march to high renown.

But south of the St. Lawrence and the lakes
All things are ripe for independence now.

Michael. How fares the army led by Washington?
Raphael, we wait to hear what you have seen.

Raphael. Michael, the great commander took his place
At duty's call more than a year ago.
Brave, stalwart men gathered in multitudes
To do his bidding with alacrity,
Or follow where he led against the foe.
But ammunition could not be obtained;
The summer passed, autumn and winter came
With only preparations for the strife.
He held the foe in Boston prison bounds,
With no way of escape but by the sea;
Yet was himself fettered by scarcity
Of balls and powder for the coming fight.
At last, in March, the royalists, alarmed,
Saw on the lofty heights of Dorchester
Artillery to belch forth fiery death,
And drive them from the city they oppressed.
Nothing remained to them but swift retreat.
Boston, set free, is gay and jubilant,
While all New England independence claims.
The patriot army proud of its success,
Hopes soon to drive the English o'er the sea.

Michael. Such baseless hopes should not be entertained.
I know that they deceive not Washington.

Raphael. The thoughtful leader scans most carefully
Each movement of his country's enemies;
He knows the conflict must be desperate.
Though crowned with laurels and by millions praised,
Boston's retreat and Charleston's brave repulse
Show him no easy path to liberty.
Keen vigilance, untiring energy,
And patient, persevering, faithful toil
Are all devoted to his country's cause.

Ariel. His countrymen must rally to his help,
Or all his efforts will be made in vain.
King George demands more armaments and men:
Twenty-five thousand brawny Englishmen;
Of hireling Hessians, fresh from Germany,
Seventeen thousand, drilled and officered;
Of silly Tories and of savage tribes
No man has numbered the vast multitudes
That England's treasury can arm for war.
To meet those countless foes the patriot chief,
In his glad hours of wonderful success,
Has only twenty-seven thousand men.
How many will stand by him in defeat,
Time yet must test by stern adversity.

Ithuriel. You spoke of a commissioner from France,
Who tendered help in money, arms, and stores.

Abdiel. France, jealous of Britannia's growing strength,
Stands with her millions ready to take part
In all that tends to lay her rival low.

Gabriel. This French alliance gives well-grounded hopes
Of speedy independence for these States.

Michael. Long months ago Virginia and the South
Severed all ties that bound them to the king.
New England still defies his Majesty.
The slow-paced patriots of these Middle States
Hold back their more enthusiastic friends.
They need angelic aid: let us assist.
Go thou, Ithuriel, to the hypocrites
Who only feign a love for liberty.
Expose their sordid, base hypocrisy;
Tear off their masks, and treat them with contempt.
Go, Abdiel, to the men who hesitate.
Rouse them to prompt, immediate action now.
Zephon, timidity demands your help.
Fill the faint-hearted with courageous thoughts.
Raphael, the great committee needs your aid
To have the declaration formed aright,

Not only as to principles and words,
But see that no expression gives offense
To any of the wise contracting States.
The slave trade is denounced in such strong terms
As Georgia never will consent to use;
Nor will New England thus condemn her sons
For trafficking in human flesh and blood.
One wants the slaves to cultivate her lands;
The other wants the profits of the trade.
The Carolinas, too, would like to have
Some changes made in those offensive words;
So Jefferson must alter those bold lines,
Or else for peace must let them be expunged.
Gabriel, to patriot, John Adams, go!
Touch with celestial fire his lips and tongue;
Give him the spirit of convincing speech,
The eloquence that men cannot resist,
That Congress may be carried as by storm.
At 2 o'clock to-morrow let us meet.

Independence Square, Philadelphia, 2 o'clock, July 4, 1776. MICHAEL, GABRIEL, ABDIEL, ITHURIEL, ZEPHON, RAPHAEL, ARIEL.

Gabriel. Comrades, the Congress now begins to vote.
The great decision soon will be made known.
John Adams was most eloquent of men:
They could not but agree to all he said.

Michael. The bell of liberty begins to sound;
The people cry aloud in tones of joy:
"Give praise to God! 'Tis Independence Day!"

BOOK FOURTH

Scene: *Trenton, N. J., December 25, 1776.* GABRIEL, UZZIEL,
ITHURIEL, RAPHAEL.

Raphael. 'Tis a sad Christmas to Americans.
Of late discouragements have been their fate.
Last August thirty thousand enemies
Drove them across Long Island, with the loss
Of a full thousand valiant fighting men.
With muffled oars they hastened to New York;
Thence up to Harlem Heights, from which they saw
Five hundred blazing homes to light their way.
Fort Washington, with its brave garrison,
Surrendered in November to the foe:
Its thousands, in vile pestilential cells,
Await their death. Fort Lee was left in haste;
Its stores were lost. The army, driv'n with speed
Across New Jersey to the Delaware,
Seized all the boats and to the other shore
In safety crossed with but three thousand men.

Ithuriel. Charles Lee was ordered to conduct his men
With haste to join the troops of Washington;
But he—vain marplot of his chieftain's plans—
Was taken by the British to New York.
He's more a Briton than American;
His army, led by Sullivan, escaped,
And joined the standard of their honored chief.
The patriots now can claim six thousand men.
Congress has fled from Philadelphia,
At Baltimore votes dictatorial power
To Washington, that he may save their cause.

Uzziel. Prospects, indeed, seem gloomy in this land.
Its destiny depends upon one man—
Upon his honor and capacity.

Who saves his country from a foreign foe
Is tempted much to save it for himself;
Or if he cannot grasp the highest prize,
And seat himself upon a despot's throne,
May he not use his sword to force a peace,
And for it claim at least the second place
In the great government that he makes strong?
He may play Cæsar if not Gen'ral Monk;
If not an emperor, a British peer.

Ithuriel. 'Twas not Virginia air that Cæsar breathed:
'Twas no Virginia mother nourished Monk.
True to his country, Washington will stand
Firm as the mountains of his native land.

Uzziel. Suspect not Washington of treachery;
Doubt not but he will do what man can do,
But when an ice-bridge spans the Delaware,
What shall hold back the British from their prey?
Then they must yield to Britain or to death,
Because the country has been so subdued
That Cornwallis starts off for Europe soon,
And Howe expects a Philadelphia home.
What think you, Gabriel, of the prospect now?

Gabriel. 'Tis desperate indeed; but Washington
Still leads his ragged troops from place to place;
Upon his side, by pow'r divine arrayed,
Are all of Europe's selfish jealousies;
Old ocean's ev'ry wave and ev'ry gale;
The deep, broad rivers of his native land—
Their ice-clad torrents and their sunny floods;
They've been his playmates from his joyous youth,
Are now his allies hast'ning to his help;
They shield him from the fury of his foes.
In league with these his country's hills and vales,
Her lofty mountains, and her fertile plains,
With all their grand majestic distances,
Fight freedom's battles in her hour of need.
Then millions of brave hearts and ready hands
Pledge each red drop that pulsates in the veins
Of liberty's unconquerable sons

To the defense of home and native land.
But best of all, his trust is in our God.
Hark! hark! what sounds are those that strike the ear?
The noise of battle floats upon the breeze;
The hated Hessians wake to meet their fate.

. . . .

At the first onset, Rahl, their leader, fell.
They die, they bleed, they beg, they plead for life.
A few on horseback fled to Bordenton,
But Trenton's garrison are prisoners,
Of death or of the troops of Washington.
The living, bound, are hurried o'er the waves
Expecting death in some most horrid form,
From men they have been told are cannibals.
There's Sullivan, there's Greene, there's Washington.
Last night they fought the fury of the storm,
The floating ice, the chilling, white-capped waves;
This morning marched to meet a sleeping foe.
Now, crowned with vict'ry, cross the Delaware,
Secure their pris'ners and their spoils of war.
This daring deed will shake the British Isle
From its strong confidence of victory.
'Twill kindle hope in ev'ry patriot's heart,
And nerve the arms of freemen for the strife.

Scene: *Princeton, N. J., at day-break, January 4, 1777.* GABRIEL, ABDIEL, ITHURIEL, UZZIEL, RAPHAEL.

Uzziel. Why wait we here? Trenton demands our care!
'Tis there the war-cloud frowns most gloomily.
There Hessians, waking from the sluggish sleep
That followed their coarse Christmas revelry,
Found Washington had crossed the Delaware
To kill or capture Trenton's garrison.
More than two thousand fell or fled away,
Or passed as captives o'er the broad, rough stream.
If the great chief had watched his prisoners,
And kept his troops on Pennsylvania ground,
He would have shunned the peril he is in;
But he returned to Trenton, and has found
Cornwallis hastening to capture him.

Raphael. By thousands British troops do concentrate
To capture Washington and end the war.
They have him where they long have wanted him,
And now can pounce upon their noble prey.
He and his troops seem hopelessly entrapped.

Abdiel. Cornwallis led from this place troops enough
To crush the little army he opposed;
They fought there yesterday till dark came down.
This morning larger numbers march from here.
They start for Trenton by the break of day.

Ithuriel. To make sure work they gather from all points,
And hope to capture full five thousand men,
With Washington and his best generals.
What noise is that waking the villagers?
The sound of battle on these classic grounds
Is startling even to an angel's ear.
Gabriel, can you inform us what it means?

Gabriel. It means the British army has been left
To beat the air in Trenton this cold day;
While Washington surprises thousands here,
And strikes the bravest of their vet'rans down.
He kept his camp-fires blazing and marched round
The num'rous army of his pow'rful foes.
The unsuspecting Princeton troops are brave;
They, with their bright and bristling bayonets,
Drive raw recruits before them from the field.
But Mercer leads his valiant veterans
And turns the bloody tide of battle back.
He falls—the conflict rages fearfully;
Death riots on the bravest of the brave,
And victory, bewildered, hesitates
To crown the brave, unflinching combatants.
But hark! A voice rings out upon the air
That stirs in patriots resistless might;
Its tones are heard where leaden hail falls fast,
And sulphurous smoke hides human forms from sight.
The target of ten thousand well-aimed balls
Cannot escape by any human means.

Abdiel, thy shield throw round him, or he falls:
Its heavenly temper from destruction saves.

. . . .

The morning breeze lifts up the stifling smoke,
And shows the bloody battle nobly won.
The British line in wild disorder broke
Before the valiant charge of Washington.
Well may that steed prance proudly o'er the field,
Displaying more of matchless majesty
Than all past ages ever yet did yield;
More virtue, valor, Christian chivalry!

Scene: *Saratoga, N. Y., October 17, 1777.* MICHAEL, ITHURIEL, ZEPHON.

Ithuriel. There is a cheering sight to kindle joy
In ev'ry home of all these colonies!
Burgoyne, in June, marched with ten thousand men,
Well-armed and well-equipped for camp or field.
At his approach the patriots fled away
From their strong places and their army stores;
But bold John Stark at Bennington, Vermont,
Whipped two detachments of his bravest men.
His Indian allies have deserted him.
Two recent battles brought defeat and loss.
Within three days starvation's work begins,
And there remains no way by which t' escape.
This mighty army now capitulates.
The proud Burgoyne, with his six thousand braves,
And six wise members of the Parliament,
Surrender to the rustic colonists.
They, with themselves, give up abundant stores,
With ammunition for the next campaign;
Five thousand muskets, forty-two brass guns,
And, worst of all, the prestige of success.

Zephon. The news of this humiliating stroke
Will startle Britain like an earthquake shock,
And make her monarch tremble on his throne.
'Twill strengthen Franklin at the court of France.
And bring about a formal alliance.

Ithuriel. Will this bring independence, peace, and joy?

Michael. Not now. Britannia claims the right to tax,
And in all cases whatsoever rule.
When the sad news of this calamity
Comes to King George, it may dethrone his mind,
But will not change his policy at all.
His right to govern people as he wills
Must not be questioned by the colonists.
Rather than this England's last ship and her last
    regiment
Must cross the ocean to keep up the fight.
When Holland, France, and Spain shall be combined
To fight the battles of her colonies,
England may wake from her delusive dreams
Of subjugation to her heavy yoke.
At present British troops claim victories
Upon the Delaware. They drive away
From Philadelphia the Congressmen.
The names of Germantown and Brandywine,
Waking sad memories in patriots,
Will, to the king and ministers, give hope
Of final victory for British arms,
And cause the flame of war to still blaze on.
The conq'rors and the conquered come this way.
What pity they should shed each other's blood!
There's Gates, there's Morgan, Starke of Bennington.
See Schuyler, Lincoln, Arnold, and St. Clair.
There Kosciusko, the brave Polander;
And there's Burgoyne, with captive officers.

Scene: *Near Monmouth, N. J., June 21, 1778.* SATAN, MARS, BAAL,
    MOLOCH, MAMMON, BELIAL.

Satan. How fare my trusty friends? How goes the
    war?
Mars. The British have lost Boston since we met;
In their attack on Charleston been repulsed;
By battles near to Brooklyn and New York
Compelled the patr'ts to retreat in haste
Across New Jersey to the Delaware,
With but three thousand ragged warriors.
The patriot chief passed o'er that freezing stream,
Leaving no boats by which his foes might cross.

The Congress fled away to Baltimore,
Giving the General dictatorial power.
Joined by a few recruits, he turned again,
Pressed on through floating ice, surprised his foes,
Defeated them, sent to the Southern shore
His numerous captives; crossed the stream again,
As if to court defeat. His feeble force
Faced a strong army and defied its pow'r;
Skirmished a day with varying success,
But, with his camp-fires burning, marched by night
To strike with consternation other foes.
Full thirteen miles away at dawn of day.
Trenton and Princeton furnished battle-fields
On which the pride of Britain was brought low.
Then came the time for haughty royalists
To flee before their ragged enemies.
Before another year had passed away
Ships bore the Britons up the Chesapeake.
At Brandywine the patriots were whipped;
At Germantown repulsed with fearful loss.
Again the Congress fled. Howe and his hosts
Seized Philadelphia, and gave several months
To merry revelry, with now and then
Heroic work, burning defenseless homes.
The patriots, meanwhile, at Valley Forge,
Half starved, half clad, unshod, stained with their blood
The snow on which they trod. But when spring came,
Reports of help from France passed through the camp,
Infusing hope and joy where suff'ring reigned.
Howe and his troops forsook their city friends,
And sought a way of safety toward the sea.
'Tis nearly time that they should pass this way.
Of Saratoga and the British force
That there surrendered you have long since heard.
I need not speak of Gates or of Burgoyne.
Thus much about the progress of the war.
What has been done in other fields of fame?

Belial. At Philadelphia, I have long held sway
O'er all the victims of degrading vice,
And many of the lofty I've debased.

Baal. Yes, not a few of the polite, the proud,
The rich, the gay, the great have fallen low,
Unhappy victims of base viciousness.
In their humiliation I delight.

Moloch. With fiendish satisfaction I have watched
The starving, freezing troops at Valley Forge,
And, gloating over Washington's distress,
Have wondered how much anguish he could bear.

Mammon. I too have done my part to crush the chief,
By tempting the most covetous to hoard
What might have bought supplies for freezing men.

Satan. A bolder, more destructive work was mine:
I turned the hearts of patriots from their chief,
And undermined their confidence in him;
Not in his virtues, but his generalship.
I told of Gates and his great victory,
Of proud Charles Lee and his accomplishments;
I led them to desire a daring chief,
Ready to take great risks and end the strife.
I puffed up Conway, with such self-conceit
That even he aspired to leadership.
The simpleton deceived and led astray
Some of the purest of the patriots.
But mortifying failure marred our plans.
The patriot leader, proof against our plots,
Sublimely tow'red above all rivalry.
But proud old Lee, still under my control,
Will sorely vex the chieftain here to-day.
I hear the booming of artillery.
Ha! ha! The tide of battle flows this way!

Mars. Hold, Satan, I must mingle in this fight!

Moloch. And I must gloat upon the sufferings
Of thousands battling on this sultry day.

Mammon. I go to gather up the spoils of war.

Belial. And I to riot amid vilest deeds.

Satan. In full retreat the Continentals come.
Charles Lee has done as I instructed him.
An English heart beats warmly in his breast;
'Tis full of rage at Washington to-day.
And yonder comes the chief to meet the foe.
He checks and turns retreating soldiery.
'Tis British troops now haste in mad retreat:
But what a vision breaks upon my view
As Washington meets Lee! Never have I
Seen such a countenance since Michael frowned
On me in our first conflict on the hills
Of my own native heav'n! Sublimely grand,
He rides in manly majesty. Sternness,
Severity, heroic rage, reproof,
Rebuke, and lofty indignation blend
With high authority in the great chief,
As he, in startling thunder tones exclaims:
"Halt, Gen'ral Lee! In God's great name I ask
Why all this ill-timed prudence here to-day?"
Lee, with insulting nonchalance, replied:
"Unless reports be false, no man has more
Of that rascally virtue than yourself."
"Go to the rear, insulting miscreant, go!"
So said the chief. "Let all the brave, the true
Forward with me to glorious victory."
Forward they go, Lafayette, Sullivan,
Charles Scott, and other heroes with their chief,
Sweeping before them England's veterans.

Scene: *Louisville, Ky., Falls of the Ohio. Sunset, July 30, 1778.*
RAPHAEL, ZEPHON, ARIEL.

Ariel. Comrades, from yonder lofty ridge is seen
A landscape, the most grand and beautiful
That charms the eye or melts the heart of man.
Th' encircling hills, radiant in sunset hues,
Seem piled in grandeur to protect from harm
God's loveliest children in this paradise.
That matchless river flows like molten gold
Between bright shores of greenest emerald,
Bedecked with flowers and enriched with fruits.

'Tis here shall rise, in the blest years to come,
Homes of the beautiful, the pure, the brave,
Of maids most amiable, and men most true.

Zephon. What men are these who seem to come from far,
Toil-worn, yet joyful, to these rustic homes?
List to their shouts of triumph as they come!
The town pours forth its happy denizens
With glad congratulations on their tongues.
See the young prattlers claim a father's kiss,
And stalwart men press loved ones to their hearts.
See joyful tears streaming from sparkling eyes,
And love's own blushes glow on beauty's cheek!
What makes these people all so jubilant?

Raphael. These are Virginia's brave and daring sons,
Sent forth by her to wrest from enemies
The broad domain that has been hers of right
Nearly two centuries, and still is hers.
Uncanceled royal charters, oft renewed,
Confirmed her title over all these lands
From the Atlantic to Pacific's coast.
When France intruded, her indignant sons
Drove the proud Frenchmen from their heritage.
When George the Third stretched Canada this way
To check the spread of freedom in the West,
They drove the land thieves of the king away
In spite of all the claims of royalty.
The Western forts surrendered by the French
Have all been used by British cruelty
To arm the Indians for a deadly strife
That spared not infancy nor womanhood.
But these frontiersmen, at Virginia's call,
Subdued her foes, and by their valor won
The nascent empire she had well-nigh lost.
The garrisons, surprised, laid down their arms,
Surrendering to rightful ownership
The vast, unmeasured region that extends
From where the mighty rivers of the West
Unite to seek the Gulf in company,

Up the broad streams each to its distant source,
With space for eighty millions of the free
To dwell securely through all coming time.
No wonder, then, that heroes such as these
Receive the plaudits of their countrymen
And wear fame's brightest, greenest laurel wreaths.
Behold George Rogers Clarke, fame's fav'rite son!

Scene: *Savannah, Ga., October 8, 1779.* SATAN, MARS, MOLOCH, BELIAL.

Mars. The dilatory tactics of these times
Fill lofty spirits with intense disgust.
Two warlike nations, mightiest of earth,
Have been at war for two and twenty months
Without a battle worthy of the name.
Their mighty fleets, though well-equipped and manned,
Avoid each other with great carefulness.
The fear of storms excuses cowardice.
Howe left the Delaware and sought New York;
D'Estaing sailed into Newport, but sailed out
Without a fight except with waves and winds;
Then sailed to Boston to repair his ships.
Leaving the Yankee army without help,
T'' escape from enemies as best they could.
The cautious Frenchman with his ships is here;
Six thousand fighting men obey his voice.
As many Carolinians are in arms,
But the slow movements of their officers
Forbid the expectation of success.
Meanwhile the war, if war it may be called,
Drags its slow movements wearily along.

Moloch. Mars, you should not belittle this great war.
Have not the Butlers led the savages
To desolate Wyoming, and destroy
A thousand happy Pennsylvania homes?
Have they not given to the greedy flames
New York's most peaceful, prosp'rous western towns?
Did not the patriots retaliate
By burning forty Indian villages?

Belial. Yes, Mars, the torch performed most brilliant
   deeds
At Norfolk, Portsmouth, and along the shores
Of the broad Chesapeake. Connecticut
Beheld the lurid flames that lighted up
Norwalk, Fairfield, and other coast-wise towns;
While cruel Tryon gazed and rocked and laughed.

Mars. That was not war. 'Twas arson, murder, theft,
Barbaric outrages on helplessness.
For deeds like these does Britain's Parliament
Vote twenty millions sterling and call out
Thirty-five thousand troops, and of marines
Eighty-five thousand more? In olden times
My heathen heroes made no wars on babes.
Men armed for battle were the foes they struck.

Satan. But, Mars, whatever hurts the human race
Gives satisfaction to malicious hate.
You say that burning dwellings is not war;
That killing babes and women is not war.
When Piggott was repulsed by Sullivan,
Losing three hundred of his bravest troops,
Was not that war? When Wayne, at Stony Point,
Conquered six hundred men and took their stores,
Destroyed their fort and bore its treasures off—
Was such a use of bayonets not war?
When Major Lee with some militia-men
Attacked the Jersey City garrison
And saw two hundred of them bite the dust,
Was not that war? Ask the whipped Tories if
It was not war that Pickens waged on them
When, near Broad River, hundreds of them fell.
What was it, if not war, when Prevost and
His forces took Fort Sunbury; when
Campbell took Augusta and Savannah?
What mean these ships, these soldiers, and marines?
They all mean war, as you shall soon admit.
These are not cowards: steadily they march
To storm the fort and drive the British out
Or die in the attempt. There is D'Estaing,

And there Pulaski, bravest of the Poles.
See Lincoln leads his Carolinians!
They vie with the brave French in gallantry.
There Sergeant Jasper hastens to the front.
The flags of France float proudly on the wall;
The banners of the patr'ts, too, are there.
But, see, the redcoats hurl them down in haste!
Pulaski falls, and Jasper, too, is slain;
D'Estaing is wounded; Britons hold the fort!

Scene: *Bank of Hudson River, September 24, 1780.* SATAN, MAMMON, BELIAL.

Mammon. What say you, Satan, to my grand campaign?
I have, without a musket or a man,
Injured the patr'ts more than tongue can tell.
Clinton, Cornwallis, Rawdon, Tarleton, Howe,
With all their troops and all their mighty fleets,
Boast no achievements equal to my own.
I have locked up the treasuries of States
Against the pressing needs of starving men,
Who battle bravely to protect their homes.
Their great commander pleads, but pleads in vain:
The miserly and covetous have joined
To paralyze the armies he commands.
Co-operation with the French is vain
Unless supplies enable troops to march
With those brave allies 'gainst the common foe.
The patriot heroes can defy armed men;
But shrink from want, starvation, nakedness
Into the rav'ning jaws of greedy graves.
The twelfth of May saw gallant Charleston fall,
Amid the thunders of two hundred guns.
Gates lost a thousand men on Camden's field;
Four thousand more were driven to their homes
By destitution's cruel tyranny.
Georgia lies prostrate at Britannia's feet:
South Carolinia trembles in her chains,
And ruin riots among Southern homes.
Give me due credit for my wondrous work.

Satan. You have my thanks for your great usefulness.

Mammon. But more I claim for labors at the North.
I've stirred the bravest troops to mutiny;
I've led to treason gifted officers.
Arnold has sold himself for paltry gold;
Britain pays down to him ten thousand pounds,
With the commission of a brigadier.
Suspicion, scowling, stalks through patriot camps,
Driving before her confidence and love.
What say you, comrades, of my great success?

Belial. I say 'twas I led Arnold to sell out.
He has with me been " Hail-fellow, well met,"
Until in morals bankrupt, he is lost.
But there he goes with Andre by his side.
They part; Andre comes nearer. See him now
Arrested by three men. He has betrayed
And overthrown himself by his mistake.
He tries to bribe his captors, but in vain.
Yes, there are Paulding, Williams, and VanWert,
Patterns of valor and fidelity,
With Andre, victim of base Arnold's guilt.

Scene: *Eutaw Springs, S. C., September 18, 1781.* GABRIEL, ARIEL.

Ariel. I watch to-day o'er pious Marion.
But what brings hither mighty Gabriel?
Words fail to tell how glad I am to meet
The honored leader of angelic bands,
The trusted guardian of most prosp'rous States.

Gabriel. I watch the closing conflicts of the war.
Light breaks upon the suff'ring colonies.
'Twill not be long till British troops retire,
Leaving the blessing of self-government
To the brave heroes of America.
I've watched the struggle since it first began;
With deep displeasure seen the cruelties
Inflicted by the British on their foes.
Of late the traitor Arnold led the fiends,
First in Virginia, then Connecticut
Was made to suffer by her recreant son.
Last January Tarleton fell upon
Morgan's division of the troops of Greene.

'Twas at the Cowpens. Furious was the fight.
The cavalry of William Washington
Was hurled at Tarleton with resistless force.
Wounded and whipped, he fled with haste and speed,
Leaving a hundred dead upon the field.
More than five hundred were made prisoners
With muskets and artillery and stores.
Cornwallis hastened to retrieve his loss,
But Greene retreated with his prisoners,
Crossed the Catawba, Yadkin, and the Dan,
Saved by the rains from fast pursuing foes.
Then, turning on his track, recrossed the Dan,
Sent Light Horse Harry Lee to find and take
Three hundred Tories who would Tarleton join.
At Guilford Court-house Cornwallis and Greene
Fought fiercely, but without a victory.
The Britons, loudly boasting, marched away,
To practice arson, theft, and robbery,
Leaving Lord Rawdon to contend with Greene.
With Rawdon Greene has fought at Hobkirk's Hill,
Torn from him all the posts he held but three.
His lordship went to Charleston recently,
To aid Balfour in murd'ring General Hayne,
And Stewart leads the battle here to-day.
The fight begins; Greene is victorious.
But see! some hungry troops have broken ranks
To feast themselves upon the spoils of war!
A fearful error! Stewart now returns;
Fighting begins again; Stewart gains ground—
He holds the field. So much for discipline!
To-morrow will compel him to retreat.
Less than two months will bring the patriots
A triumph that will lead to final peace.
See! there is Greene; there's Light Horse Harry Lee;
Yonder is Pickens; Sumter comes this way;
And here is Marion, soldier and saint.

Scene: *Yorktown, Va., October 19, 1781. Ships and camps in full
view.* MICHAEL, GABRIEL, ABDIEL, RAPHAEL, ITHURIEL.

Michael. This is the day we've long desired to see.
All heaven is jubilant, and men rejoice.

Awe-stricken hell hears all her legions mourn
And send loud groans of anguish from her depths.
Defeat adds weight to galling, dark'ning chains
Of those to whom no gleam of hope remains;
No possibility of happiness,
But fearful looking for of fiery wrath.
Satan and his dark hosts are vanquished here,
Prelusive of their final vanquishment.

Ithuriel. Here England's king and all his royal court,
And tyranny, its lordlings and its tools,
In all the lands beneath the shining sun,
Are conquered by the people in their might,
Foreshadowing triumphant human rights
Wherever men shall live upon the earth.

Abdiel. Fraternity and fellowship and love
Crown on this spot the brotherhood of man,
As seen in Washington and Lafayette,
Uniting free America and France
Under the loving fatherhood of God,
Presaging that the family of Christ
Shall soon embrace the human family.

Michael. Gabriel, will you relate what brought to pass
This wondrous triumph of the patriots?

Gabriel. When France sent her brave troops and
  mighty fleets
High hopes of speedy vict'ry were indulged;
But failure at Savannah and Newport
Was sadd'ning and discouraging to all.
While Washington planned campaigns with the French,
Arnold, the traitor, sold himself for gold,
And bargained to deliver up West Point.
Some of the ragged, freezing, starving troops
Turned against Congress and their officers,
But not against the country that they loved;
For, when the British would have bribed with gold,
They seized the spies and gladly saw them hanged.
When this was told in Philadelphia,
Some gen'rous persons sent, for their relief,

Three hundred thousand dollars of their own.
More permanent provision for the troops
Was made by a French loan on liberal terms.
Then the great chief proposed to take New York,

LAFAYETTE AT YORKTOWN.

Concerting with the French about the time.
The enemy, informed of all the plans,
Made ready to repel the allied troops.
Just then Cornwallis left the farther south,

And through Virginia led marauding bands
With arson's torch and plunder's thieving hand.
To watch his movements, Lafayette was sent.
The young French hero hung upon the rear
Of his strong enemy. His watchful eye
Perceived the faulty tactics of his foe.
He hastened to entreat his willing chief
To march with speed and capture Cornwallis.
While Washington marched southward with his troops,
Clinton, deceived, still fortified New York,
And concentrated neighb'ring forces there.
He even ordered Cornwallis to march
Down toward the sea, in readiness to sail
With all his plunderers, to save New York.
Americans and French pursued with speed.
Meanwhile, French fleets drove off the British ships,
Entered York River, bringing troops and guns,
Leaving the British no way of escape.
The siege was pressed with vigor and with skill.
Such prodigies of valor were displayed
As men of later times will celebrate.
Young Hamilton and younger Lafayette
Inscribed their names high on the roll of fame,
While older chiefs looked on admiringly
As greenest laurels dropped on their own brows.
At last, when summer's suns and autumn's frosts
Had tinged the forests with celestial dyes,
And filled with plenty all Virginia's homes,
And all her pious hearts with gratitude,
She sees her heroes reap upon her fields
A harvest of her conquered enemies,
With redcoats gayer than her forest leaves,
And treasures richer than her soil could yield.
She sees, and songs of praise rise up to God,
Till rapturous devotion, jubilant,
Fills the whole universe with sounding praise.
Lift up your voices, first-born sons of God!
Praise him for liberty to Adam's race!

> *All the Angels.* "We laud and magnify the Lord Most High,

Who was and is the source of life and love,
Of earthly and of heavenly liberty."

Raphael. Tell us now, Gabr'el, what the patr'ts gain
By this surrender of their enemies?

Gabriel. Eight thousand prisoners lay down their arms,
And give up more than fivescore mighty guns;
Surrender treasure-chests and rich supplies,
Whether just stolen or brought o'er the sea;
But best of all, they independence gain.
See there! O'Hara leads the captives forth.

Abdiel. Where is Cornwallis, that he does not lead?

Ithuriel. The earl is meanly sulking in his tent;
Humiliation he's too weak to face;
But there is Tarleton, bold and saucy still,
There many who deserve a better fate.
There go the Hessians, subjects of a prince
Who sells his subjects to get paltry gold.
'Tis well for them that they are prisoners.
Here come the conquerors; they pass this way.
Behold the noble Frenchman, Rochambeau!
There is De Grasse, Viominel, Gouvion,
Rochfontaine, DuPortail, and many more;
And Lafayette, the noblest of the French.
Behold the ragged heroes of the line!
Kings of America, now crowned with joy,
And destined soon to see the heaven of home
And be enthroned in happy, loving hearts.
There's the militia of Virginia,
Led on by Nelson, their brave Governor.
To them this is indeed the day of days
That frees their commonwealth from plund'ring foes.
Still nearer to us here are officers
Whose names belong to everlasting fame.
There is young Laurens, there is Hamilton,
There Lincoln, Knox, there mighty Washington.

Michael. Let us depart for Philadelphia,
·To see how Congress will receive the news.

Scene: *Chestnut Street, Philadelphia, October 23, 1781. Moonlight.*
MICHAEL, GABRIEL, ABDIEL, RAPHAEL, ITHURIEL.

Raphael. A messenger from Yorktown has arrived,
And thrills the town with news of victory.

Abdiel. The clock strikes ten, but joy drives sleep away.
Hear the glad watchman who proclaims the hour!
" Past ten o'clock; Cornwallis is taken."

Ithuriel. All homes and hearts glow with intense delight,
While loving gratitude gives praise to God.

Gabriel. Peace, independence, and prosperity
Now seem to dance attendance on the throngs
That tell of this grand triumph of their arms.

Michael. To-morrow Congress will be jubilant,
And give expression to a nation's joy.
Let us attend and join in thanks to God.

Scene: *Lutheran Church, Philadelphia, October 24, 1781.* MICHAEL,
GABRIEL, RAPHAEL, ABDIEL, ITHURIEL.

Michael. To-day the Congress of America
Has crowned itself with glory and renown.
It honors God and humbly seeks his courts
To offer thanks and praise for victory
To him who rules the universe in love.

Abdiel. The country under his protecting care,
Must prosper as no nation ever did.

Raphael. While these wise, pious legislators come
To lay their honors at their Saviour's feet,
I'll write their names and bid angelic bands
Guard well their steps, and lead them to the skies.

Gabriel. I almost wish permission was obtained
To let them see their guardian-angels here
Uniting with them as they worship God.

Michael. On earth man must now live by faith, not sight;
Unclouded vision shall be his above.
We must to-day remain invisible.
Let us depart and make report on high.

Scene: *Annapolis, Md., December 26, 1783.* MICHAEL, GABRIEL, ABDIEL, ITHURIEL.

Michael. Comrades, our newborn nation now takes rank
Among earth's grandest, noblest, mightiest.

Gabriel. Reluctant Britain, a full year ago,
Consented to the freedom of her child.
September saw that freedom guaranteed
By formal treaty between Holland, Spain,
France, England, and these free United States.

Abdiel. Peace reigns. A month ago King George called back
His fiercest war-dogs to their kennel homes.
No yelping cur of all his pack is left
To howl around the dwellings of the free.

Ithuriel. Heroes of independence seek their homes
To toil for bread like other honest men.
The war-worn veterans and their great chief
With many tears bedewed the parting hour.
Honor and fame attend them as they go,
And grateful thousands gladly sing their praise.

Gabriel. Great Washington to-day gives up his sword;
The chief becomes a private citizen.
Earth never witnessed such a scene before.
This uncrowned hero wears such honors now
As never king nor emperor might claim.
Behold him in his last and greatest act.

Michael. I see the modest hero giving back
Not only the commission he received,
But with it liberty and equal rights
For millions through the ages yet to come;
A land from foreign domination free;
A bright example of unselfishness
Rebuking tyranny throughout the world;
A human character pure and complete,
Time's greatest product—earth's most noble man.

BOOK FIFTH.

Scene: *Philadelphia, August 15, 1787. The Federal Convention in session.* GABRIEL, RAPHAEL, ARIEL, ZEPHON, ZOPHIEL.

Gabriel. Comrades, this great convention hesitates
To give these States a stronger government.
All efforts to agree have thus far failed;
A perfect union is impossible,
But means must be devised to pay old debts
And such expenses as necessity
Demands from such a union of great States.

Ariel. 'Tis said that a small tax of five per cent
On tonnage and imported merchandise
Would be sufficient to pay all just claims
Against the Union's empty treasury;
But selfishness devises deep-laid schemes
By which each section may enrich itself,
While making others pay the Union's tax.

Zephon. Small States claim full equality with large;
The large demand, for numbers and for wealth,
Controlling power in the new government.
The South would count their num'rous slaves as men;
The North would tax those slaves as property.
"Leave commerce free," says the rich, sunny South;
"Tax foreign ships," says the poor, freezing North;
"Give us your trade; we want your patronage."
Three States want slaves brought here from Africa;
Others would gladly stop the hateful trade.

Zophiel. "State sovereignty!" cry Mason, Lee. Yates, Ames;
Wilson and King deny State sovereignty.
Charles Pinckney asks a negative on laws
Enacted by the wisdom of the States.

(90)

To this James Madison consents, but fears,
As Mason dreads and Lee foresees, taxes
By which the North shall rob the South.

Raphael. Ames dreads consolidation. Rufus King
Opposes his New England on that point;
He joins with Pinckney, Wilson, Hamilton,
And Morris to demand strong government.
Hamilton would have a life-long Senate,
Their sons to be successors to themselves;
A President for life, to dominate
All Governors of States. These Governors

BENJAMIN FRANKLIN.

To have a negative on all State laws.
He wants to do away with all the States,
And so perfect the general government
That it can work when States shall disappear.
The British Constitution he admires;
Hereditary aristocracy
To him seems necessary to success
In giving steadiness to governments;
Hopes that an aristocracy of wealth
Will save from ruin the fair land he loves,
Nor let it sink in ruins underneath
The numbers of its low democracy.

Can such contrary views be harmonized
In one great government for sovereign States?

 Gabriel. Franklin now bids them all seek help from
  God,
And help will come in this their time of need.
By Sherman and by Ellsworth reconciled,
The smaller and the larger States agree
That in the Senate they will equals be;
But in the House of Representatives
Numbers of population shall control.
On Hamilton's advice, slaves shall be taxed;
Their masters cast their votes for three of five.
New England wants protection for her ships
To profit by transporting Southern crops.
She also wants to trade her rum for slaves
And reap rich harvests from old Afric's sands.
Therefore for gain she will not hesitate
To contract in good faith and honesty
With Georgia and the Carolinas too,
To bring them all the negro slaves they want,
If they will vote with her for tonnage laws,
By which her ships may do the carrying.
The South will get just what she always had;
New England, wealth beyond all estimate,
A golden harvest through all coming time.

 Ariel. The advocates of a strong government
Will take all they can get, and when they can
Will give wealth's aristocracy a chance
To fetter poverty's democracy.
As to the friends of civil liberty,
And all the watchful guardians of State rights,
It will be truthfully and freely sworn
That they keep all they do not give away;
Yes, keep them wrapped in paper guarantees,
Till wealth, with shining fingers, shall untie;
The sword cut up in fragmentary scraps;
Wild factions throw them to the heedless winds;
Fanaticism give them to her flames;
And despotism laugh in freedom's face.

Zephon. Does God approve of union by such means,
Of governments based on duplicity,
Of overreaching and chicanery
By those who rule the millions of mankind?

Gabriel. 'Tis not that God approves, but man is free.
The selfishness of men forbids the best.
All seek their own at other men's expense,
While God says: "Love thy neighbor as thyself."
A choice of evils, man obtains at last
A selfish union, rather than fierce wars
Between the millions of divided States.
So Franklin thinks, and so thinks Washington.
The swindling statesmen cost simplicity
Less money than the honest soldiers cost;
And soldiers are not always honest men.
Then war brings arson, robbery, and theft,
Wounds, sickness, homelessness, and sudden death,
With barbarism to enlightened lands;
And widowhood and orphanage and woe,
And hatreds such as Satan cherishes.
The work of the convention will be done,
The Constitution sent to all the States
To be rejected or be ratified.
A day's work ended, statesmen now take rest.
The weary, anxious patriots pass this way.
See Franklin, Washington, Lee, Madison,
Ames, Gorham, Pinckney, Ellsworth, Hamilton!

Scene: *Richmond, Va., June 24, 1788.* SATAN.

Satan. This is the hour, this the appointed place
At which my brave compeers attend my court.
This day's decision settles destiny,
Determines boundaries of warring States,
Or makes one prosp'rous nation of them all.
From Hudson River to the Chesapeake,
The Constitution has been ratified.
'Tis rumored all New England wears the yoke.
Even if this be so, three warlike realms
Remain to stain the land with kindred blood.

Rhode Island and New York, like a keen wedge,
Cut through the heart of the North-eastern States.
North Carolina and Virginia stand
Like solid walls to fence out and exclude
The two great States that lie still farther south.
If I can hold them so, then ceaseless wars
Shall flood the land with carnage and distress.

[BAAL, MOLOCH, AZAZEL, MAMMON, AND CHEMOSH *approach.*]

All hail! My worthy, trusted, brave compeers,
Your presence is most cheering here to-day.
Baal, what say the States you visited?

Baal. They all agree. They vote to ratify.

Satan. Moloch, how vote the States to which you went?

Moloch. They have done likewise. All have ratified.

Satan. What say you, Chemosh, as to your two States?

Chemosh. Rhode Island and New York firmly refuse
To join in this new union of the States.
But Jay and Hamilton most actively
Persuade the people now to ratify,
Though they have all the elements that make
A prosp'rous, independent commonwealth.

Satan. What of New Hampshire? Tell us, Azazel,
If she still holds out independently?

Azazel. To the new union she at last accedes;
The Constitution she now ratifies.

Satan. Say, Mammon, what of Massachusetts now?

Mammon. I found there much distrust of the new plan.
They thought the smaller States had gained too much;
Dreaded consolidation, claimed State rights,
Feared fed'ral usurpation, and the loss
Of precious liberty by despotism.

Taxation seemed to terrify their minds.
They lauded pure religion, and professed
Hot indignation against slave-holding.
Indeed, so eloquent did they become,
So violent in speech, that I did hope
They would stand up to banish slavery,
Thus bringing on incessant, bloody wars.
But Gorham, Gore, King, Phillips, Pierce, and Ames
Proved that New England gained her tonnage laws
By contract with three Southern States for slaves.
'Twas said the treasure offered for the slaves
Was better for New England than the mines
Of rich Peru, with all their yellow gold.
This golden argument would have prevailed
If all the Africans that tread the earth
Had stood in clanking chains before their eyes.
Hancock's amendments were presented then
By Samuel Adams, the great patriot;
They were adopted. The Constitution
Then was ratified, and Massachusetts
Acceded to the Union in due form.

Satan. Azazel, what has Carolina done?

Azazel. South Carolina first opposed the plan;
With proud disdain frowned on its tyranny,
Could not intrust it with her liberty;
Said if she needs must serve, why meekly bow
Obedient to New England, rather than
Wear the yoke in service to old Britain.
Claimed freedom from oppressive tonnage laws.
I thought she would reject the odious scheme,
But Pinckney told them that the Middle States,
Including great Virginia, had denied
The right to import slaves in time to come,
But generous New England had agreed
To give them slaves for the next twenty years
If they would give the Fed'ral government
An unrestricted right to tax at will
All foreign tonnage for their benefit.
He told them that they gained the right to vote

For full three-fifths of all the slaves they owned;
That Fed'ral power could never take a slave,
But, on the contrary, all States were bound
To send back fugitives their masters claimed,
Thus giving to the masters' right in slaves
The guarantee of thirteen sovereignties,
And of the Federal government combined.
He told how Greene drove out their British foes
And gave protection to their families;
How, when six States tried hard to shut out slaves,
New England's potent hand let them come in.
This wakened gratitude. She gave them slaves;
They gave the pow'r to tax the tonnage of
The foreigner, and thus monopolize
The carrying trade. The Constitution
Then was ratified. South Carolina
Acceded to the Union with her slaves.

Satan. Then nine of these disjointed sovereignties,
With four between, will give six boundaries
On which fierce wars will rage incessantly.
To-day Virginia's fateful voice will speak.
If she accedes, the others will come in
And make the Union perfectly complete;
But if she does accede, she claims the right
To secede when bold usurpation frowns.
She claims for "States," and people of the States,
All powers not granted and by words conveyed
To the new government they now create;
Claims to protect her rights and all the rights
Of her posterity to latest times
By all the strong, time-tested muniments
Of civil liberty and equity.
But despots laugh at law. Majorities
Are most despotic despots. Only force
Wielded by States can shield from Fed'ral force
The prey of sectional majorities.
One-fourth of all the Governors of States,
Backed by their troops, might lay potential hands
On rampant tyranny and fraudful greed;
Might veto domineering, selfish hate,

And hold the robber section from its prey
Until a grave convention of the States
Shall, by a three-fourths vote, give legal force
To the obnoxious measure in dispute,
Or grant relief to the oppressed by law.
Virginia'll get whatever she demands,

PATRICK HENRY.

If she secures this mighty tribunate
A fourth to veto, till three-fourths confirm,
Our bloody schemes fail of accomplishment.
Such check on selfishness held by the States
Would counteract all swindling, fraudful schemes,
And take from demagogues disunion's plea.

It would perpetuate to latest times
The peaceful union of this happy land.
We must prevent the union if we can;
If not, then see that its defects provide
Grounds for our triumphs in the days to come.
Comrades, await me here, while I look in
On these wise Solons of the wilderness.

He goes. He returns.

How greedily they swallow Henry's words!
With what complete control he sways these men!
Not Cicero, nor great Demosthenes,
Nor modern Chatham e'er possessed such power
As this great backwoods sage and orator.
Like one inspired, the rustic statesman talks.
He tells the horrors of their coming fate
In such strong language that they seem to see
Angels bemoaning their sad destiny.

[*Aside.*] I'll make the talker a true prophet yet,
As later generations shall confess.
Yet, 'twill not do to longer let him speak,
Or he may tell of means t'avert their doom.
But how to stop the torrent of his words,
Or quench the lightning of his countenance,
I find not— Yes, his voice shall not be heard;
Am I not prince of all the pow'rs of air?
Will not the winds come swiftly at my call?
I'll raise a storm to shake the solid earth;
The frowning concave rend with fiery bolts;
All elemental forces shall be stirred
To threaten men with instantaneous death.
Ha, ha! Ha, ha! They flee as shrinking from
The wrath of the divine Omnipotent.
Howl on! howl on! destructive elements,
While, in my fiendish glee, I gloat upon
The ruin and destruction I have wrought.

GABRIEL *and other holy angels arrive.*

Gabriel. Satan, why this alarming, dreadful storm?

SATAN'S DESTRUCTIVE STORM. 99

Satan. Gabriel, I'm free. Your meddling insolence
Deserves no other answer. I do not
Move at any master's word. I will it.
You poor watch-dogs of creation slip your
Gilt collars, leave your locked kennels,
And come out to yelp at your superiors.

Gabriel. Call off those fearful winds from their wild
   work.
This moment let the dreadful tempest cease;
Then, if you will, rail on with idle breath—
Yes, in an instant hush the thunder's voice,
Or feel the horrors of the wrath to come.

The fiends retire, the storm ceases.

Resistless force o'erawes the universe.
Creation's subject to Omnipotence,
Infinite wisdom rules with perfect love.
Within encircling wisdom, love, and power
Is ample scope for largest liberty
In all the hosts of angels, men, and fiends.
Here all things work together for the good
Of loving, trusting children of the Lord.
But wretches who will never yield to love,
Must feel the force of a resistless pow'r
For the protection of the universe.
Comrades, depart. Go each to his great work.
I go to mine rejoicing in the Lord.

Scene: *Eminence commanding a view of New York, April 24, 1789.*
SATAN, MARS, BAAL, MOLOCH. *They all bow low to* SATAN *except* MARS.

Mars. Hail! mighty chief! At thy command we
   come,
Faithful to thee with all allegiance due,
To execute thy grand destructive plans.
We have left naught undone that could be done.
These hateful States, resisting all our arts,
Accede to the new union. They promise
In their government protection such as
The sons of men have never known before.

Hatreds of ages still inspire our zeal,
The centuries march on with stately steps,
But to give time for sleepless vigilance
To work the ruin of man's hateful race.

Satan. Comrades, ten thousand thanks for your past zeal,
Your perseverance, and your fortitude.
With us, defeats pave paths to victory.
Though conquered often, we are ne'er subdued.

Mars. But latterly your wisest plans all fail.
These times of peace show little of your pow'r.
Next week a quiet, prosp'rous time begins,
With warrior chiefs reclined on easy-chairs.

Satan. Be patient, Mars; hear what I have to say.
These Western gales of peace and liberty
Shall scatter dragon's teeth in Europe's soil,
And from that plenteous planting shall spring forth
Millions of armed men to stain with blood
The verdure of a thousand battle-fields,
And devastate a hundred thousand homes,
Filling the world with anguish and despair.
The French are getting ready for the fray
In which half of a world will be at strife.
That conflict shall convulse most mighty realms,
Pull down earth's grandest thrones and dynasties,
And raise up heroes whose astounding deeds
Shall overshadow Alexander's fame.

. . . .

But what if I should now predict fierce wars
Between descendants of Americans?
What if, in less than fourscore fleeting years,
With more than fiend-like fury these great States
Fly at each other, and, in reckless rage,
Forgetful of the compacts of their sires,
Tread in the dust their blood-bought liberties,
Claiming despotic pow'r for States o'er States,
And over all their subject citizens!
Then hear me now. I promise more than this.
In less than fourscore years millions of men

Armed and embattled, shall tread down State rights,
Slay civil liberty, trample on law,
Outrage humanity, and to the sick
Deny through dreary years the privilege
Of buying medicines to heal disease.
The thick green venom of the sections' hate
Shall turn to gall the sympathies of saints,
And give them an intense desire to kill.
When devastation shall have done his work,
And marked his steps by ruins, ashes, graves,
Hatred shall send the basest of his slaves
To rule, to ruin, and degrade the land.

Mars. Father of lies, this seems impossible.
I doubt your pow'r, deny your truthfulness.
All lies of all the ages become dwarfed
By this false promise of false Lucifer.
Peace holds the reins under this government.
How, then, can rampant war go forth to fight?

Satan. Am I to be insulted to my face?
I reign. Nor shall Olympian Jupiter,
Backed by his num'rous family of gods,
Presume to cast contempt upon my throne.
Another word and the proud god of war
By clanking fetters shall be here disgraced.
To you, intrusive wretch, I answer not.
I shall not deign to you another word.
To these adherents of my sovereign throne
I owe the revelation of my plans.
Know, then, that this new union of the States
Has faulty parts, weak and defective links,
Imperfect joints that grate discordantly.
Man's work is tested by the touch of time,
And by my scheming for its overthrow.
Each State is now a nation in itself:
The smallest would not yield its sovereignty;
But only certain pow'rs expressly named,
Most carefully retaining all the rest;
They would not give their work a nation's name.
Yet these united sovereignties create

A fed'ral sovereign stronger than themselves.
They put into its hands both purse and sword,
Then try to bind the giant with mere words.
Divided sovereignty—Fed'ral and State,
Moved by the hatreds that the sections feel,
With clashing interests shall meet force with force,
In such malignant, bloody, cruel wars
As nations all shall stand aghast to see.
Relentless hate of sections shall send forth
The well-armed millions of a continent
In deadly strife. Fathers shall slay their sons;
Sons strike down gray-haired sires; mothers shall see
Their cherished sons go forth as enemies,
Each to destroy his brother in the strife.
To test my strategy I now predict
That upstart insolence in seats of power
Will stigmatize as traitors infamous
Virginia's bravest, noblest, purest sons,
For daring to obey Virginia's laws,
On her own soil, defending her chaste homes.
Nay, more, fanatic faction in its rage
Will give its highest honors to the men
Who copy the vile conduct of Dunmore,
Cornwallis, Tarleton, Arnold, and the rest
In giving her possessions to the flames,
All in the name of faithful loyalty.
What say you, comrades, will that satisfy?

Baal. It will, it will. I'm fully satisfied.

Moloch. I too am more than fully satisfied.

Baal. Satan, you may expect my hearty help.

Moloch. I too will help to bring these things to pass.

Satan. My trusty comrades, take my hearty thanks,
And share the glory of my great success.
In you I see unyielding confidence,
Defiant boldness, dreading no defeat,
Over all foes expecting victory.
In ev'ry contest men must yield to us!
Did we not drive out of their paradise

Adam and Eve, parents of all the race?
Did we not lead the first of woman born
To slay his brother at the shrine of God?
Antediluvians became our prey,
Till God repented that he had made man,
And gave those bold transgressors to the flood.

GEORGE WASHINGTON.

The heirs of Noah soon became our slaves,
And when to mighty nations they had grown,
We led them to destroy themselves by sin.
For ages we have walked amid the gloom
Where once in grandeur mighty nations stood.

Tyre, Carthage, Thebes, Palmyra, Babylon
Like morning dreams have passed and ceased to be.
Jerusalem, Damascus, mighty Rome
Seem shadows of their own magnificence.
We shall live on through all earth's centuries,
And in the vigor of our youth shall see
This newest of the nations share their fate.

Scene: *Broadway, New York, April 30, 1789.* MICHAEL, GABRIEL.

Michael. I bring congratulations from the skies
On the successful issue of our plans.
Our youthful nation crowns itself to-day
With governmental glory such as earth
Through all her centuries has never seen.

Gabriel. I thank you for your plaudits, worthy prince.
Great Washington comes at his country's call
To rule her factions or to fight her foes;
While Jefferson, Knox, Randolph, Hamilton
Will give wise counsels to their honored chief.
John Adams in the Senate will preside,
Ready to fill a more important place,
And Jay judge wisely in the highest court.
But see! They come, and with them Livingston,
New York's great chancellor. The book of God
There gives validity to the great oath
Which Livingston administers in form,
And Washington so solemnly assumes.
Imperial diadem or royal crown
Could add no dignity to that great man
Assuming obligations here to-day.
The thund'ring cannon makes the welkin ring,
The people cheer, the hosts of heaven rejoice,
And the great God looks on approvingly.

Scene: *State-house yard, Philadelphia, October, 1791.* SATAN, MO-
LOCH, BELIAL, MAMMON.

Satan. Once more of our achievements we may speak,
And tell of our great vict'ries over men.

Moloch. I have been stirring France to deeds of blood
That soon shall startle and amaze mankind.

Belial. And I have helped the savages to slay
The troops of Harmar, Hardin, and St. Clair,
Beyond Ohio's stream in Western wilds.

Mammon. My work has been with those who death
  distill
In Massachusetts and among the hills
Of Pennsylvania, on her sparkling streams.
My rum and whisky clients hate all laws,
Regard not man, nor do they honor God;
But Light Horse Harry Lee with Fed'ral troops
Compelled the whisky boys t' obey the law.

Satan. I have stirred strife to trouble Washington.
'Twas natural that soldiers should demand
A vig'rous government to raise supplies
Which cautious statesmen might be slow to yield.
So Hamilton most honestly desired
More pow'r for Fed'ral hands than States would grant.
I tempt him now to seize the pow'rs he wants,
And claim that though not granted, they're implied,
Or else necessitated by the force
Of public policy or dire distress.
So he creates a bank —assumes State debts
Held by the thrifty North. By tonnage laws
And tariffs robs the South, and in the North
Builds the rich aristocracy he wants
To make a strong and stable government,
According to his fav'rite theory.
Happ'ly for my success, great Jefferson
Is Southern born and of the planter class.
By the great Declaration which he wrote,
Pledged to the common people of the land,
Friend of State rights and human liberty.
Already factions gather round these men,
And vex the righteous soul of Washington.
Through many generations I will make
Their names the rallying cries of North and South,
Of speculators or of laborers,
Of State rights or of strong, rash government,
Till Fed'ral force strikes down resisting States,

And bloated wealth strides proudly o'er the poor.
I hope to bring the strifes of Europe here,
With a French party claiming Jefferson,
And England's friends supporting Hamilton.
What say you to the working of my plans?

All. Go on! go on! You have our hearty help.

Scene: *Boston Common, July, 1792.* RAPHAEL, ABDIEL.

Abdiel. Servant of God and guardian of mankind,
What loving deed has brought you here to-day?

Raphael. See you those horsemen? I attend on them.
They go to Lynn on business of our king.

Abdiel. Whence come they? On what business do they come?

Raphael. Sons of the South. New England needs them now.
With loving hearts they come to bring relief.
Their fathers sent to Boston rich supplies
When Britain would have starved her citizens,
Then came with Washington to fight her foes,
And drive the haughty Britons from her shores.
So these most gen'rous, loving Southerners
Bring to New England richer, costlier gifts,
And bolder heroes to fight fiercer foes.
There's Jesse Lee, Virginia's noble son;
He is the leader of this gallant band.
There's John, his brother, victim of disease,
Who soon shall gain his crown of victory.
From Maryland comes Freeborn Garretson
And brave George Roberts. From Delaware see
Bold Nathaniel Mills. From distant Georgia
Eloquent Hope Hull, and by his side is
Bishop Asbury, with Smith and Allen.
These men of God bring simple gospel truth
To vanquish errors which blight Churches here.
Sons of the Plymouth pilgrims leave the faith

Of their renowned forefathers, and take up
The cast-off heresies of other lands,
Deny divinity to Jesus Christ,
Say that redemption came not by his blood;
Deny that God, the Holy Spirit, works
In quick'ning, cleansing, sanctifying men;
Claim holiness by nature, not by grace;
Expect salvation by their own good works,
Or claim for scoffing men a home in heaven,
With naught of penitence or prayer or faith;
Would place Confucius by the side of Christ,
And think they stretch their charity to hope
That through the coming ages Christ may rise
To the high level of a Boston sage.

Abdiel. Say, Raphael, how did educated men
Such transcendental nonsense here embrace?

Raphael. Their fathers taught that God had fore-or-
 dained
Whatever comes to pass throughout all time,
And yet is not the author of a sin;
That God is love, and yet sends babes to hell;
That one cannot be added to the saved,
Nor one diminished from the Lord's elect,
Yet men are blamed for failing to be saved.
These contradictions trouble not the Scotch,
But Yankee brains ask: "How can these things be?"
Disdainfully they throw away the creed
Of their forefathers taught by Augustine;
Its truthful parts despise more than the false;
Then boasting of their learning and their wit.
Their fancied wisdom makes them Satan's dupes.
Of course the same gross errors suit not all,
Nor yet the same wise persons all the time;
Nor do they all cease to be Puritans,
But they are so stampeded by affright
At Calvin's errors, they'll take any thing
To get away from the divine decrees.
Socinus, Arius, or Pelagius,
The pope, Confucius, Brahma, or Buddha,

From Calvinism seem to be relief.
But from the South comes help in time of need.
New England's altar fires shall blaze again,
Lit by the torch of truth in Southern hands.
Sons of the Puritans shall hail with joy
The coming of these gospel cavaliers.
Men call them Methodists. Two years ago
Lee left his Southern home and hither came.

MARTHA WASHINGTON.

A thousand converts welcome them to-day,
And aid them in their efforts to do good.
Last week reluctant Boston warmed with love
And organized a zealous, holy Church.
Ten thousand such shall soon illume this land
With pure religion's brightest, hallowed flames,
And send to distant nations light and love
For those who grope in darkness and distress.

Scene: *Philadelphia, June 10, 1795.* BAAL, MARS, SATAN, MAMMON.

Baal. What say you, Mars, to Satan's schemes and
    plans,
Since you have seen how perfectly they work?

Mars. Let him go on. His tactics I admire.
I gladly follow his bold leadership.
I now retract my disrespectful words.
Europe will fight for the next twenty years,
And I shall revel amid bloody wars.

Satan. And these young lambs shall be old Europe's
    prey,
Devoured among her greedy, hungry wolves,
Unless the heav'nly pow'rs aid Washington.
Already Jefferson and Hamilton
Have left the cabinet for private life;
The people are for Britain or for France,
And ready to take arms on either side.
The sword of Washington and his great name
Disarm the factious, make them live in peace.
But recently, with Mammon's ready aid,
I held the chief helpless between two fires.
France sent her minister demanding help
Against the hateful foes of liberty.
Yes, France, the gen'rous friend of other days,
Roused the rash people 'gainst their government,
While Britain, with piratical intent,
Seized Yankee ships wherever they were found,
And sent the barb'rous Indians to destroy
The helpless families of the far West.
I thought the people then would fly to arms,
But Washington soon had Genet recalled
Back to his own rash country, warlike France.
To Britain Jay was sent with peaceful words.
The treaty that he made was hailed with scorn,
Was burned by mobs, assailed by orators,
Who said their country had been basely sold.
But, Mammon, you had much to do with that.
Please give the details that so hateful seem.

Mammon. Jay was most patriotic, but was met
By haughty, selfish Britons, backed by force
His youthful country could not well resist.
They proposed to move their soldiers from the
Western forts, where Indians had been armed
To slaughter babes; to leave the frontiersmen
Of that wild region; the enlarging trade;
To cease their depredations on the seas,
And pay for ships and cargoes they had seized.
But they refused to pay for stolen slaves,
As in the former treaty was agreed;
Demanded that old debts should all be paid
By those who had obtained the merchandise.
'Twas my fine hand that brought all this to pass.
When the great war began, I told the men
That war had settled all of their old debts.
When peace returned, the Fed'ral government
Agreed to the collection of those debts;
But I then told the patriots to demand
Exemption from those antiquated claims;
Then told the British not to pay for slaves,
Nor yet surrender up the frontier forts,
Until the patriots paid up their debts.
The treaty made by Jay, an Eastern man,
Paid Eastern men for stolen ships and goods,
But confiscated stolen Southern slaves,
Because old debtors died or failed to pay.
What maddens the Americans seems clear:
Wayne whipped the Indians and had peace enforced
In spite of British fraud and cruelty:
So, giving up the forts she nothing gave.
Why, then, should Jay relinquish claims for slaves?
Why raise again the question of old debts,
And fill the land with most vexatious suits?
It makes men doubly desperate to fail
In their endeavors to shake off just debts,
But so I'll tempt them to the end of time.
Satan, this trouble is not ended yet.

Satan. Nor shall it end till, roaring for more prey,
The British lion treads these shores again.

Scene: *Washington City, June 1, 1803.* MICHAEL, GABRIEL.

Michael. I hail you, happy Gabriel! News arrives
At this new seat of empire that the French
Have sold this young republic vast domains
Extending broadly westward to the shores
Washed by Pacific's peaceful, gentle waves.
The States thus gain more than a million of
Square miles of land, with mighty rivers on
Their rapid way to the vast oceans of
The East and West. This to the frontier men
Gives free access to all the whole round world,
Without leave asked of Britain, France, or Spain;
With liberal hand throws wide trade's golden gates,
And welcomes the rich commerce of a world;
Invites prosperity with wide-spread sails
To enter at ten thousand open ports.

Gabriel. Yes, Michael, but the half has not been told
Of God's great goodness to this favored land.
The Indians, whipped by Wayne, have peaceful grown;
Jay's treaty with the British, though unjust,
Caused peace to smile where war had madly frowned;
The whisky fiends of Pennsylvania
Submitted to the troops of Harry Lee,
Proving the majesty of fed'ral law;
Factions were awed by mighty Washington;
The States kept free from foreign dominance;
When France in robber tones demanded gifts,
Pinckney with stately dignity replied,
"We've millions for defense, but not a cent
For tribute to the strongest of our foes,"
And the brave States in thunder tones rolled back
The patriot statesman's grand, defiant words.
When war came threat'ningly from angry France,
The people rallied in their own defense,
And called on Washington to lead their troops.
The waves were witnesses of French defeats.
The robber ships, some captured, some destroyed,
Found foemen who could humble all their pride.
Then Frenchmen changed their rulers, and again
Peace wound her chain of love around old friends.

This strengthened the new government abroad,
And gave the people confidence at home.
It had been feared when Washington must go,
The orphaned Union would then sadly pine.
But the great man retired to private life;
The States lived on. He died; they flourished still.
'Twas feared that conflicts at election times
Would bring on anarchy and bloody strife.
Administrations changed; no blood was shed.
Then selfish faction tempted Aaron Burr
To let it steal for him the highest place;
And Burr was willing, while for days they tried
To take the presidency and its power
From Jefferson, the people's chosen chief.
But honest Bayard checked the villainy;
Against his party, let the right prevail.
'Twas well the government should stand the test,
And triumph over faction's cunning fraud.
It throttled usurpation and struck down
The tyranny that followed forms of law,
When even patriots in authority
Enacted and enforced despotic laws
Against the Constitution and the right.
'Twas proper that the ballots of the free
Should, under avalanches of contempt,
Bury those patriot tyrants of the land
In cold oblivion. Then repeal their acts,
And let the hangman burn the hateful words.
The alien and sedition laws are dead.
The party that enacted them will die.
Burr's name is hateful. Jefferson is still
The guardian of State rights, and freedom's friend,
He rules in righteousness. Authority
Not granted by the States he will not wield.
Even the treaty by which he secures
Louisiana to the land he loves
He would submit to the approval of
The sev'ral States. Happy the land with such
A ruler blessed! Thrice happy in the judge
That fills the place of highest honor in
Its highest court! John Marshall is his name.

Justice personified in him is seen.
Marshall and Jefferson, Virginia's sons,
Shall through the coming ages bless mankind,
And by the might of their illustrious names
Cause terror-stricken tyranny to quail,
And usurpation drop its mask of smiles;
While fraud, corruption, legal villainy,
Shall trembling drop their base, dishonest gains.
But see! The great Chief-justice comes this way,
And by his side the greater President:
They pass in modest majesty sublime,
Without a thread of such pretentious garb
As little greatness still delights to wear.
The honor that enshrines these noble men
Might waken envy in archangels' breasts,
If angels' breasts could envy entertain.

Michael. You grow enthusiastic in their praise;
I join you in admiring their renown,
Their unpretentious, simple, lofty aims.
But I have marveled much at the great growth
Of these United States in worldly wealth.
The fruitful soil exhaustless riches yields,
And fills the land with plenty and with joy.
The mines surrender their long hidden stores,
The forests wave a welcome to the men
That turn their lofty grandeur into gold.
Waves bear the white-winged wand'rers of the deep
From ev'ry land with tribute to these shores,
While population multiplies and spreads,
Still doubling its possessions year by year.
New settlements, blooming and beautiful,
Spring forth to join the sisterhood of States.
Vermont from her green hills came smiling down;
Kentucky, Tennessee, and Ohio,
Baptized with blood, march grandly, sword in hand,
To their high places in the stately band.
No other nation ever prospered so.
Mankind, astonished, wonder and admire.
Angels exult to see such blessedness,
And God himself smiles on the blissful scene.
Let us away where other duties call.

BOOK SIXTH.

Scene: *Tippecanoe, in the woods of Indiana, November 8, 1811.* SATAN, MARS, MAMMON, BELIAL.

 Mars. Ha, ha! ha, ha! What is it we have here?
'Tis war, but war not worthy of the name.
Napoleon's campaigns, Wellington's great fights,
Russia's rude millions, Prussia's well-drilled ranks,
Might claim applause from Jupiter himself;
But these frontiersmen and their Indian foes
May all be left to Belial and his fools.

 Belial. Take back your insult! But for knaves and fools
Your world-wide wars could never be commenced.

 Mars. True, Belial. I retract the insulting words.
I recognize the value of your work.

 Satan. Yes, fill the world with sober, upright men,
And peace would plant her olives in all lands,
Doves lay their nurselings where the eagles brood,
And harvests ripen upon battle-fields.
Ten peaceful years sages have ruled this land,
With Jefferson or Madison in pow'r.
All my malignant arts provoke no wars.
I've seen the population multiplied,
The territory doubled in extent,
The commerce increased more than seven-fold,
The wilderness explored from sea to sea,
Lewis and Clarke in distant Oregon,
As pioneers of millions who shall go
To till the lands and plow Pacific's waves.
I've seen success crown Fulton's enterprise
To yoke the steam, and make it pull his ships
Against opposing tides and wayward winds,

Seen his torpedoes dive beneath the waves,
Ready to hurl destruction at all foes
That dare invade the waters to make war.
The pirates, whipped, no longer vex the sea;
Indians, subdued, no more distress the land;
The schemes of Burr suppressed, and he disgraced;
Great Hamilton, who rivaled Jefferson,
Mourned by all parties in an early grave;
The Eastern faction growled, but dared not bite,
And I, in my malignity, looked on,
Without ability to stir up strife.
Here peace, prosperity, and plenty smiled
On Christian principles and honest men.
But I have not been idle. Mammon too
Has toiled to darken their benignant skies,
And hurl war's furious tempests at their homes.
Belial has stirred these Indians, as you see,
To deeds of treachery and cruelty;
But Harrison has whipped the savages.
Behold the ashes of their wigwam homes!
Say, Mammon, what of Britain's "lords of trade?"

Mammon. I made them agonize with envious rage,
As Yankee commerce, borne by Yankee ships,
Caused their own trade to languish day by day;
Then sent them to their rulers to demand
The driving of these upstarts from the sea
By cutting off all traffic with the French.
I moved the Frenchmen to retaliate,
And close against them all of Britain's ports.
I thought these cautious Christian men must fight
With France or England, or with both at once.
Instead of that they joined their enemies
To keep their ships confined in their own ports.
Finding they would not fight with foreigners,
I tried to raise a fight among themselves
By tempting all the selfish sons of trade
To take up arms against the embargo.
New England listens, and may yet secede
To join her fortunes with the Canadas.
John Henry thinks she will, and so does Craig,
Who now rules Canada for Britain's king.

Satan. Mammon, I give you praise for work well
  done.
I have led England to assert a right
To seize her subjects wheresoever found,
And to impress them with her own marines.
Thus ships of neutral nations now are searched
For men to fight the battles of King George.
Speaking the English language is enough
To prove them subjects of the English King.
So, in the service of these kidnappers,
Six thousand citizens of these proud States
Are held. Adding insult to injury,
I made the "Leopard" stop the "Chesapeake"
Near her own harbor, and drag from her decks
Four men to bondage, one to cruel death.
These peaceful rulers most indignantly
Ordered all British war-ships from their ports,
Then rested on in quiet dignity.
At last, when foreign trade was quite destroyed
By French and English robbery at sea,
Without a ship that dared to sail abroad,
The prudent men proclaimed "non-intercourse"
With pirate nations that destroyed their trade.
To shame them out of their inglorious peace,
I made them stand a battle on the sea.
The "Little Belt" attacked the "President"
Without a word of warning or of threat;
But as brave Rogers punished his rude foe,
Giving the British pirate deadly shots,
'Twas deemed sufficient to avenge the wrong.
So those most patient rulers still have peace;
But they shall soon have war. I'll make them fight.
Mammon, send Henry to the fed'ral court
With written evidence of England's plot
To wield New England's factions and detach
Her wordy traitors from the fed'ral league.
Belial, go to the sea-ports. Idle throngs
Need but your help, and they grow desperate.
Go wake the warlike woodsmen of the West
To deeds of valor worthy of themselves.
Bring up young statesmen to the capital:

I'll stir ambition in their youthful blood,
And war's rude hurly-burly shall begin.

Scene: *Capitol, Washington, D. C., December 25, 1812.* ASMODEUS, AZAZEL, MARS, SATAN, BAAL, MOLOCH, CHEMOSH, BELIAL, MAMMON, BELUS, SERAPIS.

Satan. A merry Christmas to my trusty friends!
Come, celebrate with me the natal day
Of David's Son, the mighty Prince of Peace;
While his meek, peaceful subjects work our will.
Roman and Greek and Protestant agree,
At least for once in perfect unity.
They all combine to take each other's lives;
They make the world one glorious battle-field;
While fishes of all oceans feast on flesh
Of Christians slaughtered by true Christian men.
Russia sees millions crimsoning her snows;
All soils are fertilized with Christian blood;
Here Protestants with Protestants contend.

Mars. Huzza! huzza! war, glorious war employs
The pious subjects of the Prince of Peace!

Baal. Huzza! huzza! his millions haste to claim
A dwelling-place with us in hell's dark depths.

All. Huzza! huzza! huzza! we welcome them!

Satan. Yes, this young nation yielded to my arts.
The Irishman, John Henry, and the plot
Which he revealed, roused hatred in the hearts
Of angry millions. Bold statesmen such as
Grundy, Clay, Calhoun hurried the timid,
Cautious, prudent, slow into rash action.
All unprepared in every thing but men,
They struck the strongest nation in the world.
As might have been expected, they have failed.
Hull basely played the coward at Detroit;
Surrendered all his men, lost Michigan,
Gave up Lake Erie, and defenseless left
The helpless people of the whole North-west.
Van Rensselaer, at Queenstown, drove the foe,

Ordered twelve hundred men to cross the stream,
And help complete the half-won victory.
New York's militia would not leave their State:
The craven cowards left their country's flag
And its defenders to the enemy.
One Smyth, still later, sent his men across,
But feared to lead the gallant patriots.
A hero leading dastard followers;
A dastard leader of brave, valiant men.
But on the ocean bravery and skill
Have given immortality to names
That shall be honored in most distant lands.
Decatur, Porter, Jones, and Isaac Hull,
Bear off the honors of the present war;
But other men shall highest honors claim
Before peace hovers o'er this land again.
Yet, comrades, all the honors won by men
Are naught compared with those we proudly wear.
Their grandest battles are but skirmishes
To world-wide conflicts such as ours are.
Our foes are stronger—yea, omnipotent—
And destined yet to triumph over us;
But we fight on through the whole course of time.
We rule all nations. I still proudly reign
"God of this world," enthroned o'er all mankind.
Yes, e'en at Christmas I rule Christian men.
Behold the great men stagg'ring through the streets!
To time's last moment earth shall still be mine,
And when the lake of fire shall blaze round me
This world of mine shall feel consuming fires.
Messiah, if he wants it for his saints,
Must it, as well as them, create anew.

Scene: *In the woods near the river Thames, Canada, October 5, 1813.*
        ABDIEL, ITHURIEL, URIEL, ZOPHIEL.

Abdiel. If tears were ever shed by angel eyes,
This wicked war would make them freely flow.
Last January Winchester's brave troops
Surrendered to their haughty British foes.
But Proctor, the most infamous of men,
Subjected them to Indian scalping-knives.

Ithuriel. So Dudley and his men were sacrificed
To savage fury at a later day.

Uriel. When gallant Chauncey and his brave marines
Drove British ships from Lake Ontario,
Dearborn crossed over to the northern shore
With troops to capture forts and army stores.
Th' exploding of Toronto's magazine
Sent death to heroes that were led by Pike;
But in the arms of victory they fell,
Crowned with the praises of the land they loved.

Ithuriel. Winder and Chandler stormed Fort George
in May.
It yet is held in spite of England's power.

Zophiel. Old ocean still is vexed with human strife,
And hurls his storms against the combatants;
But they fight on, and when defeated cry
With dying Lawrence: "Don't give up the ship!"
But not on bounding billows of the deep
Do British sailors seek for glory now.
To proud old England naval warfare means
Prowling along the shore for helpless prey,
Outraging decency and burning towns.

Abdiel. Hark! hark! I hear the sounds of horrid war,
The noise of musketry, the clash of arms;
The tramp of cavalry, the steady step
Of British infantry, and the loud cries
Of strong frontiersmen, battling for their lives.
List to the Indian war-whoop! Hear the yell
Of dying hundreds in their agonies!
See Proctor fleeing! The cruel dastard
Hastes to leave the field. His proud regulars
Flee swiftly in the steps of their base chief.
Kentucky horsemen mow them down like wheat.
See that strong Indian! Listen to his voice.
Urging his red braves forward to the fight.
That is Tecumseh, bravest of his race.'
He's badly wounded; see, the strong man falls!
As their chief dies the Indians quit the field.

See Isaac Shelby, hero of two wars,
Now civil Governor of his great State.
And there is Harrison; Virginia's blood
Throbs in his heart and mantles on his cheek,
Impelling him to most illustrious deeds.
See, at his side, the manly Colonel Croghan,
Brave young defender of Fort Stevenson.
And there is Colonel Johnson, leaning on
The shoulders of two comrades who support,
With loving hearts, their noble, bleeding friend.
And last, but most renowned of all the throng,
Behold young Perry, hero of the lake.
His naval victory, so bravely won,
Thrilled a whole nation with exultant joy,
And rendered this day's triumph possible.
This double vict'ry gives ten thousand homes
Protection against bloody tomahawks.
The playful children of the West no more
Shall check their sports to list for savage yells.
Matrons and maidens, undisturbed by fear,
Shall sing of heaven, and find it in the smiles
Of lovely innocence, secure from harm.

Scene: *Hartford, Ct., December, 1814.* MARS, SATAN, CHEMOSH, MAMMON, BELUS.

Mars. More than two years of what these men call war
Have passed with only trifling skirmishes.

Satan. True, Mars, but you're impatient of results.
You think of what is seen. I lay vast plans,
Involving millions through all coming time.
You only see some thousands march, fight, die;
Some trifling villages consumed by fire.
I cherish hatreds between North and South,
Fanning the flames that shall break out and burn
Through this broad Union in the days to come.

Chemosh. I will not hear this war belittled so;
This bird in hand is worth two in the bush.
Satan, your schemes for continental woe

May end in failure, wise as they may seem.
Mars, you may glory in great Wellington,
In Bonaparte, and Europe's countless hosts,
But don't despise this side-show of a war
Which Britain wages as with her left hand.
These hating kinsmen have struck fearful blows.
What think you of the nameless horrors seen
Near the wild banks of Raisin's bloody stream?
What of the braves by bold Tecumseh led?
What of their conquerors upon the Thames,
Led on by Johnson, Shelby, Harrison?
What of the boyish Croghan at Sandusky,
And youthful Perry, whose intrepid deeds
On Erie's waters ring around the world?
Was that a skirmish when, near Chippewa,
More than five hundred of the British fell,
Or when nine hundred fell at Lundy's Lane,
Where fame's loud trump proclaimed the honored
 names
Of Scott, of Ripley, Jessup, Miller, Brown?
What of Fort Erie's siege? attempts to storm?
Fierce bombardment for more than forty days?
Its fiery sorties and its brave defense?
When fourteen thousand men with Prevost marched,
And Downie's mighty fleet accompanied,
Up Sorel River to the Saranac?
Was that not war that forced them to retreat,
Losing one-fifth of their vast armament,
Their admiral, and nearly all his ships?
Plattsburg and Lake Champlain pronounce it war.
McDonough and Macomb wear warriors' wreaths
And write their names on glory's brightest page.
'Twas worse than war when Ross at Washington
Used arson's torch, and burned the capitol.
'Twas war sublimed, war glorified, when Smith
Marshalled ten thousand men at Baltimore
To fight at North Point for their native home.
Since that great battle ev'ry glowing star
In freedom's banner flashes forth the names
Of Baltimore, McHenry, and North Point.
In most heroic times this would be war.

Satan. Yes, Chemosh, you have wisely proved your
    point.
But, Mammon, what report have you to make
About your money-mongering clientage?

Mammon. My clients must be treated with respect.
True, they love money; others love it too,
But lack the shrewdness and the enterprise
By which New England's sons enrich themselves.
Why then should Satan coin an uncouth phrase
To fling at my most worthy clientage?
I'll not report until he takes it back.

Satan. We'll have no disputation about words.
I'll take it back; I want the news you bring.

Mammon. Well, then, when Adams ruled, and Fisher
    Ames
Was the chief orator in Congress Hall,
New England was well pleased with peace or war.
She knew her sons were wisest, bravest, best
Of all who sailed the seas or trod the earth,
And lost all patience when the purblind eyes
Of outside millions failed to see it so.
'Twas quite too bad to think of or endure
That President, Premier, Chief-justice, and
Decatur, gallant prince of naval chiefs,
Should all be Southern born and Southern bred.
And when Louisiana had been bought,
The wise men of the East declared 'twas time
To leave the Union and seek wiser friends.
When France would cripple commerce, and the sea
Saw Britain kidnap thousands of their sons,
War was demanded, but the imbeciles
Who ruled at Washington embargoed trade,
And checked the bus'ness by which men grew rich.
No wonder my shrewd clients looked abroad
For commerce that could not be found at home.
And still they seek immediate relief
In every quarter that may promise help.

Belus. 'Twas then John Henry came from Canada

To offer them Great Britain's potent aid.
They listened and encouraged him to hope
That they would meekly bear the British yoke,
Though Bunker Hill frowned on the hateful spy
And Lexington and Concord spurned the wretch,
While silent protests came from the green graves
Where lay the honored dust once nobly worn
By Warren, Prescott, Adams, Hancock, Ames;
But brave John Adams, true and faithful still,
Writing in kindness to his early friend,
Told Jefferson the law must be repealed.
'Twas done, and still they were not satisfied.
And now when war prevails and patriots bleed,
The hydra heads of faction hiss against
What they had long demanded as most wise.
With stifling breath they try to suffocate,
With snaky folds to crush the government;
Destroying credit and denying aid,
Betray the country to its enemies.
These men will go no farther. They are shrewd;
The hatreds of the sections are intense,
But their self-interest deeper, stronger far.
Theirs is not hot blood of the cavaliers,
Nor hasty chivalry of Huguenots.
They cannot hope for aught from Canada
That's worth a tithe of what they here possess.
No stretch of Fed'ral tyranny could drive
These calculating people to secede.
But, Satan, they are ready to your hand
To drive out men more hasty than themselves.
Under the Constitution they will claim
All that they want and hold all that they gain.
Others may call it legal robbery.
But they'll drive wedge and screw still farther in,
And boldly smile at their shrewd Yankee trick.
With kindly feeling and philanthropy,
Their condescending charity will stoop
To lift their neighbors to their own high plane
Of transcendental super-eminence.
If those dull neighbors venture to demur,
Audacious insults may be hurled at them.

These failing, rifles, swords, and spears complete
Their elevation to the loftier plane.

  Satan. You speak most wisely, Belus; but the world
Has many people that are worse than these,
And few that are much better can you find.
I'll use them as you say for my wise ends.
If we cannot induce them to secede,
We'll use them to make other men go out,
And then perhaps to drive them back again.
But these conventionists in Hartford met
Will give their names to infamous contempt.
As banded 'gainst their country while at war.
When they complete the work they have in hand,
And threaten Madison with what they'll do
If he does not conclude the war in haste,
'Twill be to learn of peace already made,
Without the least regard for their fierce threats.

  Mammon. Does Babylonian Belus dare to blame
The wise inhabitants of wisdom's land?
Does Satan dare to damn them with faint praise?
Such disrespect deserves, and shall receive,
The stern rebuke of one who knows them well.
This land of scholars, schools, and colleges,
Of statesmen, orators, philosophers,
Of wise inventors, and industrious men,
Shall flourish in despite of envious hate.

Scene: *New Orleans, January 8, 1815.* GABRIEL, ABDIEL, ZEPHON,
  RAPHAEL, ITHURIEL, URIEL.

  Abdiel. I hail you happy here, my friends, to-day!
Once more peace smiles upon this favored land,
Reposing in the lap of victory.
The laurel-wreath that rests on Jackson's brow
Has been well won, and now is nobly worn.
A widow's son, trained in the fear of God,
His boyhood gave its strength to freedom's cause.
Later in life he championed womanhood;
Her base detractors fled before his wrath.
When savage warriors threatened the frontiers,
And slew four hundred persons at Fort Mims,

He rushed to rescue others from such fate.
He had but acorns to subsist upon,
But gave security to helpless homes,
And wrote his honored name on grateful hearts.

Zephon. When British ships from Pensacola sailed
With troops to take Fort Bowyers' garrison,
He hastened to repel his country's foes.
Then storming Pensacola, he drove out
The enemy from Spanish Florida.
When fifty ships, with full twelve thousand men,
Came to attack defenseless New Orleans,
He martial law proclaimed, and with strong will
Compelled the people to defend themselves.
He took their cotton-bales to build a wall
For their protection from their enemies;
Sent out his gun-boats to delay the foe,
Then from the river he bombarded them;
Still later sent two thousand riflemen,
With deadly aim to slay their officers.
Then falling back behind his cotton-bales,
He smiled at their impotent cannonade,
And waited for Napoleon's conquerors.
They marched this morning, led by Pakenham;
And when he fell, by Gibbs; and then by Keen;
When he had fallen, Lambert led them off
In swift retreat from Jackson's backwoodsmen.
Eight killed and eighteen wounded was the loss
Sustained by the undrilled Americans.
Of vet'ran British seven hundred fell,
With fourteen hundred helpless from their wounds
And full five thousand pris'ners left behind.
From early dawn to nearly nine o'clock
The fight continued with terrific loss.
At each discharge the British were mowed down
By marksmen such as they had never met
Until they faced the troops of Tennessee
And stood before Kentucky riflemen.
A truce is granted by the conqueror
To let the wounded and the dead receive
All due attention from their countrymen.

Raphael. You say the war is ended, peace prevails.
Please tell me what's been gained by all the strife.

Ithuriel. The States have seen their capitol consumed,
Their coasts laid waste, their villages destroyed,
Their soldiers slain, or wounded, or diseased.
Full eighteen thousand sailors have been lost,
As many hundred ships captured or sunk.
Have paid high taxes and now owe a debt
Of fivescore million dollars, if not more.
The British have lost much, and nothing gained
But the disgrace of arson, outrages,
And high renown from Indian massacres.
Both now gain peace; yes, peace, and nothing more.

Abdiel. But then the States have freedom of the seas,
Trade unrestricted by their stronger foes,
Exemption from impressment of their sons,
And the grand record of such deeds as this
Performed to-day by Jackson and his troops
To hold in awe the tyrants of the world,
And make them fear t' offend these mighty States.

Gabriel. If men were wise, benevolent, and just,
All wars might cease, peace everywhere prevail,
And arbitration settle all disputes.
'Twere better still to organize a court
To judge of international complaints.
Each country on the globe could choose its judge
And furnish its proportion of a force
Commanded by the marshal of that court,
To properly enforce its just decrees.
Earth's armies might with safety then disband,
Producing, not destroying, property
Each nation could get help for its police
By proper application to the court,
And thus establish order in all lands.
Contiguous countries wishing to unite
Could ask the court to give them its consent.
The court could hold its sittings when and where
Occasion and convenience might demand.

Its ships and regiments might first embrace
The navies and the armies of the world,
To be reduced proportionately till
Ten thousand men would keep mankind in peace.

Uriel. Hark! hark! the hero comes! Behold the chief!
The city's saved, he honors civil law.
Judge Hall now trembles, fearing Jackson's friends,
And trembles more to hear the chieftain's voice;
But there is law, not wrath, in its clear tones:
"Judge, I have done my duty; now do yours.
The court shall be protected by the power
That did protect the city; so fear not.
If I've been guilty of contempt of court,
Inflict the penalty; it shall be paid."
The judge assessed the fine, which Jackson paid.
This grandest vict'ry of the chieftain's life—
The hero's triumph over his own pride,
The soldier's high regard for civil law,
The warrior's tribute paid to legal power—
Is the rich metal of a brighter crown
Than conq'ror ever wore on earth before.

Scene: *Pennsylvania Avenue, Washington, D. C., 1815.* ITHURIEL, ABDIEL.

Abdiel. What mean this music, these excited crowds?

Ithuriel. Decatur has returned from Barbary;
The pirates fell or fled at his approach.
Algiers, Tripoli, Tunis, well chastised,
Surrendered all the prisoners they held,
And paid in cash for their bold robberies.
The conq'ring hero and his brave marines
Bring back the long lost exiles to their homes.
Wife, children, friends, and native land agree
To make their glad hearts overflow with joy;
And there are Madison, Monroe, Calhoun,
And all the cabinet to welcome them
And to do honor to the naval chief
That rescued them from bondage with strong hand.

THE MISSOURI COMPROMISE.

Behold Decatur! modest and serene,
All heaven would delight to honor him.

Scene: *The Capitol, Washington, D. C., August, 1821.* SATAN, BAAL, MAMMON.

Satan. My honored allies, in our endless wars
Events transpire that claim our serious thoughts.
The Greeks throw off the sultan's galling yoke;
Old Spain will lose her Western colonies;
France groans beneath the Bourbon's tyranny;
A black republic called Liberia
Has been set up in Western Africa;
Jackson has whipped the warlike Seminoles,
Has chased the savages to Spanish ground,
There seized and hanged two meddling Englishmen.
England said nothing, proud old Spain complained,
But to her neighbors sold fair Florida.
I witnessed that great sale, and smiled to see
John Quincy Adams Texas give away,
While Southern statesmen kindly closed their eyes,
Or looked away in search of Northern votes.
These statesmen talk of roads, canals, a bank,
A tariff manufactures to protect;
But I make their disputes all sectional,
Make every act a triumph for the North
Or for the South. Monroe, elected twice,
Must soon retire; but the next President
Shall owe his office to a section's vote
Or to a combination between men
To give a section favors it demands.
The Union grows, new States increase its strength,
And blaze in starry brightness on its flag.
Louisiana, from the far South-west,
Met Indiana leading Illinois;
While Mississippi Alabama led,
To greet Missouri and far Eastern Maine;
But when Missouri came I raised a storm
That shook the Union with an earthquake's force.

Baal. On what pretense did you excite that storm?
She had the same right other States have had.

Satan. So I well knew, and could have proved it too,
But jealousy of sections intervened
To do for me more than I dared to hope.
I prompted supercilious piety
To claim superior philanthropy
And zeal for equal rights among all men,
Not equal rights among the sovereign States,
To claim for Congress absolute control
Of all the territories of the land,
So that Missouri could not be a State
Unless she banished slavery from her soil.

Baal. When did the States give Congress such a right,
Or any right to legislate on slaves?

Satan. Never. The Union could not have been formed
If such a notion had been entertained.
But many wish to see the States ignored,
That fed'ral force in all things may prevail.
I aid them now to take and firmly hold
All they desire in a strong government,
But never could induce the States to yield.
Still better for my grand, audacious schemes
A compromise draws a dividing line
From East to West across the continent.
That line divides two parties; fills with hate
The bosoms of a self-willed, warlike race.
That line I'll widen, make it red with blood
And glittering with swords and bayonets.

Baal. When did the people give authority
To any one to draw a line like that
Between co-equal citizens and States?
When did the States consent to such a line,
Or Southerners agree to lineal law,
That treats them as despised inferiors?
When did French residents renounce the rights
Secured by treaty with Napoleon?

Satan. Never. 'Twas King Majority enthroned.
His scepter gave to false philanthropy
To drive Missouri from the Union's door.

'Twas purblind statesmanship, with stumbling steps,
Led by ambition trampling upon law,
The rights of men, of States, and treaty rights,
All by the Constitution well secured,
Stretched out the coward hand that drew that line.

Mammon. 'Twas I that drew the contract that conveyed
New England's votes to the most southward States,
To keep the slave trade open twenty years,
And their three votes for tonnage taxing laws.
I saw the contract faithfully observed.
The slaves were brought till they were two for one,
Doubling their numbers in the twenty years.
They taxed out foreign tonnage at their will,
And so they will until the end of time.
What now is wanted? Can it be more slaves?

Belial. They want to bless the negroes by decay,
To extirpate them, let them slowly starve,
T' inclose them in a narrow boundary
And let them eat their heads off if they will.
No! no! it is not more but fewer slaves,
And fewer masters, and they very poor!

Baal. 'Twould certainly be better for the slave
To range at will, or at his master's will,
Through all th' unmeasured acres of the West.

Satan. I listen to your talk with due respect,
But marvel that you fail to see in me
The cause of wordy warfare and the strife
That now embitters sectional disputes.
I care not for the slaves, for North or South,
But fan the flames of hatred till they blaze
With all the fury of destructive war.

Scene: *Bunker Hill, Mass., June 17, 1825.* ARIEL, RAPHAEL, ZOPHIEL.

Zophiel. What means this gathering of thousands here,
With martial music and the measured tread
Of soldiers ready for the battle-field?

Raphael. 'Tis half a century since on this hill
Freemen fought bravely for their liberty.
To-day survivors of that famous fight
Meet their young countrymen to celebrate
The triumphs of the cause for which they fought.

Ariel. There's Daniel Webster, prince of orators,
Whose eloquence shall tell of noble deeds
Performed by heroes fifty years ago,
And of the principles for which they bled,
And the rich fruits of those pure principles.

Zephon. There's Lafayette, the nation's honored guest,
The friend of Washington and liberty:
Our country's friend—friend in her time of need.
This grand old hero lays upon this spot
The corner-stone of a tall monument,
Whose tow'ring top, still pointing to the skies,
Shall tell the generations yet to come
'Twas their forefathers' God whose mighty hand
Gave them the liberty that they enjoy.
Great Lafayette came back to visit now
The people that in youth he helped to free.
A mighty multitude, with happy hearts,
Have welcomed him to their rejoicing homes.
They give their benefactor fertile lands
And crown him with a nation's gratitude.
They see him shed affection's flowing tears
Upon the honored tomb of Washington.
They see the joy that lights his countenance
As he beholds their great prosperity,
Sees mines and forests and the fruitful soil
Lavish upon them richest, rarest gifts.
Old ocean rolls her treasures to their shores,
And commerce brings rich tribute to their ports.
They see how gratified he is to learn
That Porter whipped the pirates of the Gulf,
Till none remain t' alarm the sons of trade;
That Congress recognized the governments
Of all the new republics of the South
As independent nations of the earth;

That President Monroe had notified
Old Europe that she shall not colonize
A single spot of this free continent.
Now when he seeks the shores of his loved France,
Rememb'ring where his blood in youth was shed,
They send him on the good ship "Brandywine."

BOOK SEVENTH.

Scene: *Capitol, Washington, D. C., March, 1829.* SATAN, MAMMON, BELIAL, BAAL.

   Satan. Fate seems against us now, my brave compeers.
Jackson, inaugurated, spoils my plans.
He is a strict constructionist, and firm
In his determination to maintain
State rights and civil liberty against
All usurpations of the fed'ral power.
With him comes in a Senate to sustain
And strengthen him. Monopolies must die.
Protective tariffs will no longer rob
The planters to enrich the men with mills.
The bank must perish, and the treasury,
Freed from the leeches that now feast on it,
Gather no more than its demands compel
For uses that are constitutional.
Now, I had hoped that Adams would serve out
Another term, and give the greedy East
All that it asks from the depleted South;
Would strain the Constitution till it breaks,
Rending all ties that now connect the States.
This disappointment vexes me to-day.
Give your advice. Say what shall next be done.

   Mammon. Press onward in the course you have pursued.
The fact'ry lords are not yet satisfied.
The iron masters more protection claim:
They hoodwink honest men and patriots
With "The Americans against the world."
Ambition's bribes they proffer to the great,
And offer money in exchange for votes.
I pledge my clientage to your support;
We plant our money for productive crops.

FACTORY LORDS. 135

Belial. I too can tell of something you will like
My client who was once . . . .,
Now Mrs. . . ., will be snubbed, tabooed
By the *elite* of chaste society.
The pious wives of Jackson's cabinet
Will be required to recognize my pet,

HENRY CLAY AND A MANUFACTURER.

Or risk the anger of the President.
Their husbands will protect them in the right
To freely choose their own associates.
This will drive out the faithful married men,
And leave the widower of Kinderhook,
The trusted counselor of him who rules;

Waiting the day that makes him President.
The sly old fox can safely bide his time.

 Baal. But, Belial, did not the Vice-president
Expect the presidency in his turn?

 Belial. He did, but it is learned that he condemned
The Gen'ral for his course in Florida,
And his chaste wife tabooed and spurned my pet.

 Baal. Why did the President part with his friends
Rather than see your pretty pet tabooed?

 Belial. His pious mother in his early youth
Made him the champion of womanhood.
To slander female innocence and worth
Was an offense he never would forgive.
Some months ago his faithful, loving wife
Was torn from his embrace by cruel death.
The gallant hero laid her sacred form
Beneath the sod with many a tender tear.
The mem'ry of her virtues stirred the depths
Of his indignant wrath against the wretch
Whose filthy tongue had slandered her good name.
A thousand deaths of foul-mouthed slanderers
Seemed insufficient for so vile a crime.
Just then my lovely pet flashed on his sight
With tears of blushing, injured innocence,
And claimed protection from her slanderers.
A world in arms he would have then defied
And bravely, nobly died in her defense.
Satan, you smile, but all the heav'nly hosts
Had been her champions if they had seen
The lovely innocence she then displayed.

 Satan. Belial, I give you thanks for all you tell;
And, Mammon, thanks for your most sage advice.
New combinations now seem possible
That may accomplish more than I had hoped.
Yes, we have parties that are sectional,
The East against the West and planting States.
The fed'ral power arrayed against State rights.
Republican is Fed'ral newly named.

There is the bank as planned by Hamilton,
And here a party claiming all he asked,
All that he asked, but could not then obtain;
And here is Jackson, with his iron will,
His honest purpose to uphold the right,
With a strong tendency to claim that he
Himself alone is the Democracy.
I'll work the ruin of these prosp'rous States,
Accepting help from all who'll give me aid.
But there is something truly ominous

ANDREW JACKSON.

In the coincidence that brought the deaths
Of Jefferson and Adams at one time,
And that just fifty years from the great day
When independence was at first proclaimed.
How strange! The two great patriots, when young,
Labored in concert freedom to secure;
Then led opposing parties through long years,
In age became like brothers, and in death,
On Independence Day, were grandly joined.
May not this hint that union will prevail

Against all arts of devils or of men?
I hear of cars to be propelled by steam,
Gliding on iron rails with wondrous speed.
This new invention promises to be
Of priceless value to this favored land.
We must begin to study in advance
How we can make it hurry men to hell,
By accidents, by frauds, by Mammon's arts,
By all of Belial's sharp, deceptive tricks.

Scene: *The Capitol at Washington, D. C., March 4, 1833.* SATAN, BAAL, MAMMON, BELIAL.

Satan. What are our prospects now, most worthy friends?

Belial. The cabinet was scattered as proposed,
And Kinderhook's shrewd widower became
The favorite confidant of his great chief—
Was sent to England as embassador.
His rivals in the Senate called him back,
Refusing to confirm the nominee,
But that has made him the Vice-president.
He takes the oath of office here to-day,
And four years hence will be the President.

Mammon. I with success have crowned my latest scheme.
The greedy manufacturers secured
The highest tariff ever yet imposed,
Threatened disunion if it was denied,
And promised money, honor, power, and fame
To all who aided their nefarious plans.

Mars. I stirred the hot blood of the fiery South
To nullify the hateful robber law,
And got the Force bill passed to have them hanged.
I wait in hope to see the strife begin.

Baal. I gave to Hayne and Webster and Calhoun
Such oratory as earth seldom hears
To stir opposing forces into strife.
Their sections were so charmed with their mistakes
That Edward Livingston could scarce command

Attention from admiring Senators,
While he set forth truth without error mixed.

Satan. Well done! well done! co-workers with your chief,
Your great success emboldens me to-day.
But, Mars, you may wait twenty years or more
To see this peaceful country drenched in blood.
That time will come; you shall not wait in vain.
These Carolinians are very brave,
And Clay has yielded to their just demands.
The fact'ry barons have to stand aside
Till their great champion saves the land he loves.
Calhoun, victorious, sees the tariff tax
Greatly reduced through several years to come.
But see, Jackson begins his second term to-day;
The great Chief-justice hears him take the oath.

Scene: *Woods near battle-field of San Jacinto, Tex., April, 1836.* AB-
DIEL, ITHURIEL.

Abdiel. We meet again, companion of my toils.
What brings you to these far South-western wilds?

Ithuriel. The people introduced by Austin here
Have been my frequent care for many months.
I witnessed their distresses and their griefs,
And the injustice of their enemies
Before the storms of war beat on their homes;
The horrors of the Alamo beheld,
And near this place expect a conflict soon.
What can you tell me of the land we love?

Abdiel. That land still prospers, but the cholera
Has sent its thousands down to gloomy graves.
Black Hawk and all his Indian braves, subdued,
No more distress the frontier with their yells.
France sent five millions to the treasury,
And Portugal has settled her old debts.
Fire in New York laid forty acres bare,
Consuming eighteen millions of their wealth.
The politicians battle still for place
And fiercely wage unceasing wordy wars.

Death has been claiming great men for his prey:
Chief-justice Marshall, Randolph of Roanoke,
Carroll of Carrollton, and James Monroe,
Have lately been laid low in peace to rest.
Like Jefferson and Adams, James Monroe
Died calmly upon Independence Day.
May not this indicate that the great God
Makes that fair land peculiarly his care?
But hark! the sound of battle comes this way!
I go to learn the issue of the fight. . . . .
The Texans have their independence gained.
Their foes have fallen on the battle-field,
Are captured or are scattered to the winds.
See here comes Houston, hero of this fight;
And Santa Ana, captured, comes this way.
He well deserves to die a murd'rer's death,
But his release will give the Texans peace,
And crown with independence their brave State.

Scene: *House of Representatives, Washington, D. C., December 27, 1837.*
SATAN, GABRIEL.

Satan. Ha-ha! Ha-ha! My grandest work begins!
Slade of Vermont has raised my battle-cry,
And threescore Congressmen in chorus join,
Insulting all who dare to own black slaves.
They ask for votes to set the negroes free,
Just as if Congress was omnipotent,
With full authority to work its will.
But Wise, Legare, Rhett, Griffin, and McKay
Take up the quarrel on the other side,
Sustained by all the Southern Congressmen.
They handle one another without gloves.
How orderly! how calm! how dignified!
How loving! how courteous! how refined!
This hatred of the sections I'll inflame
Until all hearts shall blaze with fiery wrath.
With British emissaries I began
My fierce attack upon all Southerners.
Enthusiastic poets next assailed
Their Southern neighbors with vindictive zeal.
The smartlings of lyceums then began

To flap their unfledged wings against the South,
And with soft, gristly bills to fiercely peck
At reputations such as Washington's.
Then hireling lecturers, with caustic tongues,
Went forth to earn their bread by kindling strife;
While pulpit politicians loudly preached
Hate's cruel creed through sacred Sabbath hours.
Those insolent petitions I shall use
To fan disunion's embers into flames,
And hurl to every corner of the land
Red, sparkling brands of desolating wrath.

 Gabriel. [Drawing nigh.] Satan, I know your reasons
  for this work,
And marvel much that you have so deceived
So many shrewd, well-meaning citizens,
That at your instigation they're employed
To overturn the best of governments,
By trampling on the contracts of their sires
By which themselves have greatly profited.
Did not the British bring the negroes here,
Forcing the slave trade on the colonies?
Did not New England contract with the South
To bring them slaves for the first twenty years,
If the most southward States would vote with them
To tax the tonnage of all foreigners?
Did not the East get worthless debts assumed
Due by the States to her rich citizens,
By giving to the South the capital?
Were not these contracts made in all good faith
By sections as with sections, States with States?
Do not those sections and those States still live?
And do not those fair "bargains" bind them still?
If they would rue the contracts that they made,
Why not surrender up the price received?
If they repent of selling human souls,
Why not with tearful eyes go buy them back,
And set them free, and pay them for their time?
Judas himself brought back the price of blood,
But no place for repentance could he find.
They'll claim exemption from the punishment

Due to the sin committed by their sires;
But will this plea hold good while they retain
The profits of the contracts which they break?
Will quarrels or hot conflicts with the South
Atone for sins for which they hold the fruits?
Will they not meet before the judgment bar
Their own sins and their fathers' both combined,
Their violations of the contracts made,
Joined with the horrors of the vile slave trade?
If sympathy for slaves would break their bonds,
To buy them back is the one honest way.
If chivalry must fight to set slaves free,
Why break the solemn covenants they made
With their own kinsmen and compatriots?
Why not attack Dahomey or Brazil,
Whose right to slaves they have not guaranteed?
Who gave the Congress any right to slaves?
No master ever did, nor any State.
No State had such authority to give,
Nor could the Congress such a right assert
Without destroying justice, union, peace.
Satan, why lead these men so far astray?

Satan. Gabriel, what right have you to question me?
You speak the truth, but what care I for truth?
I'll make these meddling fellows rule this land,
In spite of compacts, constitutions, laws,
And all the compromises they have made.
Sheer, brazen impudence shall help them on,
Till step by step they rise to sovereign power,
And deluge this fair land with kindred blood.
Nay, more, I frankly tell you to your face
They'll do it all in the great name of Christ.
Go, Gabriel, lead the choruses of heaven,
But know that I still rule this lower world.

Gabriel. The Lord rebuke thee, Satan! I behold
The chains of darkness with which you are bound,
That shall confine you in the depths of hell;
While earth, no more polluted by your steps,
Shall be the home of happiness and love.

See your misguided dupes—they come this way:
Slade, Ogle, Corwin, Naylor, and the rest.

Scene: *Senate Chamber, Washington, D. C., February 13, 1840.
Henry Clay presenting a petition for the abolition of slavery in the
District of Columbia.* SATAN, MARS.

Satan. Unwilling as he is, Clay does my work.
'Tis not for his Kentuckians he claims
The right to offer these petitions here.

Mars. Why is it that petitions have of late
Become less frequent and are seldom seen?

Satan. The hands that held the pen have been outstretched
To beg fat offices, which they expect
When Harrison becomes the President.
Besides, 'twas ascertained that full four-fifths
Of Congress disapproved the action asked.
Self-love and self-conceit talk much of slaves,
With supercilious scorn; of masters much,
With hate's envenomed hiss and envy's curse.
T' annul a contract by a swindling trick,
Or rob another under forms of law,
Imparts more pleasure than the heav'ns could yield
To some of Mammon's shrewd, sharp clientage.

Scene: *Capitol, Washington, D. C., April 6, 1841.*

Zephon. How blessed this land, where peace and order
reign,
Though rulers change three times within five weeks!
Van Buren has to private life retired,
And Harrison, the people's choice, stood forth
To rule in righteousness the land he loved.
But death removed him to a higher sphere,
And Tyler takes the ruler's place to-day.
These changes have not cost one drop of blood,
Nor drawn a tear-drop from an infant's eye,
Nor brought a blush to beauty's lovely cheek,
Nor caused a widow's heart to throb with fear.

STATE HOUSE, PHILADELPHIA.

(144)

Ariel. The census shows that in the last ten years
The States have gained twice told the number that
On Independence Day defied King George.
Two new republics join the kindred band
That constitutes the great United States.
Along the lakes reposes Michigan,
While Arkansas rests by the river-side.
The warring Seminoles have been subdued:
Fair Florida no longer dreads their wrath.
The peaceful Cherokees, with sobs and tears,
Left their old home and their forefathers' graves,
And journeyed sadly toward the setting sun.
The white men paid them millions for their lands,
And gave them richer ground beyond the flood;
But gold soothed not the sorrows of those hearts
That heaved the patr'ots' sigh for native land.
The white man's contract with the white man made
Must be complied with; so the Indian marched,
Driv'n by white soldiers from their much loved homes.

Uzziel. Did retribution break the white man's banks,
Sinking two hundred millions in one year,
Driving the rich men from their palaces?
Will some Tecumseh, in the days to come,
With most despotic cruelty drive out
The peaceful whites from that same lovely land?

Raphael. 'Tis not for me to say; the future's sealed.
So of God's will, in what he here permits,
Or rather what he suffers to be done.
But yonder comes Tyler to take the oath,
And Taney to administer to him
The obligations of a President.

Scene: *Baltimore, Md., May 29, 1844. The Magnetic Telegraph.*
RAPHAEL, ITHURIEL.

Raphael. This day has witnessed such a grand event
As men have never seen on earth before.
Compared with it, all interests of these times
Must dwindle into insignificance.
The title to Van Rensellaer's broad lands;
Dorr, in the prison, or at liberty,

To vex Rhode Island with anarchic schemes;
The monument that stands on Bunker Hill;
The Bank bill vetoed, or the Bankrupt bill;
The cabinet dissolved; the boundary line
Adjusted with Great Britain peaceably—
What are they all compared with this event?

Ithuriel. Please tell me what it is of which you speak?

Raphael. 'Tis the magnetic telegraph by Morse.
He makes acidulated metal plates
Seize with strong hands the lightning's wond'rous force,
And send it as a post-boy round the world,
Over his wiry path with such great speed
As distances the swift-winged flight of time,
Or the velocity of all the spheres,
Or undulations of the rays of light.
It makes all nations neighbors, and gives each
An interest in the welfare of them all.
"What hath God wrought!" Give glory to his name!
And let all people loudly say "Amen!"
Behold the benefactor of his race,
Whose honored name shall flash around the world
And be emblazoned in the book of life!

Scene: *Washington D. C., July 4, 1846.* SATAN, MAMMON, BELIAL.

Satan. What brings you here on Independence Day?

Mammon. The interests of my clients are at stake.
They saw with undissembled pain and grief
Tyler succeed the much loved Harrison.
With wrath and indignation they beheld
Texas annexed in spite of their protests.
War followed, and they yelled with savage rage.
But here they're touched in their most tender place—
Their pocket-nerve is sorely, sadly rasped.
Four years ago Clay's compromise had brought
The tariff to the rate agreed upon;
But, to their interests ever wide awake,
My clients shrewdly got the rates increased.
But Polk defeated Clay, and then was heard
Much talk of strict construction and the like.

A tariff for protection was pronounced
Unconstitutional, and breach of faith.
To introduce it was, they said, "to lie,"
And to enforce it, "arrantly to rob."
We pleaded precedents, and boldly claimed
That from great Hamilton to Henry Clay
Protection was the settled policy
Of this great nation, and should ever be;
But they out-voted us, and will require
My much protected friends to take their hands
Out of their neighbors' purses with sad haste,
Unless the Senate holds while rich men rob.

Satan. Be of good cheer. I now am laying plans
By which protected wealth may gorge itself
At poverty's expense without control;
When war between the sections with red hands
Shall hold subjected millions by their throats
And let protection rob at its sweet will.
But there stands Polk, with Walker by his side:
They've planned a tariff that's for revenue.

Scene: *Battle-field of Buena Vista, Mexico, February 23, 1847.* SATAN, MARS.

Satan. What think you of this battle, my great friend?
Did Macedonians equal Taylor's troops?
Did Rome's famed legions make so brave a fight?

Mars. I must confess these troops are unsurpassed
By any I have seen in ancient times.
I saw on Palo Alto's battle-field,
And in Resaca de la Palma's fight,
And on the heights of Monterey displayed
Such valor as I heartily admired;
But Buena Vista bears the palm away
From all the conflicts I have witnessed yet.
The unpretending hero of this fight
Is coming this way, "Rough and Ready" still.
See at his side the husband of his child!
Though long estranged, they now are reconciled.
Jeff. Davis is the old man's joy and pride,
Whose Mississippians, a living wall

'Gainst which the tide of battle broke in vain,
Drove back the surging Mexicans to-day.
And there is Marshall, Washington, and Bragg,
Who gave the foe "a little more of grape;"
And there young Breckenridge and Crittenden,
And there the unnamed heroes of the ranks—
Let Jacob Goodson represent them all.
Hurrah! hurrah for Buena Vista's braves!
They drove five times their number from the field;
But Clay, McKee, and hundreds of brave men
Yielded their lives to win the victory.

Scene: *City of Mexico, dawn of day, September 13, 1847.* SATAN, MARS, BELIAL, BAAL.

Baal. The strife is nearly ended. War-worn troops
Enter to-day their foe's proud capital.
A war like this I never saw before.
The great republic wins in every fight.
A handful of brave men, far from their homes,
Most of them raw recruits, meet well-drilled foes,
Ten times their number, backed by millions more,
And, having conquered them, bind up their wounds,
And treat them as born brothers and true friends.

Belial. Such wars as this I have no fondness for.
I favor wars with more of deviltry.
These "goody-goody" men disturb no roosts,
They rob no sheep-folds on their pious march,
But leave their Bibles with their enemies.
'Tis said they offer fifteen millions now
For land that is already theirs by war:
This to the conquered from their conquerors.

Mars. So charmed am I by bravery in arms
That I was blind to things of which you speak.
I saw the cities of the Western coast
Surrender to Sloat, Stockton, and Fremont.
I witnessed Kearney's march to Santa Fe,
Saw it surrender to the troops he led;
Then saw him turn toward the setting sun
And at San Gabriel, with a few brave men,
Secure an empire for his countrymen;

Saw Doniphan with his eight hundred march
From their Missouri homes to Saltillo,
Fight at Bracito, cross the Rio Grande,
Capture El Paso, whip the Mexicans
At Sacramento Creek; march to Chihuahua,
Capture it and forty thousand people,
Besides troops; there with his ragged heroes
March again to find and make report to
General Wool at distant Saltillo.
I marveled at the fall of Vera Cruz;
And when on Cerro Gordo's rocky heights
Twiggs won the day, I scarce believed my eyes.
And when five thousand men so far from home
Took Jalapa, Perote, and Puebla,
With prisoners, artillery, and stores,
I said "This is but bait by which t' entrap
These bold invaders of this flow'ry land."
When unopposed the val'rous troops had passed
The Cordilleras and looked down upon
The blooming lands of Central Mexico,
I felt assured the trap would hold them fast;
But all these frowning forts have failed to check
Th' impetuous charges of resistless men.
Chepultepec was carried yesterday.
Last night, in darkness, Santa Ana fled;
To-day the conquerors come marching in.
See! There they give their banner to the breeze!
What men they are! How grandly do they march!
Would I could see them battle with their peers!
That would be war well worthy of the name.

Satan. Mars, you shall see them with their equals
 fight;
Yes, with each other in most deadly strife.
Pillow and Twiggs shall battle against Scott,
And Scott plan campaigns 'gainst his native State.
These West Point officers, now bosom friends,
Shall marshal mighty hosts with wondrous skill
To kill each other upon battle-fields.
But here they come: Scott, Butler, Pillow, Pierce,
Twiggs, Worth, Smith, Shields, and gallant Colonel Lee.

Scene: *San Francisco, Cal., August 1, 1847.* RAPHAEL, ARIEL, ZEPHON.

Raphael. Four weeks ago in far off Washington
The President, most fortunate of men,
Announced the end of war with Mexico.
Success attends his steps and crowns his plans,
Writing in lines of light his honored name.
Texas, annexed, war Christianized and made
A blessing to the men who brought it on,
Has been successful against fearful odds
In ev'ry bloody battle that was fought.
Peace comes, with graceful steps and smiling face,
To bring green laurels for heroic men
Whom he sent forth to champion the right;
And title deeds conveying vast domains,
With rocks and sands glitt'ring with shining gold,
And world-wide oceans from which commerce comes,
To crown his country empress of the seas.
There is the Golden Gate, and on this spot
Old Asia shall lay tribute at her feet.
The British treaty touched the threat'ning cloud
That long obscured the northern boundary,
Bore its fierce "lightnings harmless to the deep,"
And let the rays of friendship light the scene.
Four States have been admitted, and their stars
Are now emblazoned brightly on the flag:
Fair Florida, Texas, and Iowa
Stand with Wisconsin in the Union now.

Ariel. Raphael, such progress never has been made
By any other nation in four years.
Do you remember Smithson's gen'rous gift?
An institution bears his honored name.

Raphael. I do; and generations yet to come
Shall own their obligations and give thanks.

Zephon. Is there no drawback on these prosp'rous years,
No evil to subtract from all the good?

Raphael. No, not the least, except that chilly death

Has laid his hand on two ex-Presidents:
Jackson and Adams, both in ripe old age,
Rest from their labors and their earthly cares.

Scene: *Washington, D. C., September 19, 1850.* ABDIEL, ITHURIEL,
ARIEL.

Abdiel. Ho, comrades! this auspicious day calls forth
The glad congratulations of warm hearts
In millions of this country's happy homes.
The bow of hope and promise spans the sky,
Where storms were gathering and thunders rolled.
Clay's compromise, adopted yesterday,
Brings back sweet memories of by-gone days,
Ere Satan had stirred up the States to strife
And bade fanatic fury vex the land.
The sections once so rash abide in peace,
Encircled by the links of love's bright chain.
The country rings with cheerful, joyful words,
Ascribing highest honors to the names
Of Clay, Cass, Douglass, Webster, Bright, and Foote.
Death has called Taylor to an honored grave,
But Fillmore worthily fills his high place.
Happy the land with such wise rulers blessed,
And its fierce factions shamed into repose!
See Fillmore, Webster, Clay, and Crittenden,
Bright, Douglass, Foote, and Cass, and Dickinson!
Praise God, praise God for fearless patriots!

Scene: *Faneuil Hall, Boston, March 1, 1854.* SATAN, BAAL, MAM-
MON, BELIAL.

Satan. More than three years ago Clay's compromise
Hushed the rude storms that darkened all this land.
Since then low mutt'ring thunder has been heard,
And angry lightnings seen along the sky.
But soon a deadly cyclone shall come down,
Black with infernal malice and fierce wrath,
To overturn and desolate and crush
All it encounters in its furious course.
Yet this is what I've long desired to see.

Baal. Speak plainly, Satan, let us understand,
What is there to precipitate this storm?

Satan. The hatred of the sections, long suppressed,
Breaks forth to rend the sky and shake the earth.

Baal. New England's clergy pray to men, not God,
For help against "Steve Douglass and Frank Pierce."
Were they not born upon New England ground?

Mammon. They were! New England has no truer sons.
What is it those two potent men propose?

Satan. Self-government for men in the far West.

Baal. Self-government? For that their fathers fought.

Satan. 'Twas that New England might New England rule.

Baal. Whom would they have to rule Nebraska now?

Satan. Of course, New England. No, her clergymen,
With Sumner, Chase, Chandler, and Wade to help;
Not such New Englanders as Bancroft, Morse,
Hawthorne, Pierce, Cushing, or wise Everett.
They e'en lock Webster out of Faneuil Hall.
They want a few fanatics and their dupes
To seize the helm and steer the ship of State.
Their plans are mine; they have my hearty help.

Baal. They want to see "black feet on the white necks"
Of those whose fathers broke their fathers' yokes,
Or possibly would rather kindle flames
To burn slave-holders as they witches burned.

Belial. Or else garrote them, as the Cubans did
My friend Lopez, who went to set them free;
Or shoot them by the millions in cold blood,
And San Domingoize their lovely land.

Satan. Belial, there shall be work enough for you
And all your cronies when the war shall come,
As come it must in a few stormy months.
Insults and outrages shall stir the South
Till Southerners will haughtily withdraw,
In supercilious pride to dwell apart.

THE OCEAN TELEGRAPH. 153

Scene: *Battery, New York, August, 1858.* ARIEL, URIEL.

Ariel. Angelic rapture joins with human joy
In this great city on this glorious day.
The telegraph connects two hemispheres.
Its messages outspeed the flight of time,
And leave the rapid rays of light behind.
These people are the wonder of the world!
'Twas here the Crystal Palace grandly rose;
From here brave Perry sailed to far Japan,
Unlocking its hid treasures for mankind.
From here went Ingram who, with threat'ning guns,
Compelled the Austrians to release Koszta.

Uriel. This nation is indeed to be admired.
'Tis blessed of God and envied by mankind.
The product of her mines a single year
Would pay for Cuba, if old Spain would sell.
Her fields would feed the millions of the world,
And clothe them in clean garments day by day.
Her sons have rescued Britons near the pole,
And conquered Mormons in the Western wilds.
But see, there's Cyrus Field, Morse, Vanderbilt,
Bryant, and Greeley, Bennett, Beecher, Tweed.

Scene: *Harper's Ferry, Va., 1859.* GABRIEL, ABDIEL, ITHURIEL, URIEL.

Abdiel. What mean these crowds of grave, indignant men?

Gabriel. The most atrocious of all fiendish crimes
Was here committed by a wretch named Brown;
A crime involving treason, murder, theft,
Rebellion, kidnapping, and robbery,
Leading to arson, rape, and bloody war.

Ithuriel. Yet, strange to say, outside of prison walls
And lunatic asylums there are found
Not a few kindred spirits who, less brave,
Would canonize John Brown their patron saint.
Write poetry and sing most warlike songs
In honor of his name so infamous!

Brown and his guilty gang are to be hanged
To-day, before the setting of the sun.

Uriel. Of course such criminals must suffer death.
Do not all people execrate such deeds?

Gabriel. No; hatred of the sections longs for blood.
This country has become two hostile camps.
Grave Senators of mighty sovereign States,
Sage judges of most honored civil courts,
Poets of sweetest song and world-wide fame,

HARPER'S FERRY.

Fair ladies, loveliest of Adam's race,
And even ministers of Jesus Christ
Would gladly share the guilt of old John Brown,
But for the fear that they would have to hang.
They share his hate, but not his bravery.

Abdiel. Where is the grateful, patriotic love
That warmed all hearts when Boston was relieved,
And saw the British yield to Washington?
Where the benevolent affection seen

When Cornwallis surrendered at Yorktown?
Where is the confidence that was displayed
When Washington the oath of office took?

Gabriel. All, all are gone. They're driven from the land,
Banished by jealousy and slain by hate.

Abdiel. Are all the people thus antagonized?
Does hellish malice burn in ev'ry heart?

Gabriel. No; not one man in twenty thirsts for blood.

Abdiel. How then can twenty be controlled by one?

Gabriel. The twenty seek for pleasure, ease, or wealth,
And trouble not themselves with politics,
Except to vote as prompted by the one.
The one, an active fosterling of hell,
Is leagued with Satan to divide the States.
He makes himself a champion of the North
Against the hateful people of the South,
Whose monstrous sin it is to own some slaves,
Sold to their fathers by this champion's sire.
Of course the South has champions of its own,
Ready to battle for its right to slaves,
As guaranteed by Northern patriots.
Thus halls of Congress now are battle-fields
Where North and South contend for mastery.
When Cavaliers met Puritans in fight,
Rupert and Cromwell were not fiercer foes.
Each of the sections has a selfish few
Who climb to office by the help of hate.
They battle for their section or their State
With noisy, boastful insolence and strife.
These noisy watch-dogs always snap and snarl
Most spitefully against the South or North,
Claiming that all who do not bark with them
Are foes to God and traitors to their State.
The multitude, misled by angry tones,
Bark for their section or their sovereign State.
The evil is infectious. Demagogues
Successfully employ the same bad trick,

And feign the hatred which they never felt.
State after State has fallen into line,
And marches with its section to the polls,
Till soon fanaticism, seizing power,
Will marshal twenty States against thirteen,
And force each citizen to serve his State.
A thousand mad men thus may drive to war
The thirty millions of the peaceable,
And deluge this fair land with kindred blood.

Uriel. Was there a compact made in eighty-seven
To keep the slaves from treading Western soil?

Gabriel. James Madison says no. The ordinance
Of eighty-seven was not authorized
By sovereign States, and had no legal force
To bind the people longer than they chose.
Cass says there was no party to contract
Or make a compact with the old Congress.
It was a simple act, and nothing more,
And was not binding on the Western States.

Uriel. What of the compromise of twenty-one?

Gabriel. That was without the slightest legal force.
'Twas the hard hand of King Majority,
Stripping the Southern section of its rights,
Breaking the treaty made with Bonaparte.
'Twas robbery submitted to for peace,
So must the courts decide when called to judge.
But the strong-handed North did ostracize
All of their men who made that compromise.

Uriel. Why then do they complain of its repeal?

Gabriel. Sheer selfishness constrains them to that course.
When 'twas proposed to run on that known line
Across the continent, and give the South
The land below it, they would not consent.

Abdiel. What is it, then, they want? What can be done

To satisfy the statesmanship of hate?
Is there no remedy for this disease
That blinds men to their own best interests,
That darkens understandings, hardens hearts,
And overturns all sense of right and wrong?

Gabriel. They want all they can get, but most of all
A separation from all slave-holders,
And to see negroes cut their masters' throats,
And lustfully defile their masters' homes.
But see, there is the Governor and staff,
And there is Colonel Robert Edward Lee,
And the brave soldiers under his command;
And there the sheriff-executioner.
The penalty of law will be enforced,
But the most guilty have not yet been caught.

BOOK EIGHTH.

Scene: *Charleston, S. C., December 25, 1860.* ABDIEL, RAPHAEL, ARIEL, URIEL.

Ariel. On this glad day men celebrate with joy
The advent of the Lord in human form.
We join them, saying: " Glory be to God,
Peace on the earth, good-will to all mankind."

Uriel. Yet 'twas but yesterday that this great State,
Resolved to leave the Union in hot haste,
Dissolving all the loving ties that bound
These three and thirty sovereign States in one.

Raphael. Yes, and 'tis said twelve more will soon secede
And in a new confederation join.

Uriel. Can it be wise the Union to dissolve?
Have they the right thus to withdraw at will?

Abdiel. You ask two questions. I will answer both.
'Tis most unwise. 'Tis 'gainst the Lord's decree,
As written on his valleys, mountains. plains,
And certified by every plant that grows.
Each section raises what the other needs;
Each varying plant for union ever pleads.
Disunion is impracticable too,
So say the rivers, lakes, and gulfs and seas,
And so the waves and storms of oceans say.
Domestic commerce asks to be left free
T' enrich all sections with its benefits.
Disunion soon will lead to border wars,
And standing armies to enslave the States.

Uriel. 'Tis to avoid bad neighbors they secede,
And to prevent continued drain of wealth
From Southern States to people of the North.

Abdiel. Let us suppose all that they say is true:
That "navigation laws," "State debts assumed,"
"A chartered bank" took money from the South;
That tariffs drained its wealth from year to year;
That Southern cities dwindle and lose trade,
While millions crowd the cities of the North,
And millionaires build splendid palaces.
Admit injustice done to Southern States
By legislation on the public lands.
For argument say swindling has prevailed
In all the dealings of the North with slaves;
Say blacks were swindled out of liberty,
The South was swindled into buying them,
With pledges that the North would well protect
Their right of ownership and would send back
All fugitives that might escape to them;
That Southern men were guaranteed the right
To vote for three in five that they would buy;
Say that the thrifty North received and kept
Payment in full for all it gave the South,
Then quickly broke the contract that it made,
And will still break it to the end of time;
Add that a certain faction in the North
Is most unjust to Southern gentlemen,
And most disgusting to their high-bred tastes.
For argument, admit that this is true.
Disunion will but complicate all ills;
War multiply them twice ten thousand fold.
The selfishness of sections may cause loss
In many ways of legal robbery,
But twice ten thousand years of peaceful theft
Would cause less damage than one year of war.
As to those most offensive gentlemen,
From whom these Southrons shrink instinctively
With utter loathing and supreme contempt,
If under constitutional restraints
They are so disagreeable and bad,
What is to make them amiable and kind
When those restraints no longer hold them back?
If legal swindling makes the Southland poor,
What must it lose when hatred's backed by force?

160 *THE AMERICAN EPIC.*

Disunion offers not the least relief
From any wrongs the suff'ring South endures;
But by the force of State rights principles
Compels its honest friends to join its foes.
Resistance in the Union against wrong
Would be far safer under the old flag.

ALEXANDER H. STEPHENS.

The South has more true friends in the free States
Than can be found in all the world besides.
Disunion gives to Satan all he asks
To work the desolation of these States.

Uriel. Now tell us, is secession a State right?
Have they the right thus to withdraw at will?

Abdiel. They think they have, and so have others
  thought.
The infant West while yet in swaddling-bands,
So threatened when the East, with selfish greed,
Would trade away her pathway to the gulf
For small advantages to its own trade.
The East contended for the self-same right,
When Jefferson became the President,
And when Louisiana was acquired,
When the embargo law obstructed trade,
They asked great Hamilton to lead them out
And form a nation with its southern line
Along the Hudson or the Delaware;
But he refused to join them and secede.
John Henry came with loving messages,
Proposing union with the Canadas
Under his gracious Majesty, King George.
Near the green turf where Warren's ashes slept,
They listened with the most intense delight,
Though Bunker Hill frowned grimly all the while.
Then came the war. The country, unprepared,
Required the help of all her patriot sons
Against the foe their fathers bravely fought.
But can it be believed men of sound minds
Talked gravely in convention of the need
That sovereign States should, in the midst of war,
Obstruct the work of their own government
In its heroic battle for the right.
Yes, the great North, through the last sixty years,
Has often boldly threatened to withdraw.
It threatened when new Southern States came in;
When tariffs for protection were repealed;
When the great State of Texas was annexed;
When Mexico made war against the States;
When peace was made and much new land acquired;
And last, not least, since in these later years
The Constitution to the North has seemed
"A league with death, a covenant with hell."
Their statesmen said the Union could not last
With some free States and others holding slaves;
Yet it had lasted more than fourscore years,

From Washington and Warren to the time
When this fierce faction claimed the government.

 Uriel. What said the men who made this covenant?

 Abdiel. They claimed the right of States to interpose
For the protection of their citizens
Against encroachments of the Fed'ral pow'r;
Would grant no right to make war on the States,
Were horror-stricken at the dreadful thought
Of military force to coerce States.
Perpetual union was what they desired,
But feared 'twas utterly impossible.
They died deploring animosities
Of section against section then at work
To overturn the Union they had formed.
They claimed the right to revolutionize
Against all governmental tyranny,
And in their States saw the best means at hand
For overturning fed'ral despotism,
Hence would not give their fed'ral government
Authority to war against the States.
The advocates of a strong government
Never demanded such authority.
The States would not consent to make a thing
To arm their citizens against themselves,
To plan "A union pinned by bayonets."
Such was the union Britain had to give.

 Uriel. You say the Union never gained the right
To coerce States and force them to submit?

 Abdiel. No, never. It has troops to rise in arms
And bravely conquer all its foreign foes,
Troops to aid Governors of sovereign States
When they in need apply for fed'ral help,
Troops to suppress by force anarchic mobs
And drive fierce Indians off from frontier homes.
To enforce its laws, its courts have officers;
But to make war upon a sovereign State
The fathers never did nor would consent.
The Union has no soldier for that use.

Uriel. But what if war is made upon a State?

Abdiel. 'Twould be subversion of the government,
And despotism on its ruins built.

Uriel. What if some States should subjugate the rest,
And forcibly compel them to submit?

Abdiel. It would be such an instance of bad faith,
So base a blow at honesty and truth,
Such loud assertion that 'tis might makes right,
As to strike down morality and faith.

Uriel. But is the Union a mere rope of sand,
To be dissolved by waves of discontent?

Abdiel. No, no. 'Twas formed and lives by compromise.
Morris and Hamilton said it would take
With its strong hand the pow'rs that were denied;
But if it does, 'twill overthrow good faith
And trample moral honor in the dust.
A nation's immorality will spread
Its rank contagion widely through the land,
Tainting all classes with dishonor's breath,
Corrupting both the lofty and the low,
And teaching all to swindle and deceive,
From tricks of trade, adulterating food,
Or selling shoddy for good woolen cloth,
To the divorce court's vile indecencies;
Among the lowly and among the proud;
Smutching the reputations of high life,
The beauteous wives and daughters of the great,
The brilliant Senators, the chief divines:
From buying votes to buying Congressmen,
Or seats for millionaires in Senate halls;
From stealing money, lands, and stocks and bonds,
To stealing railroads, churches, or in time
May even steal the presidency too.
Such retributions nations overtake!

Uriel. You say the Union lives by compromise.

Without the use of military force
Can selfish men be held by such a bond?

Abdiel. They've been so held for more than fourscore
years,
And ought to be till time itself shall end.

Ariel. But if a war ensues, where rests the blame?

Raphael. The hatreds of the sections cause the strife.
Divide the blame between them as you will.
But the rash faction that's to rule the North
Will be itself a menace to the South.
'Tis revolution organized, at work,
To overthrow the union of the States
And subjugate the South to Northern whims.
No hour has passed since the first Congress met
In which its principles, if dominant,
Would not have given the Union to the winds.
The founders of the faction knew it well,
Intended it, and boast about it now.

Ariel. Will this division now take place in peace?

Raphael. I fear not. Hatred drives to bloody deeds.
The factions climbed to office upon hate;
They lose their places if men cease to hate.
In many things both of them are quite wrong:
Wrong in their hatreds, in their love of war,
In their abusive words and boasting threats:
The North most wicked in its breach of faith,
Its breaking of the covenant it made;
The South most wicked in its haughty pride,
Most silly in deciding to secede.
The North dishonest in kidnapping slaves,
Doubly dishonest when it set them free,
When with their masters it had contracted
To guarantee their right of ownership.
Yet, if it wished to see some slaves go free,
There was an honest, honorable way.
To purchase and emancipate was work
That Southern men had shown them how to do.
This broke no treaties, trampled on no pledge,

Disturbed no peace, paid back the price of blood.
If fight they must to kill some slave-holders,
Turks, Russians, Cubans worthy of their steel,
Are not far off in these fast days of steam.
Hotspurs and Quixotes may their millions slay,
Nor violate one word of plighted faith,
Such as they're bound by to Americans.

Scene: *Capitol, Washington, D. C., March 30, 1861.* MICHAEL, GABRIEL.

Gabriel. The evil that we feared confronts us now.
For more than twenty days these mighty States
Have been controlled by a minority,
Whose hold on pow'r cannot continue long
Unless they manage to provoke a war
And revolutionize the government.
This rampant faction has been born of hate,
And fed on malice from its earliest hours.
The milk of human kindness in a day
Would neutralize the venom in its fangs,
But now its horrid mother screams for blood
To gratify the longings of her brood.

Michael. Has naught been done, can nothing now be done
To counteract this bloody-mindedness?

Gabriel. Virginia grandly rose in majesty
To lay her kindly hand on maddened States,
And urge them to dismiss their enmities.
Kentucky pleaded well for unity.
A great Peace Congress met at Washington
To plead for moderation, peace, and love.
The mad-caps of the South had left in haste,
Not knowing what the Peace Congress would ask,
Nor what the selfish faction of the North
Would condescend to grant or to deny.
That faction held the purse and swayed the sword.
It chose to be defiant, and to drive
The friends of union from them in despair.
The kindly heart of the new President
Gave the peace-makers many anecdotes,

Refined or rustic, chaste or otherwise,
And wondered that they blushed but did not laugh.
His fiercer followers, with threat'ning oaths,
Demanded "blood-letting" and nothing less;
While the least furious, the mild, the kind,
Insisted that the South be northernized—
If not that day, at least in a short time.
Slaves must be free, and slave-holders condemned,
In spite of constitutional compacts:
Laws, habits, tastes, judgments, and consciences,
Or evil consequences to ensue.
They washed their saintly hands in innocence
Of their forefathers' trades that made them rich,
Forgot " the bargain " by which they for slaves
Obtained wealth greater than "Peru's rich mines."
Their contracts with slave-holders could not bind
The consciences of such malignant saints.
Their horror-stricken souls would flee in haste
From slavery's contaminating touch.
Pinckney or Gadsden or great Washington
If ent'ring the abodes of those rash men,
Would so defile the sacred sanctity
Of the old union it must be purged pure;
So sober Southerners indignant turned,
Solemn and sad with dignity, to join
Their fierce compatriots of the farther South.

Michael. Will war ensue, or will they part in peace?

Gabriel. The Southern States desire to go in peace,
And claim the right to separate at will.
The faction that now rules claimed the same right
As their forefathers have for sixty years.

Michael. Then peace and love should evermore prevail.

Gabriel. Peace might prevail, but never, never love.
Because of hate they long have wished them gone;
But if the Southern States depart in peace,
This faction dies for having driv'n them off.
If it can fill the land with bloody war,
It may live on through evil years to come
And wreak its vengeance on both North and South.

To slay a million of Americans,
And waste ten billions of the nation's wealth
In gratifying malice, would be deeds
Such as no other faction could achieve,
Such deeds as might throughout all time to come
Immortalize the statesmanship of hate.

Michael. How is it that such things are possible
Under a government by Christians made?

Gabriel. This is one government by thirteen made.
Each of the thirteen was a sovereign State.
It now is one of thirty-three composed—
Say thirty-three republics joined in one.
Each of the thirteen was a sovereign State:
Not one would yield its claim to sovereignty;
Yet each agreed to clothe with potent sway
A fed'ral government embracing all.
They would not give it pow'r to coerce States,
But let it rule their citizens at will,
And said that rule should be perpetual,
Under perpetual union of the States.
And then they gave to it both purse and sword.
And tied its hands with handsome paper twine,
Called muniments of English liberty,
And said each State was guardian of its rights,
And of the rights of all its citizens;
Yet pointed out no way by which in peace
The States could interpose to save their rights.
The fathers gave too little, or too much,
To the great central pow'r the States set up.
Wise Samuel Adams said they gave too much,
And Patrick Henry, with a prophet's voice,
Foretold the coming evils he foresaw.
Morris and Hamilton demanded more,
And said that it would take what was denied.

Michael. But what has that to do with bloody strife?

Gabriel. With less of pow'r, the States had been left free
From dread of fed'ral force and tyranny;
With more, resistance never would be risked.

Now, a fierce faction, less than half the North,
Drives off the South with its insulting threats,
And may use force to drive them back again.
If so, a sort of double sovereignty
Makes traitors of the best of citizens;
Owing allegiance to his native State,
And through it to the gen'ral government,
When they agree the citizen is safe.
But if the State secedes, and arms her sons,
And men at Washington deny her right,
Then treason dooms the citizens to death,
In spite of the most loving loyalty
To both authorities that claim his life.

Michael. How stands the President upon that point?

Gabriel. States to the fed'ral government, with him,
Are but as counties are to sovereign States.
I fear he would make war upon a State
Retiring from the Union as of right,
With no more hesitation than a State
Would subjugate a county in revolt.
'Tis possible that he has never learned
The principles on which the Union's formed.
The fire-brands of his faction are disposed
With ready hands to light the flames of war.
I fear that he will listen to their schemes,
And suffer them to glut themselves with blood.

Michael. But will the peaceful people let them fight?

Gabriel. They'll wait until some Hotspur of the South
Can be provoked to fire upon the flag;
Then call for men to rally to their help,
Defending the bright banner of the free.
An army well in hand can be increased
In many ways in spite of discontent.
The fearful will be scared into its ranks,
The brave will rush to prove their bravery,
Ambitious men to fight their way to fame,
The poor for bread, thieves for the chance to steal.
It's therefore possible—yes, probable—

That cruel war will desolate this land.
Look! There, see Chandler, Bingham, Giddings, Wade,
Thad. Stevens, Sumner, Cameron, Seward, Chase,
They are the men to curse or bless mankind.

Scene: *Charleston, S. C., April 12, 1861.* SATAN, MARS, BAAL,
MAMMON, BELIAL.

Satan. The long expected moment has arrived,
When war goes forth with desolating hand.
The Hotspurs of the South have long proclaimed
That one can whip six Northern men with ease;

FORT SUMTER.

While boastful Northern men are confident
That they in ninety days can whip the South.
Both have for years been "spoiling for a fight."
They have it now. Let them make good their boasts.
This firing on the flag will fire all hearts,
And unify the North against the South.
'Twill make the South a battle-field for years,
And every boy a soldier for his State.
What say you, Mars, have I not kept my word?

Mars. You have. You have redeemed your promises.

Satan. Go, then, and gather millions for the fray.
Bring them from ev'ry corner of this land.
From Europe, Asia, Africa, the isles,
And from profoundest depths of hellish gloom
Go, Baal, call forth all your followers.
Bring murder, arson, lust, and villainy
Of every type that earth has ever known.

Baal. I will! I will! I will! your Majesty;
And some that hell itself has yet to learn.

Satan. Mammon, go summon all your employees.
Let them serve legions of camp-followers,
Robbers and thieves by thousands in the ranks,
And captains, colonels, gen'rals by the score,
With now and then a chaplain gone astray,
Or a grave senator or sober judge,
Hast'ning on higher plunder to get rich.
Say, Mammon, are you ready for your work?

Mammon. I am! I am! my high and mighty prince!

Satan. Belial, your children call to their base work,
On battle-fields, in camps, or in the homes
Of soldiers far away from wife and child.
Stir up the slaves to lust, theft, robbery;
Invent new follies, vices, sins, and crimes.

Belial. Trust me to do my part, most potent prince.
The world shall be astounded at our deeds.

Satan. Go, comrades, drench this Christian land with blood
By Christians shed in fratricidal strife.
Rest not till millions heave their dying groans,
Till widows wail and helpless orphans cry
In twice five hundred thousand Christian homes.
Hark! hark! the thunder of the bombardment
Grows louder, more terrific than before.
Fort Sumter is in ruins! it must fall—

. . . .

The garrison comes forth with honors crowned.
There's Beauregard, the victor in this fight,
There Anderson, and Jeff C. Davis too,
And all their brave compatriots in arms.
This mad attack of Southrons on the flag
Is to the ruling faction of the North
News far too good to be regarded true
Until they have it carefully confirmed;
But when believed, they'll loose the dogs of war
To wreak terrific vengeance on the South.

Scene: *Manassas Junction, Va., July 21, 1861.* MARS, SATAN, BAAL, MAMMON.

Mars. Where are the battles and the slaughtered hosts
You spoke of when we met at Charleston last?
The city mob shot men in Baltimore.
Magruder slew a few at Bethel Church;
Morris, at Philippi, drove Southern men
As Wallace did at Romney. Blood was shed
When Garnet met McClellan, and was slain.
Rich Mountain saw a Fed'ral victory,
As did Cheat River near to Carricksford.
We have had skirmishes and swift retreats,
But nothing worthy of the name of war.

Satan. Be patient, Mars, great armies meet to-day,
Led by West Pointers upon either side,
Who will not suffer skulking to be done
By low-life cowards or by carpet-knights,
Or pot-house politicians in the garb
Of brigadier or major generals.
At Washington this is a gala day.
So confident of victory are they
That thousands come to see men play at war.
Then "On to Richmond " with but slight delay!

Baal. Hark! Listen to the cannon's thund'ring roar!
See overwhelming legions rushing on
To crush thin lines of soldiers dressed in gray!
Vast numbers will outflank on either hand
The worn and weary Southern chivalry.

Satan. What troops are those approaching from the West?

Mars. That is Joe Johnston bringing into line
Six thousand warriors who have just arrived.
What men they are! Such blood, such bravery!
Such moral force has never been surpassed.
The heterogeneous masses of their foes
Must flee or fall beneath the banded might
That fights as if one will inspired them all.
They conquer. Regulars and volunteers,
The "city roughs," " society's *elite,*"
Grave Senators and gifted Congressmen,
All panic-stricken, in confusion mixed,
With one desire—to enter Washington.

Satan. What next? what next? Tell me, thou God of war!

Mars. On, on to Washington, with haste and speed,
To strengthen its intrenchments, and call out
All Northern troops to fight in its defense!

Satan. What should Confederates do at such a time?

Mars. Capture their routed foes, or shoot them down;
Strike Washington while yet the panic lasts;
Seize forts and arms and ammunition there,
The railroads and the shipping in the port;
Capture the President and cabinet,
The Congress and all other officers;
Take Baltimore, enlist its citizens;
Hasten to Philadelphia, New York,
Boston and other cities of the East;
Call out the rabble, arm them for the fight,
And give them Southern rulers for some days,
Till the whole South could hasten to the North;
Then, turning back, meet the on-coming crowds
Of Western soldiers at well-chosen points;
Fight, or negotiate, as best might suit.

Satan. A Cæsar or Napoleon might do that,
With half the friends the South has in the North,

Or half the haters of the men who rule;
But it suits not the temper of the South
To conquer and to hold the mighty North,
If such a task were easy to perform.
What it desires is " to be let alone."
Their haughty hatred of the North forbids
The subjugation of its busy throngs.
They would not take the whole as a free gift,
Unless its denizens would emigrate
To heaven or to some other distant place.
Against all Yankees they are taken with
What an old Frenchman called " one grand disgust."
A separation is what they demand.

 Mammon. But this is folly's most absurd desire.
No Chinese wall could keep a Yankee out
Of lands he knows he is not wanted in.
Such shrewd Paul Prys would find a way to hell,
Were they prohibited from going there.

 Satan. They teach me more new tricks than I have learned
Through all the ages from all other men.

 Belus. Old Babylon had no such citizens.
Had one live Yankee landed from the ark,
This slow old world would have been spurred to speed
Such as its lazy tribes failed to attain.

 Mars. These victors will not " on to Washington."
Davis has come. See him with Johnston there;
They will not chase their panic-stricken foes.
The South has lost its opportunity.

Scene: *State Department, Washington, D. C., November, 1861.* SATAN, MARS.

 Satan. What brings you here to-day, brave, trusty friend?

 Mars. I came to stir the flames of furious wrath
Against the British here in Washington.
Wilkes is the hero of the present hour,
The idol of the people of the North.
With half a chance they'd make him President.

They talk of Wilkes, of Mason, of Slidell,
And want to sweep old England from the seas.

Satan. Have you succeeded in your enterprise?

Mars. No. Seward can defy the hated South,
And Lincoln laugh and joke at its expense;
But at the threats of Palmerston they wilt
Like fragile flow'rs before a wintry blast.
Now tell what you have done since last we met.

Satan. I crossed the ocean to the British court,
And woke to wrath the lion in his lair,
Until his roaring echoed round the world.
Then hastened back to hear the eagle scream,
And see his talons strike his raging foe.
I hoped to find quite half a world in arms—
Old England, Ireland, India, Canada,
And shiv'ring Russia joining in the fight.

Mars. You'll see the great republic cringing low
T' appease the wrath the Trent affair provoked.
Old Palmerston will get all he demands
From these puissant men in Washington.

Satan. Please tell me what the warriors of the West
Have been engaged in since the war began?

Mars. Missouri furnished soldiers for both sides;
Jackson, her Governor, was Southern born;
Price, her commander, has a kindly heart.
Brave Gen'ral Harney, grand old veteran,
The hero of a hundred Indian fights,
Was in no haste to fight his countrymen,
So they held back the fratricidal strife.
But Lyon soon let loose the dogs of war;
The Germans led by Sigel aided him.
At Boonville they began their bloody work,
Continued it at Carthage with success;
At Wilson's Creek, near Springfield, fought again,
Where Price and brave McCullough led the South.
Lyon was slain. The Germans then fell back.
At Lexington Price captured Mulligan

And his three regiments of well-armed men.
Then the command was given to Fremont,
Then Hunter, and then Halleck, in his place.
Like tops in hands of little, idle boys,
These heroes were spun round from Washington.
At Belmont Grant had skirmishing with Polk,
But nothing was accomplished by the fight.
Please tell me what the Eastern troops have done.

Satan. Along the sea-cost unimportant forts
Were captured by the navy, and some troops.
On the Potomac Baker, at Ball's Bluff,
Fell at the head of his two thousand men,
Of whom one-half were captured, wounded, slain,
By Southern men who were by Evans led.
Two hundred thousand healthy, well-drilled men,
Well fed, well clothed, and well equipped,
Confront black Quaker cannons made of wood
To keep them from bombarding Washington.
As many more drilled troops are scattered round
Between the rising and the setting sun.
What they are doing you will have to guess.
McClellan leads where Scott was in command;
Behold them as they meet the President.

Scene: *Fort Donelson, Tenn., February 16, 1862.* SATAN, MARS.

Mars. All hail! My chief, we now have war indeed.
Kentucky's mountain soil is stained with blood.
Garfield forced Marshall to retreat in haste.
Thomas at Mill Spring gained a victory,
Where Zollicoffer fell, and Crittenden
Retreated in disorder from the field.
Fort Henry, on the Lower Tennessee,
Was captured by Foote's gun-boats. Since it fell
Fort Donelson, that guards the Cumberland,
Has been besieged by thirty thousand men,
Led on by Grant, that thunder-bolt of war,
And aided by Foote's gun-boats to bombard.

Satan. How goes the siege? Can the besieged hold
    out?
There has been desp'rate fighting on both sides.

Mars. The chief commanders at the post have left,
And many soldiers have retired in haste.
Pillow and Floyd left Buckner in command,
To fight three times the number of his troops,
Besides Foote's gun-boats and the wint'ry storms.

Satan. The brave young gen'ral must give up the fort;
To hold out longer is impossible.
The firing ceases; Grant and Buckner meet.

. . . .

An unconditional surrender now
Is what the Union general requires.
This frees Kentucky from Confed'rate troops,
And gives the Union half of Tennessee,
With full ten thousand pris'ners and their arms.

    Scene: *Shiloh Church, Tenn., April 7, 1862.* SATAN, MARS.

Satan. How now, great son of old Olympian Jove,
Have we had war to-day and yesterday?
These armies lost ten thousand on each side

Mars. Yes, we had war, but they made grave mistakes.
Grant might have made the river his defense,
Till Buell could arrive with his large force;
Or, risking battle without Buell's aid,
He should have had his army well in hand,
None lost and scattered through the hills and vales
Of wooded regions near his enemies—
With scouts and sentries negligently placed.
Confederate forces, crowned with victory,
Had a rare chance to capture their whipped foes,
In spite of gun-boats, before Buell came.
War claimed earth's grandest, noblest sacrifice
When Albert Sidney Johnston was laid low.
On yesterday Confed'rates beat their foes
And drove them to the shelter of the cliffs;
To-day the Fed'rals drove them from the field;
To-morrow they will be in full retreat.
The firing ceases. Buell comes this way;
With him come Nelson, Sherman, Wallace, Grant.

CAPTURE OF NEW ORLEANS.   177

Scene: *New Orleans, April 26, 1862.* SATAN, MARS, MAMMON, BELIAL.

Satan. Welcome to New Orleans, my warlike friend!
Were you not here with Jackson in his prime?

Mars. I was. Had he been here ten days ago
My brother, Neptune, had not sent his sons,
Porter and Farragut, past all the forts
To capture this fair city. It is ruled
By one hated by women and despised
By all who honor and esteem the fair.
Can Jackson's statue look on such a man
Without a most indignant, virtuous frown?

Satan. I beg you, Mars, refrain from such abuse
Of one I number on my list of friends.

Mammon. And he is one of my best clients too,
I pray you spare him, also for my sake.

Belial. He is my fav'rite, trusty crony too.
One such to me is worth ten thousand men.

Mars. I leave him then with you, his honored friends.
But tell me what you know about the war.

Belial. I was at Pea Ridge with my Indian braves,
But there McCullough, McIntosh, and Pike
Made them behave themselves like gentlemen.
Curtis was also sober as a judge,
So sons of Belial had no chance for sport.
But twenty thousand armed on either side
Fought like young catamounts for two whole days.
Thousands were captured, sickened, wounded, slain.
McCullough, McIntosh, and others fell,
But the grand battle had no marked result.

Mammon. My clients seeking cotton claimed my care.
So with Burnside and Goldsboro I went
To capture Roanoke Island and New Berne.
Three thousand prisoners were there secured.
When Pope attacked New Madrid I was there;
Went with him down to Island Number Ten—

Saw it bombarded more than twenty days,
Until five thousand men surrendered there.
Then came with Butler up to New Orleans,
After six days bombardment of the forts.

Satan. Then you too must have learned the art of war.

Mammon. Not I, for fighting never was my trade.
But I have learned to "capture"—that's the word
Used in the army, and the navy too.
Men of all ranks have taught me that fine art,
And I am ready now to graduate.
They capture horses, cows, and merchandise,
With now and then a well-trained negro cook,
Man-servant or maid-servant, if you please.
And 'tis reported parsons steal a church
In the great name of God and loyalty.
But I must hush—the great men come this way.
There's Farragut, no blot upon his name;
And there is Porter—on his lofty brow
Hereditary honors clust'ring thick;
And General Butler spurns the ground he treads.

Scene: *Malvern Hill, twelve miles from Richmond, Va., July 10, 1862.* SATAN, MARS.

Satan. What say you now about my "skirmishes?"
I want your present views of this campaign.
Give me some lessons in the art of war.

Mars. The Shenandoah conflicts, though but brief,
Exceeded all that I had ever seen.
Never before had twenty thousand men
Performed such wonders in so short a time
Against such numbers led by noted chiefs.
Shields and Fremont were war-worn veterans,
Gen'rals triumphant over Mexicans.
Banks had fought many battles with his tongue,
Licked Abolition cohorts into shape,
And conquered troops of rampant Congressmen;
But Jackson easily outgeneraled them,
Gave their green laurels to the frosty winds,
Blending their names with his undying fame.

Satan. What think you of McClellan's strategy?

Mars. Having the railroads, rivers, bay, and sea,
He should have landed upon solid ground,
As near to Richmond as was possible,
Reserving all his force for one great fight,
And then pressed in, no matter at what cost.
His month at Yorktown, fight at Williamsburg,
Four weeks devoted to a tiresome march,
Served but to place exhausted, weary troops
Where fresh ones might have been two months before.
But toil-worn as they were, they bravely fought,
A day at West Point, two days at Fair Oaks,
Left Johnston wounded, Richmond's gates ajar,
Inviting Northern troops to march right in.
But ill-judged prudence sounded a retreat
To Malvern Hill, where victory again
Placed in McClellan's hands Richmond's bright keys.
He did not use them, but led off his troops
Some miles away, and farther down the stream.
Far less than half the blood shed at Oak Grove,
Mechanicsville, Gaines's Mill, Glendale, Oak Swamp,
Or Savage Station, or at Frazier's Farm,
Would at Fair Oaks, or even Malvern Hill,
Have placed in Richmond fivescore thousand men,
In spite of all the troops that could oppose.
The thunders that have loudly echoed here
Through the sad moments of a dreadful week,
And all the blood Virginia's soil drank in
Have been in vain. Thirty thousand deaths
Fill this broad land with tearful, sobbing grief.

Satan. Please give me your opinion in few words
Of Southern strategy and its defects.

Mars. They fight too freely, too incautiously.
Of the best soldiers earth has ever seen,
They have too few to waste such precious lives.
McClellan errs upon the other hand:
His countless troops, like apples of his eyes,
Are screened from harm. He hates to see them fight,
Lest his dear pets should sleep in soldiers' graves.

'Tis Richmond that the Union forces want.
The South has slaves and spades enough at hand
To let its sons behind intrenchments fight,
Wherever it is known the foe will come.
Why not encircle Richmond with earth walls,
The inner one outside of cannon range,
Then bid the foe come on and take the place?
See there the Northern heroes of this war!
Porter and Mansfield, Hooker, Kearney, Sykes;
And there McClellan, idol of his troops.

In March Virginia's iron Titan dared
To seize old Neptune's watery domain,
And wield his trident over subject seas:
With ten guns drove more than two hundred off,
To seek the shallow waters near the shore.
The "Cumberland" and "Congress" both destroyed,
And their rich transports blown up, burned, or sunk,
In naval warfare a new era marked.
But when the "Monitor" joined in the fight,
Virginia suffered for her sad neglect
To learn and teach the great mechanic arts.
'Twas so when Rumsey, on Potomac's tide,*
First showed a steamboat to a wond'ring world;
But skilled mechanics could not there be found.
'Twas so when Tompkins, near Kanawha's stream,†
First yoked to industry the light and heat
Of gas that came from subterranean depths.
The plodding Pennsylvanians obtained
In forty years the profit of their skill.
McCormick gave the reaper to mankind,
But sought skilled workmen in a distant State.
'Tis thus that genius gems with jewels bright
Virginia's most resplendent, matchless crown.
Transcendent glory blazes on her brow,
But lack of artisans depletes her wealth;
'Twill sink her mighty ironclads in the deep.

---

*1784. †1842.

BOOK NINTH.

Scene: *Fredericksburg, Va., December 15, 1862.* SATAN, MARS.

Satan. Ha! ha! ha! ha! this is the proudest hour
That I have known. Yes, "proud as Lucifer,"
Is what men say. Hereafter let them say:
" Proud as great Lucifer at Fredericksburg."
Behold the smoking ruins of that town;
Gaze on those thousands of unburied dead;
List to the shrieks and groans that fill the air
Is this Dahomey, Turkey, or Fiji?
No. Washington in boyhood trod this soil.
Here Patrick Henry's grateful countrymen
Escorted him t'ward Philadelphia,
When he had driven Dunmore from the land.
But now I triumph! triumph even here!
I've led a few fanatical, rash men
To fire the sections with intensest hate,
And by that hatred turned to bitterness
The richest gifts bestowed upon mankind;
Their noblest virtues vices have become;
Their excellences lead them down to death.
West Point has trained them for my hellish work,
Their education fits them for my use.
Chivalric courage dooms them to the grave;
Their hoarded wealth prolongs the dreadful fight;
Superior skill provides most deadly arms;
And piety makes conscience drive them on
To deeds that hell itself might blush to own.
'Tis war no longer; it is hatred crazed
And armed against the best of all the race.
I had not dared to hope for such results
From my most cherished, sanguinary schemes.
Inform me, Mars, about this last campaign.

GENERAL ROBERT E. LEE.
When August ended, Lee began again
To seek for enemies in Maryland

M'CLELLAN DISMISSED.

Mars. At Cedar Mountain Jackson routed Banks;
Then, hast'ning to Manassas, captured trains
And troops and stores beyond all estimate;
Fighting at Bull Run and at Centerville,
And fighting at Chantilly, caused the flight
Of Pope and his whipped troops to Washington.
There, at his own request, he was relieved.
His army, added to McClellan's force,
Followed the fortunes of that careful chief,
Who hurried back to trembling Washington,
And calmed the fears of Stanton and his friends.
When August ended, Lee began again
To seek for enemies in Maryland—
His men took Frederick, and passing on
Without resistance entered Hagerstown.
Jackson, at Harper's Ferry, captured Miles
And his twelve thousand men, with arms and stores;
Then hastened to join Lee at Antietam,
Where, after four days' fighting, Lee retired.
'Twas a drawn battle, where each army lost
More than ten thousand men and nothing gained.
Then "On to Richmond!" was the cry again
Of millions armed with very sharp steel pens.
The politicians asked McClellan's head,
Lest victory should make him President.
When ready to take Richmond, they required
Protection for themselves in Washington.
The waters all were his. He trusted them
To land him safely where a ten-mile march
Would bring him to the Southern capital.
But those bad men whose hatred of the South
And bold bravadoes first provoked the war
Required him to fight along a line
By which the foe might by a hasty march
Lay hold on their puissant carcasses.
The brave man yielded to their craven fears,
While pity for his soldiers wrung his heart,
That they must suffer for the cowardice
Of place-men who controlled their destinies.
Then they removed him from his post of power,
Promoting Burnside to the chief command.

The rest you know. There's Mosby, A. P. Hill,
Pickett, and Stuart, Early, Jackson, Lee.

    Scene: *Murfreesboro, Tenn., January 3, 1863.* SATAN, MARS.

Satan. This seems the strangest battle ever fought.
Two days ago Rosecrans was badly whipped.
To-day his troops were forced across the stream.
At three o'clock Confed'rates claimed the day,
But his well-placed, well-served artillery
Began to mow them down like ripened grain,
Until they now retire in swift retreat.
The new year's early hours are red with blood
Drawn from the veins of twenty thousand men.
Please tell me, Mars, what news from other fields?

Mars. Kentucky was last year the scene of strife.
At Richmond, Kirby Smith drove Manson out,
Then visited at Lexington, Versailles,
Frankfort, and other noted, prosp'rous towns,
And threatened Cincinnati and the North.
Then Bragg came in, by Buell closely watched.
At Munfordsville he captured prisoners;
Then, seeking to unite with Kirby Smith,
Gave Buell time to rest at Louisville,
And gather re-enforcements from the North.
At Perryville the armies met and fought.
Brave men were slain, but without marked results.
'Twas a drawn battle. Bragg and Smith retired
With great deliberation from the State,
Taking away four thousand wagon-loads
Of precious stores and many animals,
Which had been gathered during forty days.
Price was repulsed from Iuka by Grant;
Van Dorn and Price from Corinth by Rosecrans;
Sherman was whipped at Chickasaw Bayou.
You have not time for other dry details,
But must be interested to behold
Rosecrans and Thomas, heroes of this fight.

    Scene: *Guiney's Station, Va., May 5, 1863.* SATAN, MARS.

Mars. Hooker retreats; the battle ceases here.

In three days' fighting his great army lost
Seventeen thousand well-drilled veterans.
Lee is victorious, yet he has lost
More than his enemy a thousand-fold.
Jackson has fallen, and he soon must die.
In vict'ry's loving arms the hero fell,
Admired and honored by his fiercest foes.
The trump of fame sounds forth his glorious name
In every land where valor is esteemed.

Satan. Foe as I am to all the hated race,
Toiling through ages most malignantly,
To work its ruin through eternity,
I must confess he triumphed over me!
From my maliciousness extorted praise.

Mars. His last great battle was a masterpiece
Of strategy and valor well combined.
He fell not by a foeman's fatal shot.
The men who slew him would have gladly risked
Ten thousand deaths to save their hero's life.
Behold the wounded warrior on his couch
Serenely waiting the approach of death.
That open window shows his manly face.
Let us retire; see, holy angels come,
With duteous love the hero to attend.

SATAN *and* MARS *retire. Enter* GABRIEL, UZZIEL, ITHURIEL, RAPHAEL, ABDIEL, ZOPHIEL, ZEPHON, ARIEL, ZADKIEL, ISRAFIEL, *chanting:*

" Rest for the toiling hand, rest for the anxious brow,
Rest for the weary, way-sore feet, rest from all labor now;
Rest for the fevered brain, rest for the throbbing eye;
Through these parched lips of thine no more shall pass
    the moan or sigh."

"Go to the grave in all thy glorious prime,
    In full activity of zeal and power!
A Christian cannot die before his time,
    The Lord's appointment is the servant's hour.
Go to the grave; at noon from labor cease;
    Rest on thy sheaves; thy harvest task is done;
Come from the heat of battle and in peace,
    Soldier, go home with thee, the fight is won."

Scene: *Gettysburg, Pa., July 4, 1863.* MICHAEL, ITHURIEL, ZEPH-
ON, ARIEL, GABRIEL, RAPHAEL.

Michael. All hail, ye servants of the Lord Most High!
I summoned you to meet me here to-day
To wait on men in this their hour of need.
'Twas ours to meet on Independence Day
In this same State at Philadelphia
When this republic struggled into life.
We all were helpful at its wondrous birth.
Please tell me what I gave you then to do?

Ithuriel. I tore the mask from base hypocrisy,
Exposed the cloven foot of treachery.

Abdiel. I urged the slow-paced few to promptly act.

Zephon. I gave the timid most courageous thoughts.

Ariel. To the desponding I gave cheering hopes.

Raphael. To Jefferson I taught the use of words
That Georgia and New England could approve.
He had denounced the slave trade in such terms
As they could never use with self-respect.
New England would not thus condemn her sons
For trafficking in human flesh and blood.
The profits of the trade were dear to her.
While Georgia would not do without the slaves,
Nor would the gen'rous Carolinians.

Gabriel. I gave John Adams moving eloquence
That won men over to his righteous cause.

Michael. And we and all the sons of God rejoiced
To see such loving union among men;
Hoping for peace through this broad continent.
And freedom from all kinds of tyranny.
How is it with this nation we have served?
Men celebrate their country's natal day,
Not with glad greetings, worshiping their God,
But mid the ruins of a three days' fight,
Where more than fifty thousand veterans,
Killed or disabled, call for briny tears;

Or, as at Vicksburg, thirty thousand men
Are starved or slain by their own countrymen.
Are these the fruits of all our careful toil?

Gabriel. No, Michael, these are fruits of hellish hate
Between the sections of this favored land.

MINISTERING ANGELS.

Until the gospel of the Son of God
Shall drive this fiendish hatred far away,
Discord and strife and malice must prevail.

Michael. But, Gabriel, these destroying forces claim
That Christ and conscience drive them to such deeds.

Bishops and saints pray mightily to God
That slaughterers of men may have success.
Even the dying, like Mohammedans,
Claim glory in the heavens for killing men.
Their crowns are gifts from Christ, but kindred blood
Shed by their *holy* hands in this great war
Adds glory to the brightest of those crowns.
Both have high hopes of being with the Lord,
But Southern men to Stonewall Jackson go;
While the great North in the sad hour of death
Goes shouting to the bosom of John Brown.
Such silliness may hope to be excused,
But how can such malevolence escape
Just visitations of the wrath to come?

Gabriel. Michael, you state sad, mortifying truths.
A most perplexing question you propound.
But God is good and Christ for sinners died.
Satan deceives his selfish scheming dupes,
And they mislead and craze the multitude.
The hatred of the sections is indulged
Against imaginary, unknown foes.
The malice and malignity they feel
Are venomous against such fancied ghouls
As politicians paint to madden them.
When these men face to face associate,
No longer hoodwinked by the fiends that lead,
Malevolence is banished, and they love
Like brothers of one holy family.
Hancock and Lee and Meade and Stuart feel
No hellish hatred against gallant foes.
So of the war-worn soldiers of their ranks;
To know each other kindles ardent love.
Thousands of brave, unhappy sufferers
Require our aid upon this battle-field.
Let us to duty. There is Gen'ral Meade,
Attentive to the wounded and the sick;
And there is Hancock, wounded and in pain.

Scene: *Vicksburg, Miss., July 4, 1863.* SATAN, MARS, MAMMON,
BELIAL.

Satan. How goes the siege? Why does it last so long?

SURRENDER OF VICKSBURG.

Mars. 'Tis desp'rate valor upon either side
Prolongs the suff''ings of these val'rous men,
But the Confed'rates now must yield or starve.
Arkansas Post fell early in the spring,
Surrendering five thousand valiant men
To Porter's gun-boats and McClernand's troops.
Grant sought the rear of Vicksburg through the swamps,
The mud, the bayous, and the rugged hills;
Then tried to turn the river from the town
By digging deep canals to change its course.
Failing in that, he passed the thund'ring forts
With even less of harm than he had feared;
Then took with ease Port Gibson and Grand Gulf.
The Union troops gained hard-earned victories
At Jackson, Raymond, and at Champion Hills;
In a fierce conflict at Black River bridge
Whipped Pemberton, and forced him to retreat
Within the strong defenses of Vicksburg.
Grant, two days later, made a bold assault,
Hoping successfully to storm the place;
But was repulsed with loss of many men.
Since then, through more than seven bloody weeks,
The fight continues with great loss of life.

Satan. 'Tis said that thirty thousand half-starved men
Surrender on this Independence Day;
And that Port Hudson, now besieged by Banks,
Must also fall, thus op'ning to the Gulf
The unrestricted commerce of the West,
And with a wall of waters fencing off
Western Confed'rates from their brethren East.

Mammon. Then what a harvest will my clients reap!
The plunder of a hundred thousand homes,
Besides the cotton-bales and contrabands.

Belial. And the companions of my revelry
Will sport amid the wrecks of families—
White, red, and black, the lofty and the low.

Mars. The firing ceases! See that flag of truce!
Its snowy folds above the ruins float.

Peace, plenty, rest, and joy it promises.

. . . .

The torn and tattered stars and bars come down;
The stars and stripes rise grandly o'er the scene.
There's plenty now for the starved garrison.
See Pemberton and Grant and McPherson!

Scene: *Chickamauga Creek, Ga., September 20, 1863.* SATAN, MAMMON, BELIAL, MARS.

Satan. Whence come you, Mammon? whither have you been?

Mammon. I came from Charleston, where DuPont's great fleet
Was badly whipped in April of this year.
Where in July Dahlgren and Gilmore went
To batter forts and crush them into dust.
September saw Confederates retire
Within the lines of their heroic town.
Their enemies advanced their batteries
Within four miles of Charleston's wharves and stores;
Thence the "swamp angels" belched forth streams of fire
From blazing mouths on the devoted place.
But there is not much cotton we can take,
Nor many slaves as yet within our reach.

Satan. Belial, say, where have you been since we met?

Belial. From Vicksburg I went out to Arkansas;
Saw Holmes and his eight thousand badly whipped,
And from Helena driven quite away.
Saw Steele take Little Rock, and force his foes
To leave in haste with ever-quick'ning speed.
I wished for Mammon—cotton was at hand,
And I was almost tempted then to buy.
But the best day of all that I enjoyed
Was spent at Lawrence with my friend Quantrell.
It brought to mind old Sodom's wildest hours,
With memories of days before the flood.

Satan. Mars, we have something much more serious here;
The mighty Julius would have called this war.

Mars. Yes, such attacks as Longstreet made to-day,
And such as Thomas stubbornly repulsed,
Are unsurpassed in all earth's bloody wars.
The Union right and center have been crushed,
The troops killed, wounded, captured, or dispersed
The scattered fragments of great army corps
To Chattanooga in disorder flee,
Soldiers and gen'rals all demoralized.
But look at Thomas, how he holds his place,
And keeps his men in order round his flag,
In spite of war's dread cyclone raging round.
Where sunrise saw him sunset sees him still.
Protected by the darkness he'll retire,
And in good order lead his valiant troops
To help their cowering comrades organize,
And show the world "Virginia blood still tells."
With forty thousand stalwart vet'rans lost,
Darkness descends to part the combatants.

Satan. What think you now. Will Rosecrans have to yield,
Surrendering the remnant of his force?

Mars. No, Hooker comes with two strong army corps,
And Sherman also with his mighty force,
And Grant, with his high honors newly gained,
Must gather lofty laurels for his brow,
Though they may grow above bleak mountain heights,
Or hide among the curtains of the skies.
These Fed'ral troops will not surrender now;
They'll fight for victory and drive their foes.
See Bragg, Polk, Longstreet, Johnston, come this way,
With Breckinridge, Hood, Ewell, following.

Scene: *Lookout Mountain, Tenn., November 25, 1863.* SATAN, MARS.

Satan. When men fought yesterday "above the clouds,"
I was not here to witness their brave deeds.
I had expected Bragg to start the fray

And carry Chattanooga by assault.
He did give notice that non-combatants
Might be removed away to some safe place.
I missed the battle, but would see it now
Through your keen eyes—or rather hear of it
From your glib tongue. I wait—I wish to learn.

Mars. Two days ago, with quietness and care,
The troops of Hooker crossed the Tennessee,
And rested near the mouth of Lookout Creek,
Quite unobserved by the Confederates.
Day dawned upon a land obscured by fogs.
Two hours sufficed to take the rifle-pits
That swept the foot-hills with their leaden hail;
Then up the steep ascent bold thousands rushed
Onward and skyward to the jaws of death,
Crowding each other upward through the storm
T'ward the red mouths of scores of thund'ring guns
Of the fierce conflict on that tow'ring height
Between the very bravest of brave men
No words of mine can adequately tell;
But soon down Lookout Mountain's eastern side
Confed'rates fled, all tumbling down the steep,
Mingling with rocks and rifles as they rolled,
Until by two o'clock the men in blue,
Beneath their flag held all the mountain-top,
And saw their foes escape to Mission Ridge,
Where they have since been well reorganized.
Thus I've described the fight "above the clouds,"
But you can now behold it for yourself,
As if you had but loudly cried "Encore,"
And actors come again to play for you.
A larger army climbs to Mission Ridge
To drive a foe intrenched and wide-awake.
Yes, we'll have more than royal sport again,
With larger forces more distinctly seen.
See Hooker's braves descend the mountain side;
They cross the Chattanooga and ascend,
With lion leaps, far up the south-west slope
Of Mission Ridge. Sherman has boldly passed
The Chickamauga and the Tennessee.

His fearless troops, like bounding tigers, climb
The north declivity. Thomas awaits
The word that hurls uphill against the foe
His val'rous fighting host's resistless might.
Time's tardy step has left high noon behind
More than an hour ago. No order comes
For all to join in a combined assault.
'Tis two o'clock! Grant speaks the mighty word
That moves in majesty, with earthquake force,
Forward and upward the whole armament,
As if to scale the skies and capture heaven.
Such warfare mortals never waged before,
Nor all the fabled hosts that classic times
Gave to Olympian heights and groves and clouds.

Satan. Well might Confed'rates yield and flee away.
By them all Tennessee is lost and left.
The conquerors triumphant now return:
Grant, Thomas, Hooker, Sherman, McPherson.

Scene: *Covington, Ky., November 20, 1863.* ARIEL, RAPHAEL.

Ariel. Whose gallant form is that with active step
Treading Kentucky's soil so joyfully?

Raphael. 'Tis John H. Morgan, whose heroic deeds
Admiring millions gayly celebrate,
And crown with praises worthy of the name
Of him who led his troops to victories
That seemed impossible to other men.

Ariel. He walks these streets with the majestic air
Of an archangel just returned to heav'n.

Raphael. This most romantic of all cavaliers
Rode rashly on where danger led the way,
As if to court adventures fearlessly,
And throw himself into the arms of death.
Yet he was gentle to the little ones,
With smiles for beauty, and the tenderness
Of friendship toward his num'rous prisoners.

Ariel. What brings him here, and why seems he so
  glad
To set his feet upon Kentucky ground?

Raphael. He is the idol of Kentuckians:
His enemies admire his gallantry.
Last summer he attacked the great North-west
With but two thousand bold Kentucky boys;
Captured six thousand of his enemies,
Destroyed ten millions of their property,
With thirty thousand thund'ring at his heels.
But he was captured, and his enemies
Confined him in their penitentiary.
They thought that they'd disgrace their prisoner,
But most egregiously disgraced themselves
By their base treatment of a gentleman
Whose gallantry had never been surpassed.
Morgan outwitted them, and has escaped
To dazzle them with other glorious deeds.

Scene: *Pleasant Hill, La., April 9, 1864.* MARS, MAMMON, BELIAL.

Mammon. Great son of Jupiter, what brings you here?
Belial and I have business everywhere,
But battles and the like belong to you.
Had fighting here, you say, where B.... commands.

Mars. Yes, three grand armies were to meet near here,
And with the help of Porter's flotilla
Take Shreveport from Confederates with ease.

Mammon. And did they do it? And if not, why not?

Mars. Smith and the fleet took several river towns,
But here at Mansfield and at Pleasant Hill
B.... lost three thousand men and all his guns,
With rich supply trains to the enemy;
And but for the brave fighting Gen'ral Smith
Captivity had been the fate of B.....

Mammon. Was not this general many months ago
Made "commissary of great Stonewall's troops?"
And does he now serve "Rough and Ready's" son,
With equal skill in this Red River land?

Belial. Mammon, shame on you for your *badinage.*
You'll soon attack that other General B.
Remember I too claim a share in Ben.
If he loves money, he loves pleasure too.
What if they are "no generals to hurt?"
They work the wires of party with success,
And seize a share of good things as they pass.
Think not to find men great in every thing,
Nor in one spot to gather all that's great,
Nor every kind of greatness that is great,
Not e'en in that great spot that gave the world
The two great generals, B..... and B....
You'll own it has fair women and wise men,
And poets that can fight, in soft, smooth rhymes,
And pulpits that can utter words of hate,
And scores of wordy transcendentalists,
Ready in hitchy language to admit
That possibly, if properly received,
High Boston culture in two thousand years
Might make their Saviour equal to themselves!

Mars. I will not listen to the trifling talk
Of two such worthless fiends about great men
And that great spot that gave them to mankind!
What! Shall a brace of epauleted B.'s,
Or a whole swarm of callow generals,
And a few learned transcendentalists,
And some malignant, spiteful pulpiteers,
Joined with disciples of hate's horrid school,
Obscure the glory of a land that boasts
Greene, Warren, Prescott, Sullivan, Frank Pierce—
The Union's patriot heroes in their day?
And the great names of Adams, Fisher Ames,
Webster and Caleb Cushing, tried and true—
The Union's statesmen and great orators?
And Union *literati* such as Dwight,
Paine, Bryant, Halleck, Bancroft, Hawthorne, Sprague?
And great inventors, Franklin, Whitney, Morse?
And merchants whose unrivaled enterprise
Sent winter's icy fetters round the world
And brought them back transmuted into gold?

Know ye that men shall glory in that land
Long after hatred's minions, hurled from pow'r,
Shall end their spiteful, ignominious lives,
To rest in graves unhonored and unknown.
See! There is Taylor and his valiant staff.
He has chased off his conquered enemies,
And well secured his num'rous prisoners;
Has gathered his rich spoils of victory,
And now returns with his triumphant troops.

Scene: *Cold Harbor, twelve miles north-east of Richmond, Va., June 4, 1864.* MICHAEL, GABRIEL, ZEPHON, RAPHAEL, ABDIEL, ITHURIEL.

Zephon. Tell us, ye leaders of the heavenly host,
Why this fair land's so drenched with human blood.

Ithuriel. 'Tis said that Grant is losing, month by month,
Sixty or eighty thousand fighting men;
And that he now proposes to move round
South of James River, where he might have been
Two months ago without the loss of one.
Why this unnecessary waste of life?

Gabriel. The men who cursed this land with fiendish war
Keep the brave troops between themselves and harm.
Behind their well-manned forts they shudder still
At sounds of horses' hoofs borne from the South,
Though these vast armies face their Southern foes,
And die to save them from their ragged ranks.

Zephon. I understand how bravest of the brave
May die to save base cowardly poltroons;
What I would learn is, why such slaughter here?

Gabriel. When fed'ral force made war on other States,
It was against the great organic law
By which the thirteen nations became one.
'Twas usurpation, fraud, and despotism;
A rash subversion of the government;
For all the States refused to grant that pow'r.
But when fanatic fury dared to strike
The grand majestic mother of the States,

Virginia in her monumental home,
The sacred citadel of liberty,
'Twas ingrate, cruel, matricidal crime!
This sovereign State entered the Union free
To leave at will should it abuse its powers.
'Twas she gave millions liberty and law,
With Washington to guard them with his sword,
And Jefferson to write their principles
And Madison to give organic form
To their well-guarded fed'ral government,
And Marshall to apply those righteous laws
To real life in freedom's highest court.
With lavish liberality she gave
Her vast domain to make the Union strong,
Adding six mighty States to the bright band.
Virginians bought Louisiana's realm;
Traced its broad bound'ry to the western sea
That laves far distant Asia's sunny shore;
Virginians purchased Florida from Spain,
Led Texan troops on San Jacinto's field,
And re-annexed the Texan soil and men;
Virginians led the troops in Mexico
That won the lands toward the setting sun;
And a Virginian did negotiate
The treaty that conveyed those vast domains.
She tried to reconcile the headstrong hosts
That sought to kindle strife between the States.
She bore with patience insults, threats, and wrongs
Until the Northern faction spurned the hand
Outstretched by her to ward off civil war.
War came—she had no hatreds in her heart.
She fought the invaders of her sacred soil,
For principles, defending sovereign rights,
As men on earth had never fought before.
The leader of her sons called fiercest foes,
In loving tones, "Our friends, the enemy."

Raphael. Yes, and her homes, with hospitable haste,
Oft spread her feasts to feed her enemies.

Abdiel. She gave high honors to her brave compeers
Of other States who fought upon her soil;

But at the post of danger placed her sons,
To bear the brunt in many a hard-fought field.

Michael. Vainly her foes have subsidized mankind
To bring their hireling forces from all lands.
Her loving children formed a living wall
Around the immortal mother of the brave.
Four bloody years they've fought a world in arms,
Until her enemies turn to her slaves
To cry, "O help us, help us, or we fail."

Abdiel. But do not Northern armies have brave men,
True patriotic sons of liberty?
Men worthy of great honor and renown?

Michael. They do, and their brave deeds inscribe their names
High on the records of undying fame,
As witness Hancock, McPherson, and Grant,
And many of their worthy, brave compeers.

Abdiel. In other States they win great victories.
Why should they here wear laurels soaked in blood?

Michael. I answer, to avenge Virginia's wrongs,
And highly honor her devoted sons.
Give to the Fed'ral hero honor due:
He falls obedient to his honored State,
Or lives to wear the honors she bestows.
Like the brave Spartans at Thermopylæ,
He moves obedient to a law's command.
The accident of birth or prejudice
Determined where he bravely lived or died.
Give him your hearty sympathy and prayers,
But let your condemnation rest upon
The politicians who provoked the war
By trampling on the compacts of their sires.

Scene: *Atlanta, Ga., July 10, 1864.* SATAN, MARS.

Satan. How go the battles? Tell me, god of war.

Mars. Lee is in Petersburg, besieged by Grant.
Here in Atlanta Johnston is besieged.

Grant moved toward Richmond on the fourth of May;
Lee fought him in the Wilderness three days,
Then three days more near Spottsylvania.
June came. Cold Harbor saw Grant's legions hurled
In desperation against Lee's command,
Until ten thousand fell in half an hour.
Less than one month of such fierce warfare gave
Near fourscore thousand of Grant's veterans
To gory graves or to disabling wounds—
A larger number than Lee's gallant force!
The Fed'ral chief then turned toward Petersburg
To ground he might have reached without a fight.
While Grant sought Richmond o'er a bloody road,
Three thousand soldiers and a few cadets
Attacked and routed fifteen thousand men.
The men fought under Sigel; the brave boys
Were led by Breckinridge to victory.
Then to the far-famed valley Hunter came,
In expectation of submissive prey.
But Early, having less than half his force,
Drove the foul fire-fiend in hot haste away
Beyond the Alleghanies, toward the west.
At last accounts Early and Breckinridge
Had whipped Lew Wallace at Monacacy,
And scared almost to death the trembling crew
That rules the nation now at Washington.
As to these men whose movements we behold,
They marched from Chattanooga May the seventh.
At Dalton sixty thousand well-drilled troops
Were flanked by twice their number and fell back.
Resaca's two days' fighting was in vain:
On the fifteenth commenced a forced retreat.
At Dallas fighting was again renewed,
Lost Mountain next became their battle-ground.
A three days' fight led Johnston to retreat.
At Kennesaw Hood was repulsed with loss.
Five days elapsed, and June the twenty-eighth
Saw Sherman's fierce assault and his repulse;
When he would strike and storm great Kennesaw
He failed, but his flank movements drove his foe
Into Atlanta early yesterday.

Around this place will fiercest conflicts rage;
For if it yields, the South will lose car-works,
Machine-shops, foundries, arms, and army stores;
And Sherman march triumphant to the sea.
'Tis said that Johnston's Fabian policy
Is criticised by many wordy ones,
Who ask for battles—battles every day;
And that the cautious chief must stand aside
And give his place to one more venturesome.
See, there is McPherson, this army's pride.
He reconnoiters the defenses now.

Scene: *Winchester, Va., October 22, 1864.* ABDIEL, ITHURIEL, ZEPH-
ON, RAPHAEL.

Abdiel. Comrades, call forth with sympathetic speed
The swift-winged ministers of heavenly help.
The people of this valley need their aid.
With ribald mirth their enemies proclaim
That sword and ax and torch have made this land
So desolate that birds of rapid flight
In passing o'er it must provide their food,
And take it with them on their desert way.
As to the people they have doomed to die,
They say starvation is too good for them.

Zephon. Why so? Are they the worst of Adam's race?

Ithuriel. God and good angels say they are the best.

Raphael. What then is charged against these suffering ones?

Abdiel. Defense of native land and native home.
Earth has no holier homesteads for her tribes
Than docked this valley and these mountain sides.

Zephon. Why, then, these horrid vandal outrages?

Abdiel. The dastard cruelty of those who rule
The war department of a Christian land
Finds nothing that can soothe their quaking fears
While this heroic valley feeds its sons.
The name of Shenandoah strikes alarms

Through every craven heart in Washington.
Hence the great valley suffers for the frights
Her children gave to craven tyrant's hearts.

Raphael. But what avails the malice of a foe
Who wreaks his vengeance on the saints of God?
The slain wear crowns of triumph with the Lord,
The wounded have the comforts of his grace.
This fertile soil shall soon renew the wealth
Barbarian hands have given to the flames.

Zephon. How sad the thought that thousands of the brave
Shed their rich blood to fertilize these lands,
Lest cowardice should meet its dreaded doom!
How hard that one so brave as Sheridan
With arson's flames must scorch his laurel-wreaths,
And to felonious deeds train men in arms!
Behold the youthful hero of the torch:
Him pity, while you censure his vile deeds.

Scene: *Ruins of Atlanta, Ga., November 17, 1864.* MARS, SATAN, MAMMON, BELIAL.

Mars. Call you this war? or is it felony
Arrayed in all the pride and pomp of arms?

Mammon. 'Tis arson marching in a warlike garb,
And barbarism licensed to destroy.

Satan. 'Tis the accomplishment of well-laid plans,
Which I have worked for nearly fourscore years.
The hatreds of the sections I have stirred
Until they stop at nothing in their rage.
It was not thus that Scott fought Mexico,
Nor thus that Grant and Sherman learned to fight.
'Twas I that taught this modern art of war.

Mammon. This burning property finds no excuse,
Nothing to palliate such wanton waste.

Mars. My grand old heathen heroes would have scorned
To drive out widows from their peaceful homes

Or banish infancy from cradle-beds.
They fought with men—with stalwart men in arms.
Rome's worst fanatics never could have driv'n
The mighty Julius to perform such deeds.

 Satan. I marvel greatly at my own success
In banishing from peaceful, quiet homes
Defenseless thousands to far western scenes
To toil among their distant enemies,
Or die from home and much loved native land.

 Belial. And so do I. How was it all contrived?

 Satan. These Georgians are the saints of the Most High.
His angels guard and train them for the skies;
His providence works all things for their good.
But earthly retribution gave me power
To have them banished as the Cherokees,
By Georgians banished, lost their native land.

 Mammon. God gave the Cherokees a better land.
He'll make these Georgians profit by their loss!
So end in disappointment all our schemes
Against the servants of the Lord most high.

 Satan. Mammon, you have of late grown insolent.
Like other purse-proud people, you're too bold.

 Belial. Yes, that he is. He even prates against
My chosen crony, great Tecumseh S.
What if he does burn towns and cities here?
That Indian name avenges Cherokees.

 Mars. The red Tecumseh whose great name he wears
Never made war on women and on babes,
Nor fired the cities of his enemies.
A thousand Proctors, Stantons, or the like,
In vain had put red torches in his hands.

 Satan. More than four months have passed since we met here.
Then Johnston was besieged by mighty hosts.
Please tell us how the war is going since.

Mars. Johnston was superseded by brave Hood.
In three assaults upon the Union lines
The new commander lost more fighting men
Than Johnston had in quite as many months.
At last to save his army Hood marched off,
And with September Sherman entered in
And took possession of his costly prize,
In four months losing forty thousand men,
Among them McPherson, his noblest chief.
He still has sixty thousand well-armed troops
Marching triumphant eastward to the sea;
While Hood moves backward, hoping to cut off
Sherman's connection with the great North-west.
Vain hope! He leads his heroes back to face
O'erwhelming numbers of his well-drilled foes,
Led by the very ablest of their chiefs.
One only chance has he of victory:
Fanatic fury never can forgive
Thomas for being born on Southern soil.
The imbeciles at Washington propose
To move the gen'ral from his high command.
'Tis said that Grant puts Logan in his place.
If this be done, Hood may expect success.

Satan. What of the armies under Lee and Grant?

Mars. They fight like crazy fiends at Petersburg,
Where greedy, gaping graves swallow in haste
Uncounted thousands slaughtered day by day,
Replaced by victims drawn from ev'ry land.

Satan. You told of Early threat'ning Washington,
Alarming the weak rulers of the land,
Whipping Lew Wallace near Monocacy.
Was he allowed in safety to escape?

Mars. He was; and took vast quantities of stores.
Wright followed him as far as Winchester.
But Early turned and drove Wright's army back;
Then captured Chambersburg, demanding cash
To pay for buildings Hunter had burned down,

Which they refused. Then, to retaliate,
He turned barbarian, and sent a torch
To fire the town; retreated from the State,
With rich supplies of military stores.
Then Sheridan, with forty thousand men,
Defeated Early and began his work
Of desolation with both ax and torch.
Leaving his vandal task to underlings,
He sought his patrons at the capital,
To tell of all the wonders he had wrought.
Early returned, surprised the Union camp,
Scattered and drove the troops like frightened sheep,
Took their artillery and all their stores.
Then the Confed'rates stopped to rest and eat,
But Sheridan, returning, met his men,
Turned back the fugitives and made them fight,
Till they recovered the great guns they lost,
And with them won a noted victory.
Since then the war-worn valley's plundered homes
Have no defense against consuming fires.
The helplessness of outraged innocence
Sees food and barns and mills and fences blaze,
Revealing famine's ghastly countenance.

Satan. How fares the navy in these fighting times?

Mars. The Union fleets blockade the Southern coasts,
Seal up Confederate ports and banish trade.
Lieutenant Cushing sunk the "Albemarle"
In Roanoke River with a torpedo.
'Twas bravely done, and won him much applause.
In Mobile Harbor Farragut displayed
Great skill and courage as an admiral.
Lashed to his flag-ship's rigging he remained
Till forts and ships and monster iron-clad rams
Pulled down their flags and Mobile was his prize.
Confed'rate ships have fought most gallantly,
Destroying commerce at a fearful rate,
Making their flag the terror of the seas,
But gaining nothing for their sinking cause.
Yet "Alabama," "Sumter," "Florida,"

And other softly spoken Southern names
Sent consternation among Northern ships.
When Semmes met Winslow on the coast of France,
A foeman worthy of his steel was found.

THE "SUMTER" CHASED BY THE "IROQUOIS."

An hour of battle ended in defeat
To Semmes, who saw the "Alabama" sunk.
An English yacht saved the brave captain's life,
But Winslow on the "Kearsarge" won the fight,
And proudly walked his deck a conqueror.

BOOK TENTH.

Scene: *The Capitol, Nashville, Tenn., December 16, 1864.*

Mars. From this proud Capitol how grand the view!
Rome's seven hills by seven multiplied
Could never match what we behold to-day;
Nor had the Tiber, in its hour of pride,
Such sparkling waters as the Cumberland,
Nor all antiquity a braver man
Than he whose statue will adorn these grounds.
His heroism might have well sufficed
For twice ten thousand ordinary men,
With quite enough to make a Cæsar left.
The recollection of his glorious deeds,
Inspiring generations yet unborn
With patriotic valor, shall raise up
Defenders of his much loved native land
Against all foes throughout all time to come.

Satan. What of the living issues of these times?
What can you say of yesterday's great fight?

Mars. Thomas, the conq'ring hero of the day,
Is much the ablest gen'ral of the North,
But never fully trusted by the men
Who rule to ruin this great government.
To serve them he had trampled on State pride,
Fought for the North and her compatriots,
Gave his Virginia talents to their cause,
Won vict'ries for them, saved them in defeat,
Endured Virginia's blushes and her frowns,
Through sadd'ning years of sanguinary war.
The rulers, hating his brave Southern blood,
Had issued orders, and had sent them on,
Dismissing Thomas from his high command.

Satan. How could he lead the army if removed?

Mars. His generalship had taught him when to strike
And vict'ry taught the prudent messenger
That orders from his master came too late
To vanquish such a victor and disgrace
The hero of so many gallant deeds.
Hood had come north, indulging in high hopes;
At Franklin fought with Schofield, who retired
Behind intrenchments Thomas had thrown up,

GENERAL HOOD'S HEAD-QUARTERS NEAR NASHVILLE.

While Hood made ready to begin the siege,
Thomas moved from his works and routed him.
Hood and his men fought bravely to the last;
But yesterday his bleeding, shattered ranks
Turned sadly southward, fleeing from their foes,
With five and twenty thousand comrades lost.
Thomas and Schofield, coming up the walk
Meet Andrew Johnson, the war Governor.

Scene: *Columbia, S. C., February 20, 1865.* ABDIEL, ITHURIEL,
ZEPHON, RAPHAEL.

Abdiel. War fills the earth with most atrocious crimes.
The righteous suffer and require our aid.
I followed Sherman's forces to the sea,
And saw Hardee, with fifteen thousand men,
Forsake Savannah and retire in haste,
While Sherman's forces proudly entered in.
I've seen the sky lit up with hellish flames,
And heard the shrieks of outraged innocence,
And helped in many a case of sore distress,
But never witnessed aught that equals deeds
Of lawless villains in this commonwealth.

Ithuriel. I found the saintly Bachman in the hands
Of ruffians who wore Union shoulder-straps.
God's aged servant suffers their abuse
Because he shielded helpless womanhood.
I had them captured by the good man's friends
And brought to beg for mercy at his feet.
He spared them, and refused to have them slain.

Zephon. I turned away the furious tongues of flame
That threatened to consume the lowly home
Where faithful Dinah trusted God and prayed.

Raphael. I saw Hardee leave Charleston with his
    troops;
And from devouring flames I rescued men,
And saved fair women from ills worse than death.
The old flag floats in triumph o'er this State
But to protect base bummers, thieves, and brutes,
Turned loose to prey upon defenseless homes.
How long, how long will Sherman's Christian men
Permit their troops t' indulge in such black crimes?
Northward the army moves in grand array,
While conflagrations blaze along its march,
And fiendish men stray from its serried ranks
To carry consternation to sad homes.
Behold the hell-hounds searching for their prey!

Scene: *Bentonville, N. C., March 19, 1865.* MARS, BELIAL, MAMMON.

Mars. The oft defeated army still fights on.
This morning Johnston, who commands again,
Attacked his enemies and would have gained
A glorious victory but for the fight
Made by brave troops by Jeff C. Davis led.
They held the field and saved the scattered hosts.

Belial. No wonder Johnston hoped for victory.
Hosts of base fellows of the vilest class
Went off from Sherman's army to attack
Weak women, little children, and poor slaves.

Mammon. And larger numbers of my thieving friends
Were absent laying hold on property.
Kirkpatrick's cavalry rode forth in pride
To strike at Hampton on the eighth of March;
But they were driv'n for refuge to the swamps,
And hardly managed to escape on foot,
Saved by a part of Slocum's army corps.
Two more strong army corps approach this place.
See! their successful leaders come this way.
There's valiant Terry, whose brave forces took
Fort Fisher after B. F. Butler failed;
And there is Schofield, late in Tennessee,
When Thomas scattered Hood's most valiant troops.

Scene: *Steps of the Capitol, Richmond, Va., Sunday morning, April 2, 1865.* GABRIEL, RAPHAEL, ITHURIEL, ZEPHON, URIEL.

Raphael. How lovely is this sacred Sabbath-day!
How bright the sunshine, and how green the hills
Reflected by James River's crystal flood!
See swelling buds adorning ev'ry tree,
And song-birds making charming melody.
The sound of sweet-toned bells invites to prayer.
The little ones already sing God's praise,
And lovely women lead their joyful songs.
The aged and infirm send up to heav'n
Devout thanksgiving for celestial gifts.
The pris'ners and the wounded call on God
For gracious help in this their time of need.

14

The pious slaves, with rich religious joy,
Crowd to the temples of the living God.
Blessed with the liberty that Jesus gives,
Their human bondage lightly bears on them.
So much of grace pervades this atmosphere
It seems a happy half-way place to heav'n.
And this, in spite of vast beleaguering hosts
That gather to destroy these Christian homes.

Ithuriel. Yes, and the war grows fiercer hour by hour.
Six thousand men were captured yesterday
From the defeated army of the South.
'Tis whispered Petersburg must shortly yield;
And when it falls, Richmond must share its fate.
But see! the ministers of God go forth
To lead the worship of good citizens
In all the sanctity of godliness.
There's Duncan, Doggett, Minnegerode, and Hoge;
And there is Burrows, an adopted son,
True to his foster-mother to the last.
Promiscuous crowds now pass on solemnly,
Gazing intently upon Washington,
Whose statue seems to bless them from its height.

Uriel. There is the President, with form erect;
He seeks support from Him who governs all.
God help that honored heir of many woes!
This day Grant orders a severe assault
By such a force as never charged before.

Zephon. And must these saints surrender to their foes?

Gabriel. 'Tis possible. " God chastens whom he loves."
Let us unseen go worship where they meet.

Scene: *Richmond, Va., noon, April 2, 1865.* SATAN, MAMMON,
CHEMOSH, BELIAL.

Satan. Ha, comrades, this religious calm soon ends!
Strange people are these pious Southerners!
I moved my people greedily for gain
To bring barbarian slaves to this fair land,
Hoping to so demoralize the whites
That with their servants they would sink to hell.

But the black wretches soon were taught to pray
And hymn the praises of the Lord most high.
Another generation would have swept
Th' improving Ethiops far from my control,
While those who ruled them gracefully displayed
Devotion, piety, and holy zeal,
With morals pure and manners so refined
As won the admiration of mankind.
I gave them war and drenched their land with blood;
And yet while millions threaten them with death,
They pray and sing and preach, and offer Christ
To ev'ry ragamuffin in their camps.
And Richmond with the "Bummers" at her doors,
Still goes to Church and keeps the Sabbath-day.
I'll let her know hell hates such worshipers!
Her pious homes, consumed by raging flames,
Shall give her children to the midnight storms.
I'll wreak my fury on the whole broad land,
My foot-prints now are seen in battle-fields,
In countless graves and trenches of the slain,
In piles of ruins and in rising smoke.
Proud, patient people look upon it all,
And say they trust in God for better days.
But they shall yet " curse the great God and die."
Some shall be banished to far foreign climes;
The gloom of dungeons others shall enshroud,
While iron fetters cramp most honored forms.
Worse still! worse still! these pious polished saints
Shall have for rulers through long, weary months
The lowest, vilest, most outrageous tools
That earth or hell or the whole universe
Can furnish to my hand to govern them.

Mammon. Ho! Satan, did you see that messenger,
Who at the Church called out the President?
Lee is retreating now from Petersburg.
Richmond must also soon be given up,
And there will be much booty to divide.

Belial. And there will be disorder here to-night.

Baal. And fires will blaze extensively around.

Chemosh. The worshipers desert the churches now

Belus. The rulers are assembling in hot haste.

Mammon. The treasure chests go rumbling toward the cars,
Guarded by trusty soldiers with due care.
There's Davis, Breckinridge, and their small force,
Bound for Amelia Court-house to meet Lee.
Thence to seek Johnston and combine their strength.

Satan. But I have counteracted their design.
Starvation will confront them at that place,
To Danville I have forwarded the trains.
To-morrow enemies will triumph here.
Soon the whole South must yield to conquerors.

Scene: *McLean's Orchard, Appomattox Court-house, Va., 1 o'clock, April 9, 1865.*

Uzziel. Contending armies still surround our steps
And dying groans are heard on ev'ry hand.

Abdiel. The strife grows fiercer as if near its close.

Ithuriel. At Deatonsville Lee lost six thousand men,
At Farmville burned the bridges in his rear,
Sent Longstreet to secure the Lynchburg road
To give his starving troops a safe retreat;
But Sheridan was there to drive him back,
And close the only pathway of escape.

Raphael. Then must the dauntless hero soon submit.

Zophiel. Already the conditions have been named
On which the troops of Lee lay down their arms.
The gen'rous magnanimity of Grant
In this his hour of triumph and renown
Is admirable, and deserves high praise.
Lee's dignity and grandeur in defeat
Crown the illustrious hero of the South
With the completeness of a character
By grace refined, by suff'ring perfected.
Behold the foremost men of this broad land!
Grant leads the millions of a conq'ring host;

Lee, in adversity, stands forth confessed
The noblest product of the centuries—
A peerless, modest, brave, heroic, grand,
Unostentatious Christian gentleman!
Earth has no soldier worthy to receive
The battle-blade of such a man as Lee.
Grant knows it. He will never claim that sword!
But leave it to be wielded by the hand
Of him from whom he learned in joyous youth
With stainless hand to grasp the spotless prize
Fame offers to the valiant and the pure.

THE HOUSE WHERE LEE SURRENDERED.

Scene: *Ford's Theater, Washington, D. C., April 14, 1865.* SATAN, BELIAL.

Belial. Satan, what next? Your war must shortly end.
Johnston's and Kirby Smith's and other troops
Must soon surrender and go home to work.

Satan. Yes, and the Fed'ral army will disband;
But my great conflict with the pow'rs above
Knows no cessation, nor an hour of truce;

I now propose a bloody tragedy
To startle angels and astound mankind.
An actor here, who from his infancy
Has been familiar with the tragic stage,
Has long sought opportunity to seize
The President and all his cabinet,
And hasten with them through the Southern lines
As pris'ners to negotiate for peace.
Of course he failed; but his poor silly dupes,
Hare-brained and stage-struck, wait upon his will,
Ready to deal out death if he commands.
The conquered South in hopeless ruin lies;
Its rulers even now are fugitives.
This actor's best loved friend was doomed to death
For a most daring feat performed by Beall
Upon the waters of the Chesapeake;
The President refused to save Booth's friend.
Booth's crazed, and I have instigated him
To act the assassin on this very night,
While his copartners in this dreadful crime
Seek noted victims in their quiet homes.
Behold the actor, with a deadly aim
To slay the nation's most important man,
Kindling to fury all the wrathful flames
That now between the angry sections blaze!

GABRIEL *enters.*

Gabriel. Horror of horrors! blackest of all crimes!
A bold assassin slays the President.
Quite unfamiliar with theatric scenes,
I'm here too late to save him from his fate.
Satan's malignity has triumphed here.

Scene: *Durham, N. C., April 18, 1865.* MICHAEL, UZZIEL, ARIEL.

Ariel. Nine days have passed since Lee's brave veterans
Laid down their arms and homeward turned their steps,
In peace to tread the paths of poverty;
Will Johnston still in bloody strife engage,
Aiming by swift retreat toward Mexico
To prop the throne that Maximilian claims?

Michael. He will not.   Never will Americans
Uphold an Austrian despot on these shores.
But if they would, the forces led by Grant
Hedge up all roads that lead troops westwardly.
When Lee's surrender sealed the Southland's fate,
Her sons determined blood should cease to flow.
Troops of the South fought for their principles;
Failing to win, they nobly claim their place
Under the flag 'neath which their fathers stood,
And standing firm defy a world in arms.

Uzziel. 'Tis said that Sherman offers Johnston terms
By which his soldiers become citizens,
Restored to all the rights that were secured
When British foes were driven from this land.
O'er Lee and Grant the flower of chivalry
Bloomed in the light of Christian principle,
And men wore superhuman dignity.
Now Sherman to the troops of Johnston gives
The conquered all the rights that conq'rors claim.
He uses language such as charmed mankind
When Thomas Jefferson still lived and wrote
Of civil liberty and equal rights.
Sherman, the hero, shows wise statesmanship,
With scholarly perfection unexcelled.

Michael. 'Tis Breckinridge whose classic statesmanship
Deserves the plaudits you to Sherman pay.
The Fed'ral chieftain first denied the right
Of a civilian to take any part
In the affairs of military men,
But when reminded that his visitor
Had been an active Major-general,
And of the War Department had been chief,
He kindly condescended to permit
The great man to be present and assist.
Then did the might, the majesty of mind
Assert its natural supremacy,
As Breckinridge dictated Sherman's terms
In the most polished language of the schools,
Until the hero marching toward the sea,

Charmed by the blandishments of Breckinridge,
Declared that with but one more social drink
He had commanded his entire consent
To give his conq'ring army to his foe,
And yield himself a pris'ner of war.
But as it is under the great man's lead
The Fed'ral gen'ral plays the dictator
To elevate the men that Johnston led;
And who shall venture to deny his right,
As a supreme commander in the field,
To dictate terms to his own prisoners?

Ariel. 'Twas fortunate that Breckinridge was here
To be the advocate of worthy men.

SATAN *approaches.*

Satan. Ha, Michael! I yet rule this lower world;
I rule to ruin your most hopeful plans.

Michael. But, Satan, in his day of mighty power
The President, like Sherman, is most kind,
And much disposed to pardon all his foes.

Satan. The President! He has been dead three days,
And I control the madness of these times.
Fanatic fury drives to bloody deeds,
Wreaking its vengeance upon multitudes;
It e'en hates Sherman for his last kind act,
And soon will wrest all power from his hands.
Lincoln would have restrained it; he is gone.
It would hang Lee and Johnston if it could,
And millions of the people of the South.
This Breckinridge, with all his wondrous gifts,
'Twill to the ocean drive in a frail skiff.
But, Michael, I've no time to waste on you:
This is my most important harvest time.

Michael. Perverted talents, as in Satan seen,
Are quite enough to make archangels weep.
Capacities for good, in men unused,
All run to waste because of enmity.

A hundred thousand filled not Johnston's place
When he no longer was in high command;
Yet this great nation ostracises him,
And would if fiercest foes were raging round.
Such is the fruit of war between the States;
So Breckinridge, a statesman from his youth,
Will soon be banished from the land he loves.
Uncounted generations of the past
Hereditary virtues have sent down
To give in him " assurance of a man "
Possessed of every needed excellence.
With Buena Vista's laurels on his brow,
Wit, genius, learning, talents in his brain,
And oratory flowing from his lips;
Honors came crowding thickly round his steps,
And fame proclaimed his greatness in his youth.
He distanced competition, and looked down
On every rival of his grand career,
Until the highest place was in his reach
That any nation ever had to give,
And then lamented that they had not more
To lavish on the object of their love.
But fiery factions blazed around his path,
And drove him from his highway of renown
To give a section talents that belonged
To every foot of his dear native land.
True to his friends, he fought their battles well,
When fiercer partisans had ceased to fight,
Upheld their government until it fell
A pile of hopeless ruins at his feet.
Then sent his kinsman of the silv'ry tongue,
Most eloquent of all his country's sons,
With true Kentuckians to guard the way
Of his great chieftain through the forest's gloom;
Till Davis chose seclusion as his guard,
And was betrayed by darkness to his foes.
Kentucky's hero grandly gave himself;
No other had so much to sacrifice
On friendship's altar for his countrymen—
Youth, health, wealth, office, power, promotion, fame—
But Breckinridge gave all to honor's cause.

Scene: *Capitol, Washington, D. C., May 30, 1865.* GABRIEL, ITHU-
RIEL.

Gabriel. Once more peace walks the earth with grace-
ful steps,
Most gently stretching forth her loving hands,
Releasing pris'ners and disarming foes,
Disbanding armies and conducting home
Husbands long banished from their loving wives,
Sons to their parents, lovers to fond maids,
And fathers to their little, prattling babes.
On yesterday the new-made President
Proclaimed amnesty to Confederates,
Except a few conspicuous characters.
They'll hasten to repair the waste of war,
And with the hand of industry invite
Prosperity to visit their abodes.

Ithuriel. But will it come since laborers are free?

Gabriel. Our God has done so much t' enrich these
States,
No enemies can keep their people poor.
Two questions have been settled by the war:
The slaves are free, the Union permanent.
If it's oppressive, there's no remedy;
To this rash revolution all submit.
Secession and disunion now are dead,
And with them negro slavery expired.
This change admitted, other things remain
As they have been for nearly eighty years.
The North made war for union, so she said,
And freed the slaves in order to success.
She has succeeded, and of course the States
Are in the places which they tried to leave.
So Lincoln said, and so says Johnson now.
This was the theory on which the war
Was prosecuted to its bloody end.
Men who believe that States might freely leave
Of course denied the right to drive them back;
But if the Constitution gave the right
To coerce States and force them to remain,
Or drive the straying wand'rers back again,

'Twas to the very places that they left,
With all their rights and duties unimpaired;
If not, coercion was atrocious crime.

Ithuriel. But you forget that Satan heads the gang
Of desperadoes that now rule the land;
You'll not expect consistency in them,
They would have deposed Lincoln, had he lived
T' oppose their furious onslaughts on the South.
To them the Constitution and the laws
Seem "leagues with death and covenants with hell"
When they protect the people of the South
Against malicious, furious, fiendish rage.
Johnson has hated aristocracy,
Proclaimed himself the champion of the poor;
Has loved the Union, and has risked his life
In its defense among its enemies.
He may be rash and rough, but he is brave,
And will uphold th' authority of law;
What seems to him his duty he'll perform
In spite of whatsoever may oppose.
Vindictive cruelty may sometimes hurl
Unnecessary insults at his foes,
And suff'ring, too, if they're of high degree;
But to the lowly he is ever kind.
Behold the poor man's ever faithful friend!
Th' unpurchasable champion of the poor
Boldly defies the hosts of Mammon led
In this proud capitol, where capital
Controls the legislation of the land,
And dominates obsequious cabinets.

Scene: *Richmond, Va., May, 1867.* ABDIEL, ARIEL, ZOPHIEL, ZE-
PHON.

Abdiel. What brings my faithful comrades here to-day?

Ariel. We come th' escort of one who needs our aid;
Two years have passed since Davis ceased to rule
The noblest people earth has ever seen.
Since then this chosen ruler has become
A great vicarious suff'rer for his class
And for the people over whom he ruled.

Zephon. How so? And why should he such suff'rings bear?

Ariel. Some think t' avenge the wrongs of negro slaves,
And vindicate the government of God.

Zophiel. Did not our God give laws to govern slaves?
And did not that convey a right t' enslave?

Ariel. God did give laws to govern human slaves,
But not a law to make of freemen slaves.
Man kidnaps man: thus slavery begins.
The kidnapper was wicked, and his prey,
Per possibility, more wicked still.
The rude barbarians became merchandise
By commerce taken to plantation homes.
The master can be fiend-like, if he will,
And suffer for the sins that he commits;
Or, like the friend of God, great Abraham,
May train the servants born in his own house
To be the valiant soldiers of the Lord.
The law of God to masters and to slaves
Proposes to bestow upon them both
The glorious freedom of the sons of God.

Zophiel. Where rests the guilt of human slavery
As it existed in the Southern States?

Ariel. For more than fourscore years the British king,
And his rich lords of trade forced negro slaves
Upon the people of their colonies.
Virginia protested; but the rude blacks,
To make the British rich, were sent in droves.
The far-famed "bargain" which New England made
With Georgians and with Carolinians
To bring them slaves for fully twenty years,
Doubled the numbers of the servile race.
In spite of protests from the other States
The East received millions of yellow gold
For black slaves bought with rum, and in exchange
For souls of white men unto Satan given.

Zophiel. Did not the mad men of the North predict
An insurrection of the Southern slaves,
Filling the land with arson, murder, lust,
And nameless horrors such as Hayti saw?

Ariel. They did. It was not soldiers, arms, nor forts
Kept their predictions from becoming true;
Nor politicians nor patrolling guards
Preserved the sanctity of Southern homes.
'Twas Christian love among religious slaves
That neutralized barbarian viciousness.
The saintly women of the sunny South,
Gentle, refined, meek, modest, pious, pure,
Most beautiful, most lovely, and best loved
Of all Eve's fairest, fascinating train,
Have claimed the sooty children of their slaves
For virtuous heirs of immortality:
Meek, humble followers of Jesus Christ.
John Brown and his most fiendish followers
In vain have hoped for San Domingan scenes
Among the true disciples of the Lamb.

Zophiel. If slavery thus Christianizes slaves,
Why not enslave the whole of Africa?

Ariel. So thousands argued against common sense.
It did not save the slaves of other lands:
'Twas Christianity that Christianized.
The Methodists and Baptists of the South
Have brought more Africans to Jesus Christ
Than have been gathered upon heathen ground
Of all earth's tribes by all earth's ministers.

Zophiel. You charge the guilt of Southern slavery
Against Great Britain and New England States;
Does no part of it rest upon the South?
Men of the South once hated it, but now
They all have learned t' embrace it lovingly.

Ariel. Yes, Zophiel, to those slav'ry-hating men
Its horrors and its profits all belonged;
But the great guilt of gross mismanagement
Rests on the South with more than mountain weight.

The South loathed slavery till the mighty North
Would wriggle out of all the covenants
Made with slave-holders in more honest times,
And called their benefactors criminals.
Then hatred seemed to drive out common sense;
Then Southern men defended slavery.
They said it was a blessing sent from God,
A blessing to the master and the slave:
Each son of Japhet owed it to the Lord
To capture and enslave some child of Ham,
To the great glory of the Lord most high.
This theory was never practiced there,
But something worse grew out of hellish hate
Between the sections of a Christian land.
To charge God with the guilt of slavery
Was most insulting to the Holy One,
But the domestic slave trade was far worse.
When Southern men sold slaves to Southern men,
The slave might often choose his own new home,
And keep his loved ones in his neighborhood;
But this depended on a kindly heart:
Law must not meddle with a master's rights:
So said defiant Southern gentlemen.
They left their slaves without a word of law
To shield them from the Northern rich man's greed,
But when the sheriff sold for Northern debts,
The highest bidder took the human soul,
And sundered all the slave's most tender ties.
No matter if the loving master plead,
Or wept, or cursed to see his playmate sold:
Away from parents, children, wife, and home,
The property must bring its highest price.
In spite of cries and tears from anguished hearts
The slave was exiled far from all he loved.
The suff'rers by this lack of kindly law
Were not barbarians brought from Africa,
Nor hardened criminals, well steeped in crime,
But colored Christians born and taught of God.
The possibility of such hard fate
Robbed the gay slave of much hilarious glee.
" Old master's" home was his blest paradise;

To leave it, banishment from Eden's joys.
Thousands for sale begged men to purchase them,
To keep them near the families they loved.
And when they failed to find a purchaser,
Lest they should flee to swamps, or Canada,
Were thrust into damp jails and bound in iron
To go in agony they knew not where.

    Abdiel. These helpless suff'rers from infernal hate
Between the ruling sections of the States
Did God forget and fail t' avenge their wrongs?

    Ariel. I need not talk of retribution now;
But slaves are free, and more than all the wealth
They ever earned has been destroyed by war.
Thousands of wealthy, honored Southern men
Have begged for bail to stay in their own homes,
When low-bred despots, proud of hate-born rule,
Arrested them with spiteful tyranny.
And tens of thousands, fearful of arrest,
Have dodged the hated "home guards" day and night,
Or slept in prisons, fed on prison fare.
Hundreds of thousands, men of ev'ry rank,
Left happy homes to sicken in the camps;
Or way-worn trudged through dank, malarious swamps;
Or pined in prison far from friends and home;
Or died by thousands battling with fierce foes.

    Abdiel. Was this t' avenge the wrongs of suff'ring slaves
On those who might have shielded them from harm?

    Ariel. I did not say so, but the white man's lot
Was not unlike what the sold slave's had been.
Such seeming retribution threatened all
Whose hate of Yankee meddling left their slaves
So unprotected by the civil law.
But there were some conspicuously known
Who suffered much from arbitrary pow'r.
Those times saw Henry Clay's beloved son
Dragged from his happy home and family

To the chief city of his native State,
And exiled in the care of hireling guards,
As many decent negroes oft had been;
Saw her chief-justice flee to Canada,
As pious, sober slaves with haste had fled;
And the chief pastor of the proudest sect
Hasten away to dwell in Toronto;
Her loved ex-Governor, a Union man,
Dragged from his bed at night by armed men,
And hurried off to damp Fort La Fayette,
Deprived of all the decencies of life,
Thence carried to Fort Warren to reflect
On men who won the liberty he lost
For failing to appreciate and laugh
At obscene jokes from one whose will was fate.
So a slave trader might have shown dislike
Toward one too pure to relish his coarse wit.
Another Governor, who fought three years,
Commanding Union troops in active war,
Was exiled from his State into a wild,
And left to wander without purse or sword,
As destitute as any negro slave,
Fleeing from traders who bought human souls.
His grave offense was voting for his choice
Among the men who would be President.
I might proceed to tell of thousands more
Whose sufferings were such as negroes bore
As the result of lack of human law
To save them from unnecessary woes,
But I forbear to state more instances.
Undignified contentions now prevail
Between the Congress and the President.
While they contend about prerogatives
And how the conquered States shall be controlled,
The Southland suffers from the worst misrule
Bad negroes and worse white men can inflict.
Plantation government, by blacks or whites,
Was not considered half so villainous.

Abdiel. Can there be retribution in the fact
That white men must endure misgovernment?

Ariel. I did not say so. You may judge of that.
I said that he who ruled by their free choice
The noblest sons and daughters of their race
Is a vicarious suff'rer for his class
And the proud people he was called to rule;
That this great man has borne indignities
And sufferings beyond comparison
With any borne by other Christian men.
A price was set upon his honored head;
He was accused of most atrocious crimes,
Was hounded through the land that honored him.
Mad millions loudly clamored for his blood,
And sung of hanging him upon a tree.
Chased through the forest paths of three great States,
Th' illustrious fugitive at dawn of day
Was torn from much loved family and friends,
And rudely hurried to the Chesapeake.
Fortress Monroe became his prison house,
Made strong by his own care in happier days.
There the meek invalid was doomed to wear
The iron fetters of despotic rule.
When the sick suff'rer saw the manacles
And the rough men to fetter his weak limbs,
Astonishment almost suspended thought.
Soon indignation gave him such great strength
That men and shackles were thrown off with ease,
And manhood's majesty defiant stood
Proof against degradation by his foes.
Exhaustion followed effort. There he lay,
The helpless victim of infernal hate,
With iron on his limbs and in his soul.
The tread of sentinels drove sleep away:
No quiet moment visited his cell,
No secret corner hid from watchful eyes,
By day or night this modest gentleman.
Brave sentinels abhorred the cruel task
That made them seem like Gorgons or foul fiends,
With horrid looks converting men to stone.
The army surgeons in the name of God,
Humanity, and their great science plead
For one whose virtues had made them his friends

Two years' subjection to tyrannic whims
Have failed to crush the patient sufferer.
He comes to-day demanding liberty
Or a fair trial through the courts of law.
They hold him still for trial. He gives bail.
He never will be tried. He's innocent.
No law condemns the victim of hell's hate,
So his worst enemies must now admit.

Abdiel. If God avenged the wrongs of negro slaves
Upon the honored men of Southern States,
Did that excuse or justify the wrongs
Inflicted upon Davis and his friends,
And on the humbler millions of the South?

Ariel. No, no! Stern retribution follows fast
In footsteps of wrong-doers of all grades:
Some in this life, more in the life to come.

Scene: *Senate Chamber, Washington, D. C., May 26, 1868.* SATAN,
MARS, MAMMON, BELUS, BELIAL.

Satan. Comrades, the rulers of this continent
Have fallen upon most unhappy times.
Davis was hunted, captured, bound in iron,
Accused of crimes, confined two years, gave bail,
And then demanding trial was denied.
In Lincoln's hour of triumph he was shot,
Mourned by the men who were his enemies.
The Mexicans dethroned their emperor,
And doomed him to the penalty of death.
'Tis said that Johnson, who is now impeached,
Will be expelled from his high place to-day
By the rash men who rule to ruin here.

Belial. They've met their match in this their President.
I've watched my big-brained crony from his youth.
He seldom fails in what he undertakes.

Belus. What have these men against their President?

Mars. He was as rough and ready as themselves,
Able to comprehend their vicious schemes
And counteract the shrewdest of their plans.

At duty's call he vetoed their bad acts,
And turned out Stanton from his cabinet.
He wished to rule the country four years more
And end unconstitutional misrule.

Mammon. He need not lose his office for a day:
If they hate Johnson, they love money more.

Satan. Halt, Mammon, and be careful how you talk!
Most Senators may be quite sinful men
And like myself may glory in their deeds,
But hint not that such great men can be bought.

Mammon. I dare not speak against your chosen friends,
But may assert that they have all grown rich.
The silly honesty of early times
Has long been numbered with the things that were.

Satan. Mammon, imprudence is your fault of late:
You tell our party secrets out of school.
While we await the Senate's action here,
Let us rehearse the hist'ry of these times.
The buying of Alaska was an act
To be remembered to the end of time.
But I shall watch for opportunities
For war between Great Britain and the States
About their frozen boundaries and trade.

Mammon. The grand old party we have served so well
Has proof of our devotion to its cause.
With Douglass or with Bell for President,
There could have been no war between the States.
We beat them by divisions in the ranks
Of the majorities opposed to us.
When we had beaten them, some kindly words
Would have hushed all the storms of discontent.
We spoke them not, but let the storm rage on.
To serve our faction and preserve its life
Has cost ten thousand millions in hard cash
And sent a million to untimely graves.
Was such a party cheap at such a price?

Satan. To us it was. We need its services
To curse the country to the end of time.
If dying it should cease to work our will,
Another like it never could arise
To secrete so much venom in its hate.

Mars. Its miscreated, monstrous government
Of subjugated people in the South
By ten black Legislatures of ten States.
With lighter-colored Governors to match,
Five military rulers with their troops.
Over five districts under epaulettes,
Fifteen coarse Congressmen to crown the whole.
Is complicated, military, mixed,
Kaleidoscopic and yet quite unique.
Solon, Lycurgus, Numa, Draco, Laud
Could never have imagined such a scheme.
Stanton and Satan must have hatched it out.
Own up now, Satan, tell the truth for once.

Satan. What if we did? Who had a better right?
See! see! the crowd! The Senate now adjourns.
Johnson's acquitted. Yes, he comes this way,
With Evarts, Seward, Stanberry, and Chase.
See yonder Butler, Stephens, Chandler, Wade,
Sumner, and Morrill, Sherman, Morton, Hoar.

Scene: *Boston, Mass., November 12, 1872.* GABRIEL, ZEPHON, AB-
DIEL.

Zephon. What means this burning mass of merchan-
dise,
This crumbling granite and this melting iron?
Here blazes eighty millions of heaped wealth
On threescore acres of rich Boston's ground!
A year ago Chicago saw fierce flames
Consume two hundred millions at one time,
Spread over more than three square miles of land.
The great North-west has been so scorched by flames
That dwellings, factories, stores, merchandise,
Green, growing crops, and rich, ripe, luscious fruits,
And even vegetables under ground
Have been devoured by the hungry heat.

I've seen it all, and asked myself the while
Whether their boisterous glee and joyful shouts
O'er flames that blazed upon Atlanta's hills,
Or lit the skies o'er Georgia's villages,
Or gave unfading glory to the land
Where flows the Shenandoah's sparkling stream,
Has aught to do with these calamities.

Gabriel. 'Tis not for us to judge the sons of men,
Or pour out retribution on their heads.
I saw th' unseemly mirth of which you speak.
These blazes bring to mem'ry their offense,
But kindle not in them a thought of guilt.
'Tis ours to aid all peoples in distress.
These troubled ones demand our hearty help.

Zophiel. Such losses industry will soon retrieve,
And enterprise convert them into gains.
But only grace can build good character
Amid the ruins by sin's cyclone made.
If States may swindle States and compacts break,
To profit by collective villainy,
Shrewd citizens will rulers imitate,
For fraudful States raise fraudful citizens,
Till rank corruption fills the land with fraud.
Wat'ring lean cattle just before they're weighed
Suggested wat'ring railroad stocks to sell,
And thus get two for one by a sly trick.
"Black Friday" gave slick scoundrelism wealth,
But covered the great business world with gloom.
Commercial ruin came from cornering gold,
But gave twelve millions to two swindling men.
Tweed and his comrades steal from rich New York
Uncounted millions, and insulting ask:
"What will you do about this trifling thing?"

Abdiel. But worse than this, "The Credit Mobilier"
Taints the great Congressmen with basest fraud.
From sea to sea the railroad has been laid
On the crushed ruins of their characters,
And yet with brazen fronts they claim respect
Without a blush for their ill-gotten gains.

So universal is corruption now
That thieves and swindlers most adroitly cling
To all departments of the government.
No methodistic honesty can shield
Nor West Point lofty honor well protect
The President himself from the shrewd thieves.
They wind themselves into his confidence,
And cast the shadows of their crimes on him.

Gabriel. 'Tis sad to see so much dishonesty,
Such universal grabbing after gold;
But I predicted this great greed for gain
When hatred seized the reins of government
And, spurning constitutional restraints,
Drove madly over all the rights of States.

Zephon. This wondrous country still grows rapidly
In spite of sins and gross mismanagement.
The broad Pacific ocean from afar
Sends geetings to th' Atlantic hour by hour,
And both stretch out strong arms of shining steel
To grasp hands over this broad continent.
Thirty-eight millions in their peaceful homes,
Under one flag in thirty-seven States
May bid defiance to their ev'ry foe.
The States are all once more in Congress halls,
With Senators and Representatives.
The ruling faction, hoping to secure
By negro votes a longer lease of power,
Has made the blacks voters and citizens.
This gives more Congressmen to Southern States
Than they have ever had before the war.
These will be white men chosen by white men,
Pledged to support a white man's government
Over the negroes and their Northern friends.
What will the ghost of Sumner say to this?
And how will his live friends ward off the force
Of the reaction of their boomerang?

BOOK ELEVENTH.

Scene: *Centennial Building, Philadelphia, Pa., May 10, 1876.* MI-
CHAEL, GABRIEL, UZZIEL, ITHURIEL, RAPHAEL, ABDIEL, ZO-
PHIEL, ARIEL, ZADKIEL, ISRAFIEL, AZARIAS.

Michael. Comrades, with joy I meet you here to-day
Amid these works of nature and of art,
Gathered together out of many lands.
These signs of peace and progress call for thanks
To the great Giver of all perfect gifts.

All. " We give thee joyful thanks, most gracious Lord,
For all that thou has done for Adam's race
And for thy blessings lavished on this land ! "

Gabriel. The storms of war were low'ring darkly round
When we beheld this youthful nation's birth.
We've watched it through a hundred years of growth,
And now see giant strength and wisdom joined
With beauty's blooming, glowing loveliness.
This exhibition well rewards our care.
While we await the coming multitude,
Please tell of great events of recent date.

Uzziel. England has paid for damages at sea.
To the rich commerce of America
By war-ships that went out from British ports,
Of dollars fifteen millions and a half!
What would King George the Third have said to that?
England concedes to the United States
The channel boundary which they had claimed
Near to Vancouver's Isle and Fuca's Straits.
Grant wanted San Domingo's sunny isle,
But Sumner was the marplot of his plan.

Israfiel. Proud magnates of this land by death laid low
Await the resurrection trumpet's sound.

Stevens and Stanton, Seward, Sumner, Chase,
Wilson and Greeley, Thomas, Canby, Meade,
Brave Farragut, and matchless Robert Lee—
All silently sleep now in quiet graves,
Unnoticed by the busy, bustling world.
Still this great country lives and flourishes,
The noblest nation in the universe.
Hark! Martial music floats upon the air!
Four thousand veterans escort their chief
And make the welkin ring with their huzzas.
Behold the living magnates of to-day!
They come to act their parts in this grand scene!
See the embassadors of foreign lands,
The judges of earth's highest civil court,
The honored Governors of sovereign States,
Great Senators and Representatives,
Naval and military officers
Of highest rank and most successful deeds,
Distinguished visitors and citizens,
Thousands of women in their loveliness,
And gleeful childhood's artless innocence.
Who enter? 'Tis the modest President.
He takes his seat, and at his side is seen
The Emperor and Empress of Brazil.
Music rings out! Th' enchanting notes are hushed.
Prayer lifts its voice—the suppliant prayers of all
Ascend to heav'n from Matthew Simpson's lips.
 . . . . Hear Whittier's hymn! It sounds as if inspired.
To Hawley Welsh presents; and he to Grant
The grounds and buildings and their grand array.
Grant kindly welcomes all, and then declares
The exhibition open to the world.
Then with Brazil's great emperor to help,
Starts the grand engine that with giant force
Propels broad acres of machinery.

Scene: *Pittsburg, Pa., July, 1877.*   CHEMOSH, SATAN, MOLOCH,
   BAAL, MARS, MAMMON, BELIAL, BELUS.

Satan. Comrades, what think you of those hellish
   flames
That on red wings soar upward toward the heav'ns?

Baal. Their tow'ring grandeur fills me with delight!
Moloch. They promise flowing streams of human blood!
Belus. I am reminded of old Babylon,
Tyre, Nineveh, Ecbatana, and Troy,
Long buried 'neath the ashes of their homes!
Belial. I think of present pleasure in rough sport!
Mars. I ask for valiant legions to shoot down
The wretches who disturb the public peace!
Mammon. I mourn such waste of so much precious wealth!
Satan. Here is the "aristocracy of wealth,"
And the "Democracy of numbers" too,
That Alexander Hamilton desired.
The aristocracy of wealth conspired
To cut down labor's earnings ten per cent.,
Which meant less food, less clothing, and less fire
In the rough huts of squalid poverty,
That millionaires might faster heap their hoards.
The maddened toilers in the Southland, taught
By honored officers to light the torch,
Apply it now to Northern property.
See in those flames the red, rich, ripening fruits
Of Sherman's tactics, Hamilton's finance.
But this destruction is the poor man's loss;
The rich will make him pay the damages
In taxes, lower wages, higher rents,
More costly clothing, fire, food, furniture.
Less wealth must mean less comfort for the poor.
The rich can always buy what they desire.

Chemosh. These railroad riots and destructive fires
Spend all their fury on the prosp'rous North;
The long lines stretching southward are secure.

Baal. War taught the Northern workmen how to burn
The property of men they do not love.
That lesson Southern men are slow to learn;
Even the negroes, though exhorted long
To burn up Southern property, refuse.

Mammon, you study questions of finance,
Please tell us whether capital's increase
Is detrimental to the lab'ring poor?
Whether the poor have any thing to gain
By the destruction of a rich man's wealth?

Mammon. No; wealth's increase is gainful to all men,
And wealth's destruction subjects all to loss.
Some get an unfair portion of the gain,
And others share too largely in the loss.
The strife between labor and capital
Is ruinous to both, and ought to cease.
If either party grows dissatisfied,
Let operatives and machines work on
At such fair rates as a just court may fix.
Thus, without quarrels or the loss of time,
Production still proceeds to increase wealth.
Work the machines all day and all night long—
Three sets of operatives, each eight hours.
Overproduction never need be feared,
With free trade in the markets of the world.
If public faith is pledged to certain men
For their protection against foreigners,
Take off the tariff, lay a bounty on
T' indemnify confiding citizens.
Add the just bounty to the general tax,
Let the whole Union and each separate State
Pay their whole tax into one treasury,
From which the States or counties would draw out
An equal sum for ev'ry citizen.
The only other tax to be assessed
Would be by cities for their purposes.
To raise the money for that gen'ral tax,
Double the duty and the excise on
Tobacco and intoxicating drinks.
From ev'ry dollar of the capital
Of money-making trusts and syndicates,
And other corporations of the kind,
Collect three mills in each and every year.
Raise the deficiency from capital
Over one thousand dollars in amount.

Chemosh. But what of State rights in a plan like this?

Mammon. The right of all to tax the capital
That hides itself from States in which 'twas earned
In the great cities where the wealthy live.
Amend the Constitution to that end.

Mars. Tell us what else the nation yet can do
To save its millions from its millionaires,
And thus avert the ruin that impends?

Mammon. With no taxation on the lab'ring poor
By tariff, excise, or to license trade.
Tax heavily the filth, the wastefulness—
Disease and crime in alcoholic drinks,
Till prohibition drives them out of use.
Wash with soft soap at least three times a day
The mouths of minors who defile themselves
With snuff, tobacco, or with nicotine
In any of its varied, filthy forms.
Thus to the poor would soon be saved with ease
Two hundred millions paid in tariffs now;
Eight hundred paid in bounties to the rich.
Because of tariffs on the things they make;
Eight hundred more from alcoholic drinks,
And full two hundred from tobacco saved.
Two billions yearly thus saved to the poor,
And a round billion taxed upon the rich,
Would make the poor grow richer ev'ry year
Without depriving wealth of luxuries
Or bringing one rich man to poverty.
To help the poor rise up in affluence,
Compel all children to attend the schools
From fifth or sixth up to their fourteenth year;
From fourteen to eighteen, to learn some trade,
Profession, calling, business, or pursuit.
Make vagabonds, tramps, vagrants, swindlers work;
Convicted criminals keep well confined,
And give them food and clothes and constant toil.

Belial. Ho, Mammon! you had better now turn saint.
Add exhortation, preaching, prayers, and smiles,

And music to relieve their leisure hours.
Your money-mong'ring statesmanship would leave
No worthless character in all the land,
Nor one disciple of destruction's school.
If Satan does not keep close watch on you,
You'll turn the head of every devil here,
And then turn pastor of a thrifty Church
(An independent, liberal Church, of course)
Among the wealthy people of New York,
Chicago, Boston, Brooklyn, or Detroit.
But go on with your lecture on finance
Till Satan comes with more important work.
You could give lessons even to Jay Gould.

Azazel. Why not divide all wealth in equal parts
Among the people of a prosp'rous land?

Mammon. It would not stay divided for an hour:
The thrifty men could soon seize sev'ral shares,
The spendthrift hasten to be poor again.
'Twould clog the wheels of progress and destroy
The fruits of many years of industry.

Belus. But as the rich grow richer, and the poor
Still more dependent on machinery,
Will not the fate of Babylon and Rome
Descend upon a land of helpless slaves,
Dependent on a few with purse and sword?

Serapis. These people boast of their intelligence:
So did old Egypt in her days of pow'r,
But basest of the nations she became.

Mars. They glory greatly in self-government;
But so did Athens, Sparta, Thebes, and Rome.
Wealth in few hands led to their overthrow;
It purchased slaves and fawning sycophants,
But patriotic valor to defend
The failing fortunes of a sinking State
Was something wealthy rulers could not buy.

Mammon. This great republic had its destiny
In its strong hands for its own weal or woe.

It placed the yoke of hatred on its neck,
And used its strength to drag the car of war
Through gory fields to fame's enchanted grounds.
Peace came, and my shrewd minions seized the reins,
Gilded the yoke, and drove the nation on
To serve an aristocracy of wealth.
Of all the millions spent in hatred's war
One-half went to the purses of my friends.
One dollar in the public treasury,
Drawn by the tariff from the toiling poor,
Puts four into the pockets of the rich
In higher prices for protected goods.
'Tis said they now make merchandise of votes;
That one in four of voters is for sale,
That Legislatures sell themselves for gold,
And senatorial honors can be bought.
'Tis said the presidency, if not sold,
Was hocus-pocused from th' elected man,
To keep the grand old party still in place
The nation's treasures to manipulate,
Strike freedom down and fan the fires of hate.
But let the truth be told. *The non-elect*
To whom the highest office in the world
Was given by the nation's great mishap
Was the best man, or rather the least bad,
Of the bad money party's chosen chiefs.
'Tis a great pity that a man no worse
Should have to bear his party's infamy.

Satan. Ho, Mammon! You've grown wondrous wise
  of late.
You're quite a statesman and philanthropist.
Why not to free trade and free public schools
Add free libraries, lectures, lyceums,
Free fruit on all the road-ways of the world,
And dwellings free from sale for tax or debt?
Have done with your nonsensical debates!
'Twas other business brought us here to-day.
What might be and what will be differ much.
With flames like these we'll fill this boasting land.
Society's great social pyramid

Grows broader at the bottom day by day,
And at the top richer and heavier.
By combinations, trusts, and syndicates,
And higher tariffs to enrich the rich,
We'll heap up gilded greatness till the poor,
Crushed and despairing, overturn it all,
As did the French a century ago.
See you that Scotchman? Once he was quite poor;
But tariffs piled up riches at his feet
Until he buys an old, historic home,
In honest times giv'n by a grateful State
To show her love for a great general.
Pile on the tariff, let the trusts combine,
And such a princely fortune will be his
That he'll hobnob with princes in their realms,
And have proud statesmen share his toadying.
Let us away. Chicago claims our care.

Scene: *Washington, D. C., December 5, 1879.* ITHURIEL, ABDIEL, ZADKIEL. *On Currency.*

Ithuriel. 'Tis said that silver was demonetized
In such a quiet, underhanded way
That Senators and Representatives
Could not learn when or why or how 'twas done,
But the effect was soon well understood.
Less currency took money from the poor
And gave it to their wealthy creditors,
While trade constricted, wilted, withered, shrunk.
But when the people learned what had been done,
They forced the emissaries of the rich
To issue silver currency again
In coins such as their honest fathers used.

Abdiel. When war was raging, paper currency
Was often borrowed by the government,
To be repaid in paper promises:
But when war ceased the shrewd old bond-holders
Demanded gold for paper promises;
And politicians gave them all they asked,
Thus doubling all that debtors had to pay
And doubling the receipts of creditors.

Zadkiel. Millions of money known as trade dollars,
Though they were largely over "standard weight,"
Of more intrinsic worth than "standard coin,"
Were in the people's hands, and when suppressed
Caused them the loss of twenty cents on each:
Thus have base sharpers filched from multitudes.

Ithuriel. So the great banking law gave to a few
Int'rest on bonds, on notes, deposits, drafts;
And left the people subject to the whims
Of six and thirty thousand selfish banks,
To lend them much or little, as they please,
T' expand or contract currency at will,
With naught to regulate their waywardness.
In speculative times they've funds to lend,
Expanding the expansion more and more ;
But when a crisis comes, as come it must,
They make the pressure more and more severe;
Sad borrowers, begging from door to door,
Find no relief from hopeless bankruptcy.
Far better would it be to separate
All banks and banking from the government.
They talk of an elastic currency—
'Tis flexible to make the bankers rich
At the expense of losing multitudes—
A currency to stretch in prosp'rous times,
And to contract when scarcity prevails.

Abdiel. A stable currency is what men need,
Subject to no contraction nor control;
Enlarging as the people multiply,
And mines give up their silver and their gold.
This can be gained by banishing bank-notes,
And ev'ry form of currency but one,
That issued by the public treasury;
In notes of ev'ry various size required,
From hundred thousand dollars to half-dimes;
But never to exceed in its amount
Four times the money in the public vaults,
Nor fifty dollars for each citizen.
Backed by the specie and the government,

These notes would pass most current round the world.
Were any lost, 'twould be the nation's gain,
Nor would the wear of coin cause any loss
To circulate this people's currency
Use it to pay expenses, purchase bonds,
And satisfy all public creditors,
Replenishing the treasury with coin.

Scene: *Elberon, Coast of New Jersey, September 19, 1881.* RAPHAEL, ISRAFIEL, ZADKIEL, ZOPHIEL, ZEPHON, AZARIAS.

Azarias. The patient suff'rer is at last relieved.
Death, the deliverer, to his rescue came.
On him the healing art exhausted skill,
Trying in vain its choicest remedies.

Ariel. Affection's gushing sympathies on him
Lavished their kindest, tenderest ministries.
Mother, wife, children, multitudes of friends,
Vied ardently in fond devotedness.

Raphael. He was a model husband, father, son;
Was much devoted to the sciences,
To art, to oratory, and to law;
And literary lore was his delight.

Israfiel. In arms and statesmanship he had success,
And reached the highest station under heav'n.

Zadkiel. Th' assassin's bullet killed all enmities,
Turning his fiercest party foes to friends.
His agonizing pains struck censure dumb.

Zophiel. The millions of a nation sore bereaved
Lament the loss of their chief magistrate,
And Europe's royalty in sympathy
Sends letters of condolence o'er the sea.

Zephon. Six months ago the Czar of Russia fell,
A victim under an assassin's hand.
Thus despots have been slain in foreign lands
Through many years with mournful frequency.
But these self-governed people were exempt
From deeds of violence against their chiefs,

Till old John Brown was made a model saint,
And murder was the highway to renown.
Such teachings tend to multiply Gitteaus.

Zophiel. Death reaps rich harvests of distinguished
men
Without assassin's blades or minie-balls.

Zephon. Death's doings need not be reported here
To prove assassination's uselessness;
But if you will add Morton, Hooker, Black,
Brave Custer, Chandler, Phillips, Carpenter,
With thousands killed by Scio's earthquake shock;
But give your highest honors to the names
Of Bryant and Longfellow, sons of song,
Whose rhymes ring grandly through the universe.

Scene: *Concord, Mass., 4 P.M., April 30, 1882.* ARIEL, RAPHIEL.
The Burial of Ralph Waldo Emerson.

Ariel. The length'ning shadows of this April day
Fall mournfully upon an open grave
Where soon shall rest the honored form of one
Whose death sends sadness to ten thousand homes.
To bury him, behold what hundreds come
Of Boston's *literati* and *elite,*
With eloquent orations, solemn songs,
A tender sonnet, poetry sublime,
Inspired Scripture, fervent prayers to God,
Spring's fairest flowers, her greenest laurel wreaths.

Raphael. He had hereditary genius, wit,
Gentility, refinement, and good taste.
Learning, philosophy, and poetry
Unitedly twined honors round his brow.
Graceful and honest, his mild manners won
Respectful admiration from mankind.
Admiring thousands followed where he led,
And, fascinated, copied his defects.
His brief, concise, unfinished epigrams
Gave them a halting, stumbling, hitchy style,
In which t' express his nebulous conceits,
And throw obscurity round what he taught.

His " nature," " spirit," " soul," and " over-soul "
To them meant pantheism undisguised,
Or inspiration of the Quaker sort,
Or Swedenborgian dreamy mysticism,
Leading away from Christ, from God, from heav'n
Toward ill-defined and vague uncertainties.

RALPH WALDO EMERSON.

Better for him and his wise followers
The iron creed which his forefathers held;
But better still the truth of God as taught
By the Redeemer of the human race.
Here is firm footing; here is solid ground
On which the humblest of his children build
The principles of sound morality

And glorious hopes of endless blessedness.
O God, in thy great goodness, give the learned
These blessings lavished on the ignorant!

Scene: *Baltimore, Md., 1884. Methodist Centennial Conference.* RA-
PHAEL, ARIEL, ZEPHON. *Theology.*

Ariel. What brings these thoughtful, prayerful people
out?

Zephon. They come to celebrate th' important day
That gave this nation its first bishop here,
And organized its purest, strongest Church.
A hundred years have set the seal of God
On their devotion to his sacred cause.

Ariel. What say these men to those misguided ones
Who in their hard hearts say: " There is no God?"

Zephon. When pressed by such, they modestly reply:
" Whence came this universe of wondrous worlds,
The marshaled legions of a countless host,
Marching in majesty, with tireless step,
In glory and in grandeur through the skies?
How was the gay and gladsome world attired
With sparkling gems and robes magnificent,
The embodiment of beauteous loveliness,
As if to claim th' admiring love of heav'n?
Whence conscious life in all its varied forms,
Its grand gradations, its mysterious force?
And man the worshiper? whence his desire
To trust and to adore, if there's no God?
Whence his astonishing perceptive pow'rs,
His quick and lively sensibilities,
His lofty reason, his potential will,
If there's no God in all the universe?
What is eternal, if it is not God?
What are the leading links in the long chain
Of secondary causes?" The reckless,
Vain agnostic proudly says he knows not,
And, sneering, says he does not want to know.
Perhaps he fears a rival on the throne
Where self receives the homage of his heart,
And hence concludes to know no other god.

Raphael. But a wise scientist must know it all,
Or seek to know it all, and teach it too.

Zephon. "A fev'rish mass of phosphorated brain,"
He says, " spins, spider-like, a misty web
Of philosophic thoughts of evolution."
What he calls evolution he asserts
Makes lifeless law by dull, dead force evolve;
" Hot, hissing, blazing, embryonic globes"
" Evolved from yielding luminiferous ether,"
Or from "primordial hydrogen, molded
In some atomic vortex" deep and wide.
Whence came the ether or the hydrogen
Our wise men do not condescend to tell.
But evolution hardens those hot globes
To rocks, to metals, or to ocean's bed;
" Decomposition clothes their surfaces
With soil or water, and the sun gives warmth,"
"Atoms infinitesimal" become
The "protoplastic germs of quick'ning life"
No microscopic glass has yet revealed.
Ten thousand ages pass, and these become
Distinctly "animalcules." Then slowly
Through interminable centuries in
Leisurely succession, wriggling into
Being, come " maggots, worms, minnows, monkeys,"
And even great philosophers themselves,
As evolution's last, completest work.

Ariel. In forty weeks God's providence evolves
From one infinitesimal live germ
The various metamorphoses required
To make a full-fledged infant scientist.

Zephon. Yes, that is true, but hear the argument:
"This evolution of all things," they say,
" Proceeds from natural, unchanging law,
Inherent in unliving or dead force
That in unconscious or dead matter dwells.
How could a changeless and unvarying law
Cause variations in its own effects?

According to this fancied theory,
At ev'ry step of evolution's march
Through ages past resistless law cried, "Stop!"
And evolution had no pow'r t' evolve.
Immutability must ever be
Omnipotent, in an unliving law,
Forbidding progress and preventing change.
Under the rigid reign of changeless law
Eternal fires through nature's boundless realm,
If kindled once, must ever burn and blaze.
If burning globes were formed, unvarying
Law would bid them burn forever. Lifeless,
Unchanging law would, in a lifeless world,
Eternize lifelessness and death enthrone.

Raphael. All law implies a maker of the law,
Authority, intelligence, and will
To modify, suspend, enforce, repeal.
This theory still lacks the Christian's God
To give and to administer its law;
But needs him most to make its universe,
And people it with living worshipers.

Zephon. Unliving law, inherent in dead force,
Could never from dead substance life evolve,
Nor from unconscious nothingness evoke
A living, conscious, active intellect.
Life comes from life, comes from the life Divine —
Life unoriginated, underived,
Eternal, self-existent, infinite!
Without whom nothing did or could exist.
Receive in faith this great foundation fact,
And they may build what theories they please.
They are but thoughts. They may be true or false.
Take, if they must, a past eternity
For evolution under changeless law;
But drive not God out of his universe,
The God who made it and pronounced it good.
Think of that period in the distant past
When only God filled all immensity.

He, the sole Self-existence, the I Am,
No atom, force, law, motive, purpose, plan,
Nor possibility but in himself.
Then of, and by, and for himself alone,
Creation's mighty fabric was produced.
For of him, to him, through him are all things.
He was the All! He now exists in all,
Yet quite distinct from all created things.
He still supports and governs what he made.
He is the Father. All depend on him,
His arms embrace them and his pow'r protects.
Pervading space, filling immensity,
His awful voice has frequently been heard,
His pow'rful presence ev'rywhere is felt,
Yet nowhere seen by any eye of man;
For no man hath at any time seen God.
No man hath seen him, nor can any man
Behold the omnipresence of the Lord.
Too broad for human sight, ubiquity
Defies all finite pow'r his form to scan.
No creature is ubiquitous. Give one
The speed of thought and perfect holiness
Attracting him to the Most Holy One;
Of omnipresence, what could he perceive?
Only so much as might be manifest
At one small point in universal space,
In one brief moment of fast fleeting time.
The infinite beyond remains unseen.
A natural impossibility
Denies to sight divine ubiquity.

Raphael. But have not men seen and conversed with God?

Zephon. Yes; God, the Son, hath often talked with men;
Adorned their feasts with his loved countenance;
Revealed himself to Adam, Abel, Cain,
Seth, Enoch, Noah, Abraham, and Job,
To Isaac, Jacob, Moses, Joshua,
And many other saints of ancient times.
Yes, his delights were with the sons of men.

'Twas he became incarnate, wore the flesh,
And shed his blood to save a sinful race.
He conquered Satan, death, and left the grave,
To reign till ev'ry foe shall be subdued.
'Tis He in his humanity shall judge
The countless millions of angelic hosts,
And men in his eternal likeness made,
In glorified humanity enthroned,
Shall rule in righteousness the universe,
Through all the cycles of eternity.

Raphael. And does the Holy Ghost reveal himself
To sight as well as to the throbbing heart?

Zephon. The Holy Spirit manifests himself
In dove-like hoverings of lambent flame.
So he was seen by Moses on the Mount
Of Horeb, when the bush burned unconsumed;
And upon Sinai, when the prophet's face
Bore off its borrowed brightness to the camp.
Isaiah beheld him when the triune God,
Throned in the temple, sent him to his work.
When at the baptism of the Son of God
The Holy Ghost descended on his head,
'Twas in a glorious, dove-like form he came.
At Pentecost in cloven tongues of fire,
On apostolic heads his brightness shone.
Thus, while ubiquity's too vast for sight,
The unembodied Father is not seen.
But Deity is manifested by
Th' eternal Son and by the Holy Ghost.
Doubtless the Son in human form divine,
The Holy Ghost in dazzling glory bright,
Did manifest supreme Divinity
From the first moment when created light
Made motion, form, and color visible.

Ariel. Are there not some who still deny the Son
The worship due to his most honored name,
And say the Holy Ghost is not divine,
And call triunity irrational?

Zephon. There are, but Christ claimed worship and
The adoration of inspired men. [received
He's an impostor if he's not divine;
Triunity is not irrational;
We reason from the known to the unknown.
Nature abounds in things that are triune.
In God's own image man was made triune;
He craves companionship and pines away
If left with none to banish loneliness.
Yet Arians leave their unitarian God
Through all the cycles of eternity
That passed before the universe was made,
Self-doomed to solitary loneliness.
They make immensity his prison-house,
With none to share the horrors of his fate.
They own that God is love, but love requires
An object, its affection to receive.
Love passes over to the object loved.
What was there for a unitarian God
To lavish love upon before the dawn
That ushered in creation's natal day?
He of necessity must then have been
A God of uncompanioned solitude,
In isolated selfishness enthroned.
Not so the Christian's God reveals himself!
Our God is love. Triunity in him
Ineffably unites loving and loved
In infinitely joyful fellowship.
Three real persons most distinctively;
Yet in their nature, essence, substance, one.
Alike, eternal, good, immutable,
Omnipotent, omniscient, holy, just,
Their omnipresence through the realms of space
Necessitates eternal unity
In the divine, the purely spiritual.
Our God is love. Compassion for the lost
Gave the divine, eternal Son to die,
Redemption to provide for Adam's race.
He through the ages calls his ransomed home.
Man's access to the Father's through the Son
By the felt power of the Holy Ghost.

Ariel. Some men assert that from eternity
God did most freely and unchangeably
Wisely ordain whatever comes to pass;
That all events in him originate,
All destinies depend on his decrees,
Established ere he made the universe;
That one cannot be added to the saved,
Nor one diminished from the number lost.
They say contingencies, if once allowed,
Might overturn his righteous government,
Dethrone the Lord, and wreck the universe.

Zephon. He has not so revealed himself to us.
God does not ordain all that comes to pass.
Sin comes to pass which he could not ordain,
For he prohibits sin and threatens death
To all who violate his righteous law.
He has no secret will to set aside
The teachings of his own inspirèd word.
The sovereignty of God is absolute,
His universe is under his control,
His wisdom and his power are limitless.
By his decree angels and men exist,
Created free to freely serve their God.
This finite freedom, if unlimited
Except by its inherent weaknesses,
Finds ample scope for its free exercise
Without endangering the throne of God.
Unfettered, finite freedom's loftiest flight
Falls far below th' encircling infinite.

Ariel. They say if he does not ordain, he knows,
And that foreknowledge certainly implies
Fore-ordination by the all-wise God.

Zephon. Not so. Fore-ordination is the cause
Of all that ever has been fore-ordained;
Fore-ordination causes the thing known,
But knowledge causes not. 'Tis what's foreknown
Causes the knowledge and must govern it,
But though foreknowledge does not cause what's known,
The absolute foreknowledge of events

Implies the certainty of what is known,
Because the Lord can never be deceived.
Th' event will be as certainly foreknown.
All that depends on human liberty
Can only as contingencies be known,
Uncertainty of action must forbid
All certainty of knowledge of the act.
Contingent, as they were, on human wills,
There was not any thing to know till man
Freely determined what that thing should be.
And the same man might freely change again
From evil unto good, or bad to worse.
God knows all things precisely as they are;
His knowledge is exact and accurate.
Some things he knows as fore-ordained by him
Before the race of man began to be.
Of these his knowledge is most absolute.
Such was his purpose to create mankind
With freedom to obey or disobey.
Such is redemption's glorious mystery.
The gen'ral judgment, the triumphal reign
Of our great Saviour over all his foes,
And the enthronement of his honored saints,
With him in glory through eternity.
Some great events were fore-ordained and known
For years before they actually took place.
Such was the deluge. Such was Israel's march
From Egypt to the glorious promised land,
And Judah's from the plains of Babylon,
When sent by Cyrus, the "Elect of God."
But many things were as contingent known,
Because dependent on free agency.
So " God repented that he had made man
When man had sinned and grieved him at his heart."
To Israel made his " breach of promise known,"
And let them perish in the wilderness.
So disobedient Saul was doomed to death.
So David's sin brought punishment and grief:
His penitence found mercy with the Lord.
So Hezekiah's life was lengthened out,
And Nineveh's destruction was postponed.

So Judas fell from his apostleship
To depths of degradation and despair,
While humble Peter's penitential tears
Obtained forgiveness from his loving Lord.

Raphael. Thus ev'ry sinner who has been forgiv'n
Illustrates the great principle involved.
God changes not. He ever is the same,
Nor does he change his purposes or plans.
But when men change, he gladly welcomes them
With changed relations toward his government.
When men with gracious freedom turn from sin
To seek salvation through the Saviour's blood,
Then God beholds his ransomed with delight,
Welcomes the prodigal in loving arms,
And says the dead's alive, the lost is found.
He knew them once as sinners doomed to death;
He knows them now as heirs of endless life.

Zephon. God the immutable can never change,
But his foreknowledge of contingencies,
His knowing all things as they really are,
His unrestricted freedom from control
Provides for mercy through atoning blood
And leaves him free to show that God is love.
Love from the Father, Son, and Holy Ghost
Brings to the penitent from Calvary
Grace, mercy, peace, and everlasting life,
While justice, holiness, and truth approve.

Raphael. Our God is free! Most absolutely free!
No mythologic fate is over him,
Nor is he chained to an "Eternal Now"
Forbidding action and restraining love;
Nor, as a false philosophy asserts,
Is a concatenation of events
Held in his hand to help him govern worlds,
Lest they escape beyond his wise control.
Nor did he from eternity enact
Augustine's and John Calvin's stern decrees,
Ordaining whatsoever comes to pass,

Forbidding hope to millions ere they lived,
And dooming little infants to be damned.
Fore-ordination binds not loving hands,
Foreknowledge fetters not the Saviour's feet,
Omniscience does not drive omnipotence
To the performance of a task prescribed.
No bondage to eternal prescience
Forbids eternal love to save mankind.
No despot attribute's resistless force
Withholds from men the saving grace of God.
He freely governs those whom he made free.
His knowledge of contingencies is such
That by his all-wise, comprehensive plan
Man's finite freedom through its grand career
Is unobstructed by the infinite.
The freedom of the infinite provides
For all emergencies that can arise
From finite freedom's largest liberty.
Most freely in his own free government
Over the free, in his free likeness made,
Divinely free the mighty sovereign rules!

BOOK TWELFTH.

Scene: *Washington, March 4, 1885, at the Capitol.* ABDIEL, ZO-
PHIEL, ISRAFIEL.

Abdiel. A nation changes rulers here to-day.
The party that was dominant goes out,
Producing scarce a ripple on the stream
Of its unequaled grand prosperity.

Zophiel. Great Washington's completed monument
Looks down on the new ruler as he takes
The solemn oath that binds a President
The Constitution and the laws t' obey,
Support, enforce, and rightfully maintain.
But Washington's example wields a force
More potent than laws, oaths, or penalties
To lead successors into rightful paths.

Israfiel. Short-sighted men imagine that they see
Impending ruin, like an avalanche,
Descending and o'erwhelming this fair land,
Whenever their own party's overthrown.
The party falls, the country flourishes;
It thrives and gladdens in the smile of God
In spite of all the tricks of selfishness.
The gifts of God enrich a prosp'rous land,
And make it an example to the world.
Thrift, enterprise, invention, science, art
Unveil the treasures that have long been hid
In air, in earth, in waters, and in mines,
Until, o'er rivers bridged, through mountains drilled,
Trade heaps up treasures brought from ev'ry land,
And opens avenues from shore to shore
Till the Pacific "hears" the Atlantic "roar."

YOSEMITE FALLS.

NEVADA FALL.

Abdiel. But is there nothing gained by all the strifes
Of noisy parties seeking offices?
Does all the waste of time, of money, zeal
By politicians bring no lasting good?

Israfiel. In a free government the watchfulness
Of parties over parties serves to check
Extravagance and rashness, and detect
Dishonesty among the men who rule.
The "ins" are tempted to lay hold upon
The treasures that are under their control;
The "outs," though not more honest, are inclined
To publish and expose the plunderers,
And hasten to eject from office those
Whose hands have robbed the public treasury.
This selfish watchfulness results in good.

Zophiel. Between the parties of the present time
The tariff has been cause of much dispute,
But the protected classes are too strong
To loose their hold upon their victims yet.
Hundreds of millions of ill-gotten gains
Serve well to gain a thousand millions more
T' enrich the rich, and make the poor more poor.

Abdiel. This new administration promises
Reform in civil service, and much else
That tends toward honesty and uprightness.
But when did office-seekers prove sincere?
The hatreds of the sections Cleveland hates,
He will encourage unity and love;
Will know no North, nor East, nor West, nor South,
But one broad banner waving over all
The dwellers in the country that he loves.

Zophiel. From statesmen let us turn our thoughts away
To those who subjugate to man's control
The broad domains of nature's untrod realms.
The telephone, by mute electric force,
Conveys the human voice hundreds of miles
On paths of wire to seek the list'ning ear.

The phonograph catches the life-like tones,
Imprisons them so that they may be heard
In song, or speech, or cheerful dialogue
Through days, months, years, or centuries to come.
Electric lights drive darkness far away
From streets, from dwellings, churches, halls, or shops,
Kindling bright sunshine in the darkest nights.
Electric motors easily propel
Swift gliding cars, or drive machinery.
From depths profound come gas to light the towns,
Smelt ores, make glass, cook food, and warm the homes
Of millions in the cities of the land.
How wonderfully blest of God are those
Who claim this country for their dwelling-place!
Cleveland and Hendricks, walking, come this way.

Scene: *Riverside Park, Overlooking Hudson River and New York City, August 8, 1885.* UZZIEL, ITHURIEL, ZADKIEL.

Uzziel. What means that solemn, mournful cavalcade,
Inspiring awe along the crowded streets,
Awakening grief in millions of sad hearts,
And sending sorrow through a weeping world?

Ithuriel. It is the obsequies of General Grant
That drape in mourning all the eye can see,
Hushing to stillness all irreverent sounds.
The soldiers that he led to victory
Are moving slowly toward their hero's grave,
And the great gen'rals against whom he fought
Pay willing honors to their conqueror.
They come like true, brave brothers of the brave,
To honor and lament their countryman,
And pledge themselves to gallantly defend
The union of the country that he loved.
Henceforth the hatreds of the sections lie
Forever buried in the grave of Grant.
Men of all sections see in his career
Inspiring lessons, as they fondly turn
To boyhood's ventures, manhood's first success
Upon the battle-fields of Mexico;
The trials of his life till Donelson

258   *THE AMERICAN EPIC.*

Gave to his name the charm of victory;
The rapid strides by which he rose to pow'r,
The honest struggles of the President
To stem corruption's overwhelming tide,
The true Republican in foreign courts,
The honest victim of a sharper's tricks,
Toiling with failing strength to pay his debts
And make provision for a widow's wants;
The long, brave battle with disease and death,
The patriot's love for his whole native land,
Give Grant the tribute of a nation's tears,
A place within all memories and hearts,
As his old comrades lay him in the grave.

Zadkiel. Behold the peaceful heroes as they come!
Hancock superbly leads the solemn pomp,
Conducting the great chief to glory's grave,
Followed by those who knew and loved him best—
Fond, faithful mourners of his household band;
Then as pall-bearers, Sherman, Sheridan,
Logan, Jones, Porter, Rowan, Boutwell, Hoyt,
Childs, Drexell, and two mourning gentlemen
Who wore the gray when armies bravely fought;
Johnston and Buckner, with sincere respect,
Join their old enemies to honor Grant,
And mingle tears with Union veterans,
Who crowd by thousands round their hero's tomb.

Scene: *House of Representatives, Washington, D. C., 6 P.M., October 1, 1890.* MICHAEL, GABRIEL.

Michael. Comrade, we've watched the glorious destiny
Of this great people more than sixscore years.
We've seen weak colonies become great States,
With thirty times the number that rose up
To protest against British tyranny.
Sixty-three millions under one grand flag
Defy the power of a world in arms.
We've seen the expansion of their peaceful rule
From Mexico's warm Gulf to arctic seas.
All climates, soils, mines, waters now combine
To pay their tribute to these mighty States.

What can a nation need that this has not?
Peace and prosperity with magic force
Shall draw the people of this continent
Till in an equal union bound by love
All parts of this vast hemisphere unite.
Yes, from the northern to the southern pole
And from the centers of surrounding seas
The stars and stripes of freedom soon shall float.

Gabriel. Your vision of the future is sublime.
It may be realized in years to come
If Satan does not triumph over man.
But we have witnessed his malign control
Of millions thirsting for each other's blood,
Till nothing seems impossible or hard
To be accomplished by this foe of man.

Michael. What are his latest shemes to overturn
This blessèd home of human happiness?

SATAN, *rushing forward.*

Satan. Michael, I'm here to answer for myself,
And hurl defiance at your heav'nly hosts.
I claim this world as mine. Its Prince! Its God!
O'er its proud millions I still reign supreme.
What right have you to prowl through my domains,
Skulking in these high places where I rule?
You ask what are my latest schemes and plans?
Know then that I veil not my grand designs,
But boldly execute my sovereign will
Before the faces of my enemies.
I have for servants mighty ones of earth,
Who stop at nothing when I lead them on,
As witness Reed, McKinley, Lodge, and Quay.
With such as those to back me, I am bold.

Michael. Satan, I've heard before your boastful words
And witnessed your malignant practices.
You would dethrone th' Almighty if you could,
And on the ruins of his universe
Erect mid dismal horrors your dark throne.
But chains of darkness limit your career;

Omnipotence restrains malignity.
You have not power to work your wicked will.
Forbear, bravado, lest by wrath divine
To outer darkness you should be consigned.

Satan. Michael, I laugh to scorn your silly threat.
Malevolence, forgetful of all dread,
Impels me on to triumph over men;
And proudly, grandly I disdain to fear
All possibilities of punishment
Or unknown horrors of most dismal fate.
Know then that Europe's nihilistic bands
I'll move by desperate, destructive deeds
To overwhelm this land in anarchy.
By socialistic communists I'll drive
Away life's gentle, Christian courtesies
And undermine domestic blessedness;
Banish all Sabbath laws and Sabbath rest,
And fill the holy day with revelry,
Dragging the toil-worn laborer from his home,
His church, and life's most sacred sanctities.
I'll move Rome's zealous priests to strike the schools
Where patriotic Christian men unite
To banish bigotry's malign control
And teach the young to walk in wisdom's ways.
The demagogues of this free land shall move
To place the children under the control
Of princes of a dethroned despot's court.
Yes, your republicans shall bow around
The thrones of haughty red-clad cardinals,
And give them money to enthrone again
Rome's cast-off tyrant on her seven hills.

Michael. Satan, the decent people of this land
Will hang your anarchists and nihilists.
They'll make your communists behave themselves,
Or limit socialism to prison bounds.
The public schools, time-tested and approved,
Will be sustained in spite of ev'ry foe.
Americans may mumble Latin prayers
And toady round the slaves of priestly rule,

With loss and harm to no one but themselves.
Satan, you are the sland'rer of mankind:
"Accuser of the brethren" is your name.
Why throw suspicion upon Catholics?
Carroll, of Carrollton, with patriot zeal,
Stood by his country in her hour of need.
Taney and Emmett were bold Democrats,
Upholding Jeffersonian principles.
If you seduce their co-religionists,
And show through them your ugly, cloven foot,
To trample upon sacred human rights,
As you have often done in other lands,
Your dupes will hear indignant thunders roll,
And feel the flashes of the people's wrath.

Satan. Your optimistic views of human life
Throw their red rose tints over this fair land.
Indulge them while you can. It suits me well
To hear of your high hopes. I'll blast them all
And rule to ruin your most hopeful pets.
Another means of ruining the race
Is by the tyranny of appetite.
By votes of silly negroes and the scum
Of Europe's pauper hordes and criminals
I'll fasten on this country the vile trade
In filthy liquors, that sends to the grave
Eight hundred thousand victims in ten years;
That fills asylums with mad lunatics,
Crowds jails and prisons, packs the poor-houses,
Sends mis'ry to twelve hundred thousand homes,
Hangs ripened fruits of crime on gallows trees,
And fills the land with deeds of violence.
Nay, more, to prove to you that I still rule,
Grave judges, Senators, and Governors
Shall be degraded victims of strong drink;
Shall drag their lofty honors through the filth
Of pot-house politics, to lead the hosts
That trample on all law in hot pursuit
Of public plunder and illicit gain.

Michael. Satan, the happy people of this land
Have grown familiar with your villainy.

Soon they will be too wise to vote for such
As you would elevate to seats of pow'r.
The accursed traffic by which men get drunk
Will be prohibited and have to cease.
This old device of yours against mankind
Has slain its millions, may slay millions more,
But men will not forever be deceived.
The trade is doomed; 'twill be prohibited.
Go, braggart, seek for plans you have not tried.

Satan. Michael, you are the braggart. I prevail
In every conflict with the hateful race.
In spite of all the teachings of all time
And all the heavenly help that they receive
The sons of Adam will be drunkards still.
Hereditary appetite's too strong for law,
Too strong for will, for conscience to control,
Will make them slaves to poisonous alcohol.
The hatreds of strong parties I've inflamed,
Hoping to see a furious civil war,
With ev'ry voting place a battle-field.
The party that made voters of the slaves
Are sadly disappointed when they see
Blacks represented by the men they hate.
They know that large majorities of whites
Vote solidly against them ev'ry time.
Their only hope of carrying "close States"
Is based upon the solid negro vote.
New York, New Jersey, and Connecticut,
Ohio, Indiana, Illinois,
Theirs only by the grace of colored men,
Will soon to them most hopelessly be lost.
Hence they are desp'rate to gain Southern States.
They'll have them if they have to fight for them.
Hence an election force bill is proposed.
A host of saucy, meddling officers
Are to attend at ev'ry voting place
To keep the meddling party still in pow'r.
The President's appointees are t' appoint
These officers to teach men how to vote,
And how to skillfully manipulate

Compliant, rascally "returning boards."
When these my "men of seven principles,"
"Five loaves and two small fishes," raise some fights,
A new rebellion will be then proclaimed,
And dogs of war let loose against the South.
Local self-government is what men want;
This they demand all over this fair land,
And when they see these myrmidons of pow'r
Rudely assailing this most cherished right,
'Twill stir the fires of strife, both North and South
And kindle flaming war from sea to sea.
Michael, my plans o'erwhelm your faculties;
Your utter helplessness provokes contempt
For you and the poor subjects of your care.
Beware, beware! I'll fill this land with blood.

Michael. Satan, the people rising in their might
Will vanquish your rash meddlers at the polls.
An avalanche of votes shall fall on them,
And bury them 'neath infamy and scorn.
Five weeks shall see Lodge, Hoar, Houk, Chandler, Reed,
Rebuked by an indignant, mighty host
Of peaceful patriots through the ballot-box,
And Lodge's Force bill take its place by right
With alien and sedition laws of old.
A few malignants shall not stir up strife
Among the peaceful people of this land—
Yorktown, Long Island, Bunker Hill forbid.
Men have grown sick of sectional disputes;
Nine-tenths of all good citizens rejoice
To live in love, and let all hatreds die.
Self-interest on the part of Northern men
Will settle the race question in the South.
Mischievous intermeddlers must retire,
Or ruin the investments Northern men
Have made by millions in the great Southland.
Negroes may legislate in Congress halls
To give Republicans majorities,
But a black government on Southern soil
Would sink the capital invested there.
Besides all this, most noble Northern men

Despise the silly hate of demagogues
Between the people of the same grand race.
They saw their brothers of the South grow poor
Through eighty years of tributary trade,
By which the thrifty North was much enriched;
They saw the entrance of the iron wedge
That severed friendship, broke the bonds of love,
And drove those brothers from their Union's home.
They saw them strive to separate in peace,
Accept stern war, fight bravely for their cause—
More bravely than men ever fought before—
Pity their pris'ners, beg for fair exchange,
Which Stanton would not grant on any terms;
Beg the rich North to send its surgeons down
With medicines for its own suff'ring men,
Asking no aid for Southern helplessness.
Saw their brave brethren conquered and subdued;
The woe that waits the vanquished frowned on them.
The South in ruins smiled at poverty,
And welcomed toil as its hard heritage;
Yet saw its fruits of labor wrenched away
By thieving blacks, by alien scoundrels led;
Then, rising in its manly majesty,
Cast off barbaric hordes and rascal rule,
Obtained from heaven renewed prosperity,
And stands to-day the peerless conqueror
Of earth's most dread, malign adversity.
Since bled by tariffs, and by pensions robbed,
Sees the great North grow rich at its expense.
Ireland to landlords, Poland to the czar,
Nor conquered provinces to ancient Rome,
Never so much of tribute could have paid.
And so the wealthy, the triumphant North,
Owns Southern railroads, mines, and furnaces,
Banks, factories, plantations, farms, and stores,
With dividends sent duly to the North.
The North men own hotels and palaces,
All occupied by North men half the year,
Then watched by North men till North men return.
The South looks on admiringly to see
Northern magnificence and wealth displayed,

CONFEDERATE MONUMENT AT NASHVILLE.

And, toiling on, begs most imploringly
For more and more of wealthy Northern men
To bring still more of Northern capital;
Invites and welcomes Northern working-men
To build up homes in its mild Southern clime,
Hails them as brethren of one family.
The Southron's trust in God, his fortitude
While boldly fighting with adversity,
His patient industry, his enterprise,
His Christ-like, his divine forgetfulness
Of dreadful suff'ring wrongfully endured,
His most sincere, undying confidence
That Northern men, rebuking tyranny,
Will, from high places of authority,
Drive out his bitter, unrelenting foes—
All, all with most resistless potency
Appeal to Northern magnanimity
For help against fanatic, furious hate.
Nor will th' appeal be vain. Election day
Will see the millions of the mighty North,
With gen'rous sympathy, indignant rush
To hurl their ballots against despotism,
And free their Southern friends from Reed, from Lodge,
McKinley, Ingalls, Cannon, and their dupes.
'Twill shake the tyrants with an earthquake shock,
And disappoint your base malignancy.

Satan. Gabriel, there's millions of ill-gotten wealth
At my disposal to secure results.
We can buy votes enough in the close States
To overcome your large majorities.
We'll do it, and we'll rule with heavy hand
In spite of Northern magnanimity
And sympathy for noble Southerners.
But even if we lose November's vote
Our famous Congress will have three months left
In which to drive our hated Force bill through,
And any legislation we may need
To keep the country under my control.
They'll pass the Force bill, and insult the South,
And rob the treasury to pay their tools,

If the next Congress should by two to one
Condemn our grand old party's sad misrule.

Michael. If they should be so steeped in tyranny
As to despise the people's spoken will,
It will but seal their everlasting doom,
And give them to undying infamy.
Satan, in spite of your malignity
This country still shall flourish, and its sons
Shall triumph over you and all your dupes.

Satan. But, Michael, here in this broad capital
This very hour my grandest scheme prevails
Against all common sense, all scholarship,
All science, all economy, and thrift,
All friendships of the nations of earth,
And the best judgment of earth's shrewdest men.
McKinley's Tariff bill is now a law;
In this my friends have pleased me quite too well.
So much taxation people will not bear;
But the rich manufacturers had paid
Into the party's great corruption fund
Such mammoth sums beyond all precedent,
We could deny them nothing that they asked.
They saw their chance and piled the tariff on
Beyond all reason, or propriety.
In vain we warned them not to kill the goose
That laid for them so many golden eggs.
They answered that they had a bird in hand
Worth more to them than two in any bush;
That they were now determined to make hay
While summer suns shine on Republicans:
And so the monstrous bill was hurried through,
From which they hope for many, many years
Of peaceful plunder to enrich themselves.
See! Harrison comes forth, followed by Blaine,
By Windom, Tracy, Proctor, Miller, Rusk,
Noble and Mason, and McKinley too,
Proud author of this famous Tariff act.
The President has signed the robber bill,
Now wealth shall glut its rav'nous appetite
At the expense of pinching poverty.

Michael. He signed the warrant of his party's death.
McKinley is its executioner.
Yes, this is "the beginning of the end"
Of the bad party called Republican.

Satan. Michael, your wish was father to that thought.
The party lives to work my sovereign will.
'Twill still live on to give protected wealth
A longer lease of pow'r to rob the poor.
The excise and the tariff ev'ry day
Take a round million for the treasury.
To raise that million the taxed people pay
Four millions to protected industries.
Domestic manufactured merchandise
Costs that much more than they would have to pay
But for the tariff and the excise laws.
Thus do the rich heap up increasing wealth,
The poor sink down in deeper poverty.
When wealth was well divided in this land,
Each workman hoped that he would become rich;
But now the millionaires, trusts, syndicates
Can dictate wages, prices, and rewards,
Till a poor man must starve or beg or steal,
Or take for wages wealth's most grudging dole
For the hard labor of his horny hands.
Soon this oppression becomes heavier,
And hopeless toil sees wondrous stores of wealth
Most temptingly appealing to desire,
Yet for the hardest and most constant work
Can earn no right to share the good he sees
Beyond a pittance to sustain his life.
Will not strong hands lay hold on luxuries,
Despising all the rights of property,
Giving to anarchy and lawless rage,
The rich inheritance of these great States,
And laying all their glory in the dust?
Yes, I shall see destructive forces here
Spoiling the grandeur of this capitol,
Shall revel 'mid the ruins I have wrought.
With fiendish exultation I shall gloat
Over archangels driven from the earth

And helpless, hopeless human sufferers
Enduring unimagined agonies.
Michael, draw off your legions to the skies.
Leave your broad banners trailing at my feet,
Go hide within the battlements of heav'n,
Flee mourning over realms that you have lost;
Go, leave me in my glory here to reign!

Michael. Satan, your silly boasting I despise;
No threats of yours can daunt whom God protects.
Corruption's legions cannot rule this land
By their unprincipled, compliant tools.
Sheer selfishness drives them to nominate
Men of a nobler class for offices
Demanding honor and integrity.
How wonderful it was to see pure men
Like Cleveland and like Harrison succeed
In winning office through conventions swayed
By many of the most unprincipled,
Who ever sold themselves for offices,
Or bartered honor for advantages.
Such honest, upright, honorable men,
Selected by the selfish or corrupt,
Prove heav'n's own watch-care over this fair land.
So down to latest times shall God preserve
This noblest of the nations of the earth.
Your robber tariff soon will be repealed.
The people in their might and majesty
Will soon rise up against your tyranny.
The senate and the representatives
Will pass a tariff law for revenue,
Will take the hands of rich monopolists
Out of the purses of the laboring poor,
Will build up commerce with a whole round world,
And send the white-winged argosies of trade
To ev'ry port beneath the smiling heav'ns.

Satan. Michael, the hist'ry of the human race
Is but the record of my victories.
Go seek for Babylon and Nineveh,

Tyre, Sidon, Troy, Carthage, Palmyra, Thebes,
The Greeks, the Romans, and the Saracens!
I gave them to destruction, and they fell.
Think you these people but of yesterday
Can stand against my strong, resistless might?
The greediness of gain that here prevails
Will undermine the virtue of these States.
Such selfishness indulged in ancient times
Extinguished all the glory of old Rome.
The rich men and their sons monopolized
The good things of the empire until wealth
Corrupted young patricians and left none
To fight the battles of imperial Rome
But foreigners and rude barbarian hosts.
The men who would have formed a living wall
Between their country and its enemies
Had vanished from the places that they loved.
They slept in death, while rich men and their slaves
Became the prey of vile barbarians.
But selfishness seeks only its own good;
It heaps up wealth no matter who may lose.
A hundred millions wants a hundred more,
A thousand would another thousand add.
For this high tariffs tax the toiling poor,
Wages reduced give lab'rers scanty food,
Scant clothing, fuel, books, and ev'ry thing.
The very rich grow richer hour by hour,
The very poor more num'rous every day.
When these two classes cover the whole land
Then anarchy or slavery must prevail,
And your great nation takes the downward grade
By which old Rome passed onward to decay.
Michael, the evils that o'erthrew old Rome
Are actively and dang'rously at work.
They'll give your millions to destruction soon.
I'll drive my chariot over their remains,
And hell shall celebrate their obsequies
By crowning its great chief with honors won
In battles with the proud Americans!
At my grand triumph I would gladly drag
Gabriel and Michael at my chariot wheels.

Michael. The Lord rebuke thee, Satan! I behold
Like lightning your descent to deeper depths
Of degradation and disgraceful crime.
Go, wretch! [Satan disappears.] The curse of God
 abides on you
Until the sentence of the day of doom
Consigns you to the "pit that's bottomless,"
The "outer darkness," and the "lake of fire."

Gabriel. Michael, that foe of God and men departs.
Let us now profit by his boastful threats.
The people will rebuke his guilty dupes
And banish them from their high seats of pow'r.
Tariffs and force bills we need dread no more,
Nor Reed's pretentious, petty tyranny.
But wealth and poverty in hostile ranks,
Increasing their great armies day by day,
And alcohol disguised in tempting drinks
Are evils that demand most watchful care.

Michael. Yes, Gabriel, danger threatens at these points,
And selfishness will counteract our plans;
But we must lift taxation from the poor,
And help them to control their appetites.
Yes, we must now with watchful, honest care
Double the duty and the excise on
Tobacco and intoxicating drinks
Till prohibition drives them out of use.
From ev'ry dollar of the capital
Of money-making trusts and syndicates,
And other corporations that get gain,
Collect three mills in each and ev'ry year.
If more is needed for the public use,
Collect it from existing capital.
Less than a thousand dollars should not pay
A cent into the public treasury.
A hundred thousand should pay double tax;
One million should pay double that again,
Over ten millions double that high rate.
Except tobacco and intoxicants,
Let nothing pay tariff or excise tax.

If there must be protected industries,
Protect by bounties from the treasury
To cheapen what the poor man has to buy.
All moneys for the nation or the States
Should through collectors of one class be paid
Into the nation's common treasury.
Thence draw by States according to the sum
Of population on the ground of each.
Cities and towns would only have to tax
For municipal purposes alone.

Gabriel. But, Michael, how would that affect State rights?

Michael. 'Twould give the States a right to find their wealth
Now hid in the rich cities of the land,
Or swallowed by incorporated trusts.
Let the robbed people understand their rights,
Amend the Constitution, and thus save
Impoverished millions from shrewd millionaires.
The common people pay the taxes now
By tariff and by excise laws, and pay
The manufacturers four times as much
In higher prices for their merchandise.
Reverse this: lift the burden from the poor,
Let wealth pay taxes and pay bounties, too,
So that protected industries may thrive.
'Twould save the poor two billions ev'ry year
Without denying wealth its luxuries.
A court of equity's authority
Could hold the scales of justice evenly
Between hard labor and stern capital,
Assigning each its just and rightful share
Of profits from their joint activity,
And thus avoid most wasteful, costly strikes.
Thus might the poor grow richer year by year,
Hushing the loud complaints of poverty,
The rich become true brothers of the poor,
Fearing no evil from invet'rate hate.

Gabriel. Michael, corruption in high places seems
Too strong to yield success to your wise plans.
The selfish rich will strive by bribery
To hold the advantages they now possess
For gath'ring up the coppers of the poor.
They'll madly work 'gainst honor, justice, right,
To hoard up wealth that they can never use,
Nor many generations of their heirs.
You'll find it hard to stem so strong a tide.

Michael. But, Gabriel, this great nation reads and
 thinks;
It reasons well upon its own affairs;
It rules its millions through the ballot-box;
It will not suffer low-lived, vile saloons
To prey upon its vitals as they have.
'Twill not permit ten thousand wealthy men
To undermine the people's liberties
And trample on the millions of the free.
It will not wait till revolution rends
The glorious fabric which the fathers built;
But, peaceably and quietly, will find
A remedy for ev'ry threatening ill.
With optimistic vision I foresee
Prosperity and greatness for this land
In spite of selfishness and Satan's schemes.
Parties may change, factions may gender strife;
But Christian character shall grandly rise
Above corruption's overwhelming tide,
And steer the ship of State in safety on
To peaceful ports, secure from every storm.
This people, mightiest that earth has known,
Shall tower in grandeur and magnificence
Sublimely over an admiring world
Till Christ shall come to reign in righteousness.

INDEX.

A court to prevent losses by workmen and employers, 234, 271.
A court to prevent war, 127.
Adams, John, 56, 61, 68, 104, 124, 137.
Adams, John Q., 129, 134, 151.
Adams, Samuel, 32, 33, 56, 60, 95.
Africa, 22.
Agnostics, 243.
Alabama, 129.
Alabama claims, 231.
Alamo, 139.
Alaska, 227.
Alcoholic drinks, 22, 105, 234, 235, 270.
Alexander, 62.
Alexandria, 58.
Alien and sedition laws, 113.
Allen, Ethan, 63.
Allies of Washington, 70.
America a greater Britain, 8.
Anarchy, 260.
Anderson, Major, 171.
Andre, Major, 82.
Angels, 3, 187.
Annapolis, 89.
Arianism unnatural, 248.
Arius, 107.
Arkansas, 145, 190.
Arkansas Post, 189.
Arnold, Benedict, 82.
Arson: Dunmore, 59; Tryon, 80; Arnold, 82; Lord Ross, 127; Sherman, 201; Sheridan, 201; Hunter, 203; Early, 203.
Asbury, 43, 106.
Atheists, 243.
Atlanta, 198, 201.
Augustine, 107, 251.

Babylon, 62, 248.
Bachman, 208.
Baker, 175.
Ball's Bluff, 175.
Baltimore, 52, 69.
Bancroft, 152.
Bank, 146.
Banks, 178, 183, 194.
Bankrupt law, 146.
Bayard, 113.
Beattie, 38.
Beauregard, 171, 172.
Beecher, 153.
Bennett, 153.
Bethel, 171.
Bingham, 169.
Black Boomerang, 230.
Black Dinah, 208.
Black Friday, 229.
Black Hawk, 139.
Black River Bridge, 189.
Blenheim, 32.
Bonaparte, 122.
Boonville, 174.
Boston massacre, 36.
Boston Port bill, 50.
Botetourte, 25.
Bracito, 149.
Brandywine, 75.
Brahma, 107.
Breckinridge, John C., 191, 199, 212, 215, 216, 217.
Breckinridge, W. C. P., 217.
Bright, J. D., 151.
Bristol, 52.
British boundary, 146, 150.
Brown, General, 122.
Brown, John, 153, 188.
Bryant, W. C., 153.
Buckner, 176, 258.

(273)

274 INDEX.

Buddha, 107.
Buena Vista, 147.
Bunker Hill, 61, 131.
Burgoyne, 73.
Burks, 20, 56.
Burnside, 177, 183.
Burr, 113.
Butler, Ben F., 178, 195.
Butler, Wm. O., 149.

Cabinet dissolved (Jackson's), 138.
Cadets, 199.
Calhoun, 118, 128, 138.
Calvin, 107, 251.
Camden, 20, 30.
Cameron, 169.
Canada, 55, 65, 123, 124.
Cass, 151.
Catharine of Russia, 23.
Cedar Mountain, 183.
Centennial of Independence, 231.
Centennial of Methodism, 243.
Centerville, 183.
Cerro Gordo, 149.
Champion Hills, 189.
Chandler of Michigan, 169.
Chandler of New Hamp., 263.
Chantilly, 183.
Charleston, 29, 47, 52, 81, 158, 169.
Charlotte, Queen, 31, 37.
Chase, 152, 169.
Chatham, 8, 20, 26, 31, 34, 38, 56.
Chapultepec, 147.
Chauncey, 120.
Cherokees, 145, 202.
Chickamauga, 190.
Chihuahua, 149.
China, 23.
Choiseul, 29.
Christmas Christians, 118.
Clarke, George Rogers, 79.
Clay, Henry, 118, 139, 143, 147, 151.
Clay, Henry Jr., 148.
Clay, James B., 223.
Clinton, 81.

Clive, 23.
Coercion of States, 162.
Cold Harbor, 196, 199.
Columbus, 8.
Compromise of 1821.
Compromise of 1850.
Confucius, 107.
Conspiracy against Washington, 76
Contracts North and South, 92.
Cordilleras, 149.
Cornwallis, 70, 72, 83, 87.
Corruption, 163, 229, 230, 237.
Covington, Ky., 192.
Cowper, 38.
Currency, 238.
Curtis, 177.
Cushing Caleb, 195.
Cushing Lieutenant, 204.

Dalrymple, 32.
Damascus, 62.
Daniel, 9.
Dahlgren, 180.
Davis, Jefferson, 147, 173, 210.
Davis, Jeff C., 171, 209.
Dearborn, 120.
Decatur, 123, 128.
Declaration of Independence, 68.
De Estaing, 79, 81.
Defects of the Constitution, 101.
Demagogues, 155.
Destitution, 81.
Dickinson, John, 45, 52.
Donelson, Fort, 175.
Doniphan, 149.
Dorr, 145.
Douglass, 151, 157.
Downie, 122.
Dudley, 120.
Dunmore, 57, 58.
Dupont, 190.

Early, 184, 199, 203, 204.
Elberon, N. J., 240.
Electric lights and cars, 257.
Ellsworth, Oliver, 92.
Embury, 42.
Emerson, 241.

INDEX.   275

Emmett, 261.
England, 8.
Europe, 22.
Eutaw Springs, 82.
Evolution, 244.
Ewell, 191.

Factions confounded, 151.
Fair Oaks, 179.
Farragut, 177, 178, 204.
Federal Constitution, 92.
Federal convention, 90.
Federal soldiers honored, 198.
Field, Cyrus, 153.
Fillmore, 151.
Fires in the North, 228, 232.
Florida, 129, 145.
Floyd, 176.
Foote, 175.
Ford's Theater, 213.
Fort Sumter, 169.
France, 12, 24, 29, 34, 73, 75, 81, 84, 85.
Frankfort, Ky., 184.
Franklin, 48, 49, 73, 92, 93.
Frederick, 183.
Fredericksburg, 181.
Fremont, 175, 178.
French agent, 64, 67.
French officers, 87.
French Revolution, 100, 104.
Fulton, 115.

Gadsden, 54, 56.
Gage, 49, 54, 56, 59.
Gaines's Mill, 179.
Garfield, 175, 240.
Garnet, 171.
Garrettson, F., 106.
Gates, 74, 75, 76, 81.
Genet, 109.
George the Third, 6, 16, 26, 30, 31, 35, 37, 39, 45, 48, 49, 55, 59, 60, 64, 74, 89.
Georgia, 14, 18, 58, 79.
Georgians banished, 202.
Germantown, 75.
Gettysburg, 186.
Giddings, 169.

Glendale, 175.
Golden Gate, 150.
Goldsboro, 177.
Goldsmith, 38.
Goodson, 148.
Gore, 95.
Gorham, 95.
Government, 167
Grant, 175, 176, 189, 190, 196, 198, 199, 201, 210, 212, 213, 215, 231, 232, 257, 258.
Gray, 38.
Great Kennesaw, 199.
Greene, 71, 82, 83.
Grenville, 10, 15.
Gridley, 63.
Grundy, Felix, 118.
Guilford C. H., 83.
Guinea's Station, 185.
Gulf Stream, 12.

Hagerstown, 183.
Halleck, 175.
Hamilton, 86, 93, 104, 109, 116, 132, 161, 167, 233.
Hampton, 209.
Hancock, John, 54, 60, 95.
Hancock, W. S., 188, 198, 258.
Handel, 38.
Hanover, 37.
Hardee, 208.
Harney, 174.
Harper's Ferry, 154, 183.
Harrison, Ben, 60.
Harrison, Ben Jr., 266, 268.
Harrison, W. H. 116, 121, 143.
Hartford convention, 121.
Harvard, 13.
Hatred of masters, 152.
Hawley, 232.
Hawthorne, 152.
Hayne, Gen., 83.
Hayne, Senator, 138.
Helena, 190.
Henry, Fort, 175.
Henry John, 116, 117, 123, 161.
Henry of Navarre, 24.
Henry, Patrick, 17, 18, 56, 57, 64, 97, 98, 167.

276 INDEX.

Hill, A. P., 184.
Hoar, 263.
Holmes, 190.
Hood, 191, 203, 207.
Hooker, 180, 184.
Houston, Samuel, 140.
Howe, 70.
Hudson, Fort, 189.
Hudson River, 81.
Hull, 118.
Hull, Hope, 106.
Hull, Isaac, 119.
Hunter, 175, 199.
Hunt, Robert, 13, 43.

Illinois, 129.
Independence Day, 68, 186.
India, 23.
Indians, 12, 105, 120, 125, 139, 145.
Indiana, 129.
Iowa, 150.
Italy, 24.

Jackson, Andrew, 125, 126, 128, 134, 139, 151, 206.
Jackson, Miss., 189.
Jackson, Stonewall, 178, 183, 185, 188.
Jalapa, 149.
Jamestown, 11.
Japan, 23.
Jasper, Sergeant, 81.
Jay, John, 56, 104, 110, 111.
Jefferson, Thomas, 17, 56, 68, 106, 109.
Jessup, 122.
John Street Church, 39.
Johnson, Andrew, 207, 218, 226, 227, 228.
Johnson, R. M., 121, 122.
Johnson, Samuel, 31, 38.
Johnston, A. S., 176.
Johnston, Joseph E., 172, 179, 191, 200, 203, 209, 214.
Jones, 119.
Junius, 45.

Kearney, 148.

Kentucky, 114, 165.
King, Rufus, 95.
Knox, 87, 104.
Kosciusko, 74.
Koszta, 153.

Lafayette, 77, 84, 85, 87, 132.
Laurens, 87.
Lawrence, 190.
Lee, Charles, 67, 76, 77.
Lee, Jesse, 106.
Lee, L. H. Harry, 80, 83, 105, 111.
Lee, R. H., 17, 56, 57, 64, 93.
Lee, Robert E., 149, 157, 182, 183, 198, 199, 213.
Legare, 140.
Leopard and Chesapeake, 117.
Lewis & Clarke, 115.
Lexington, Ky., 184.
Lexington, Mass., 59.
Lexington, Mo., 174.
Lincoln, A., President, 165, 168, 174, 214, 218, 219, 224.
Lincoln, General, 74, 81, 87.
Little Rock, 190.
Liverpool, 52.
Livingston, Chancellor, 20, 56, 104.
Livingston, Edward, 138.
Lodge, 265.
London, 6.
Longstreet, 191.
Lordlings, 49.
Louisiana, 111, 197.
Louisville, 77, 184.
Lyon, 174.

Macomb, 122.
Madison, 91, 93, 128.
Magnetic telegraph, 140.
Maine, 18, 129.
Malvern Hill, 178.
Manassas, 171.
Mansfield, Gen., 180.
Mansfield, Lord, 75.
Marion, 83.
Marshall, 113.
Mason, 174.

Massachusetts, 95.
McClellan, 171, 179, 180, 183.
McClernand, 189.
McHenry, Fort, 122.
McIntosh, 177.
McPherson, 190, 193, 200.
Meade, 188, 232.
Mechanicsville, 179.
Mexico, 148.
Michigan, 145.
Mill Spring, 175.
Missouri, 129, 130.
Mississippi, 129.
Monmouth battle, 77.
Monroe, 128, 129, 133.
Monterey, 147.
Morgan, Col., 74, 82.
Morgan, John H., 193.
Morris, 163.
Morse, 140.
Munfordsville, 184.
Murfreesboro, 184.

Nashville, 206.
Natural gas, 257.
Napoleon, 111, 114, 130.
Nebraska, 152.
Negroes, 19.
Nelson, Gen. 176.
Nelson, Gov., 87.
Netherlands, 34.
Newbern, 177.
New England, 13, 14, 24, 55, 59, 66, 106; clergy, 152.
New Orleans, 125, 177.
New Jersey, 69, 71, 74.
New York, 18, 104, 153
Nimrod, 31.
Nineveh, 62.
Norfolk, 52, 59.
North, Lord, 50, 64.
North Carolina, 58, 65.
Nullification, 138.

Ocean telegraph, 153.
O'Hara, 87.
Ohio, 114.
Ordinance of 1787, 156.
Otis, 37.

Palmerston, 174.
Palo Alto, 147.
Paper promises paid in gold, 238.
Patriot army, 3,000 strong, 69.
Peace Congress, 165.
Peaceful statesmen, 1, 15.
Peace in 1815, 127.
Peace with amnesty, 218.
Peace with independence, 89.
Pemberton, 190.
Pennsylvania, 71.
Perote, 149.
Perry, 121, 122.
Perryville, 184.
Persia, 23.
Petersburg, 203.
Philadelphia, 51, 68, 88, 90.
Philippi, 171.
Phonography, 257.
Pickens, 80, 83.
Pierce, Frank, 149, 152.
Pike, 120.
Pinckney, 93, 95, 111.
Pittsburg, 232.
Plymouth Rock, 13, 14.
Polk, Gen., 175, 191.
Polk, President, 146, 147, 150.
Pope, 183.
Port Gibson, 189.
Porter, Commodore, 178.
Porter, Fitz John, 180.
Portugal, 139.
Prescott, 63.
President and Little Belt, 117.
Preston, Capt., 36.
Price, 174.
Princeton, 71.
Proctor, 120.
Prussia, 23, 24.
Public schools, 260.
Pueblo, 149.
Pulaski, 81.
Pulpit politicians, 141, 152.
Purse and sword, 262.
Putnam, 98.

Quantrell, 190.

Randolph & Bland sell forty negroes, 59.
Randolph, Edward, 104.
Randolph, John, 140.
Rawdon, 83.
Raymond, 189.
Republicanism is revolution organized at work, 164.
Resaca de la Palma, 147.
Retribution, 17, 21, 197, 209, 219, 223, 224, 225.
Richmond, Ky., 184.
Richmond, Va., 21, 44, 56, 209, 216.
Ripley, 122.
River Thames, 119, 120, 121.
Riverside Park, 257.
Roanoke Island, 177.
Robbery by law, 147.
Rome, 62.
Romney, 171.
Rosecrans, 184, 191.
Rousseau, 24.
Rusk, 266.
Russia, 23, 115.

Salem, 51.
Saltillo, 149.
San Francisco, 150.
San Gabriel, 148.
San Jacinto, 139.
Santa Fe, 148.
Saratoga, 73.
Satan at Fredericksburg, 182.
Satan's call to war, 170.
Satan's grand plot, 100, 101, 102, 105, 110, 123, 125, 129, 130, 131, 134, 137, 140, 141, 142, 152, 153, 154, 155, 156, 157, 167, 169, 170, 201.
Satan's great storm at Richmond, 98.
Satan's soliloquy, 21.
Savannah, 79, 208.
Scott, 122, 149, 175.
Secession claimed as a right, 162.
Secession unwise, 158.
Sectional hatred, 131.

Settlers of States, 14, 15.
Seward, 167, 174, 227, 232.
Shelby, Isaac, 121, 122.
Shenandoah, 178.
Sheridan, 201, 204, 212.
Sherman, Roger, 92.
Sherman, W. T., 176, 191, 199, 200, 202, 203, 208, 215.
Shiloh, 176.
Sigel, 174, 199.
Silver demonetized, 538.
Simpson, Bishop, 232.
Slade, 140.
Slave freed by Mansfield, 50.
Slave trade, 19, 50, 59, 68, 92, 95, 186.
Slidell, 174.
Sloat, 148.
Smith, John, 43.
Smith, E. Kirby, 184.
Smith, Samuel, 122.
South Carolina, 58, 82.
South Carolina Constitution, 95.
Spain, 12, 89.
Stamp act, 8, 15, 26, 26.
Stanton, 183, 227, 232.
Stanton and Satan, 228.
Stark, 73.
Statesmanship of hate, 157, 165, 167.
St. Clair, 74, 105.
Steel, 190.
Stevens, A. H., 158, 160, 162.
Stevens, Thaddeus, 228.
St. John's Church, Richmond, Va., 56.
Stockton, 148.
Strawbridge, 42.
Stuart, 188.
Sullivan, 59, 69, 71.
Sumter, Fort, 169.
Surrender of R. E. Lee, 212.
Swamp angels, 190.

Taney, 145, 261.
Tariff, 90, 135, 139, 147, 266.
Tarleton, 82, 83.
Tax, corporations, syndicates, and trusts, 234, 270.

Taylor, Z., 147, 151.
Tecumseh, 120, 140.
Tecumseh, White, 145, 202.
Telephone, 257.
Terry, 209.
Texas, 129, 139, 150.
Thames, 119.
Thomas, 175, 184, 191, 193, 207, 232.
Tippecanoe, 115.
Toronto, 120.
Townshend, 27, 30, 34.
Tracy, 266.
Trade dollars, 239.
Trenton, 71.
Trinity Church, 18, 39.
Tripoli, 128.
Tunis, 128.
Twiggs, 149.
Tryon, 80.
Tyler, 145.

Vagabonds, 235.
Valley Forge, 76.
Van Buren, 138.
Van Rensalear, 145.
Vandalism, 317, 318.
Vanderbilt, 153.
Vermont, 114.
Versailles, 184.
Vicksburg, 189.
Virginia's benefactions, 196, 197, 198; conditions on acceding, 96; wrongs predicted, 44, 98, 100, 102; heroism predicted, 44; efforts to prevent war, 165, 197; heroism in war, 172, 197, 198; destruction of enemies, 181, 196; hospitality, 14, 197.
Voltaire, 24.

Walker, R. J., 147.
Wallace, Lew, 176, 199.
War Christianized, 150.

War with left hand, 122.
Warlike Christians, 118.
Warren, 62, 124.
Washington, D. C., 111.
Washington, George, 17, 46, 56, 57, 61, 64, 70, 71, 73, 76, 77, 87, 89, 103, 104, 109, 113.
Washington Monument, 255.
Washington, William, 83.
Wayne, 80, 111.
Wealth: all lose by its destruction, 233.
Webster, Daniel, 132, 138, 151, 152.
Wellington, 122.
Welsh, 232.
Wesley, Charles, 11, 38.
Wesley, John, 11, 64.
West, 38.
Westminster Abbey, 5.
Whitefield, 40.
Whittaker, 43.
Whittier, 232.
Wilkes, Commodore, 174.
Williams, Paulding, Van Wert, 82.
Williamsburg, 16.
Wilson's Creek, 174.
Winchester, 119.
Winder, 120.
Windom, William, 266.
Windsor Castle, 27, 48, 49.
Winslow, 205.
Wisconsin, 150.
Wise, 140, 157.
Wolfe, 43.
Wool, Gen., 149.
Worth, 149.
Wyoming, 79.
Wythe, 17.

Yale, 13.
Yorktown, 83.

Zollicoffer, 165.

Servant of God and Guardian of mankind.

(280)

QUESTIONS.

BOOK FIRST.

The figures refer to the pages upon which the questions are answered.

FROM what nation did our States spring? Great Britain. With what event does authentic British history begin? Julius Cæsar's conquest, B.C. 55. After the Romans left (A.D. 410), what peoples oppressed Britain? (6.) With what results? What change had taken place when George III. reigned? What city is the British capital? (6.) Where do the British erect monuments to distinguished men? (5.) When did Columbus discover America? October 11, 1492. To what nation did he give it? Spain. Who first landed in North America? John Cabot and his son Sebastian. In attempts to plant colonies, what Englishmen failed? Gilbert, Raleigh, and Grenville. Where and when was the first permanent settlement made? Jamestown, Va., May 13, 1607. Who were leaders? Gosnold, Smith, Rev. Robert Hunt, Newport, and Wingfield. By whom were they assisted? Lord De La Ware, Sir Thomas Gates, and Sir George Somers. What did they take to Virginia? Europe's highest civilization. What became of most of these sons of England's nobility and gentry? They died prematurely. When the survivors became inured to hardships and toil, what followed? (12.) What took place long before the "Mayflower" left Holland? (13, 14.) What is said of the New Englanders? (14.) Of colonists of other States? (14, 15.) Of a nation in embryo? (8.) Of separation from Britain? (8.) Of William Pitt? (8.) Of George III.? (10.) Of Grenville's Stamp act? (10.) Of the Western Hemisphere? (11, 12.) Of the Indians? Of the French? Of Spain? (12.) Of the Stamp act in the North? (15.) Of Virginia's happy condition? (15, 16.) Of the House of Burgesses, May 1, 1765? (16, 17.) Of the Union? (18.) Of the year 1765? Of Britain's officers in New York? (18.) Of King George. (18, 19.) Of the Venal Parliament? (19.) Of the wealthy nobles? (19.) Of America's friends? (20.) Of prominent New York patriots? (20.)

BOOK SECOND.

WHAT is said of Britannia? (22.) Of Europe? Of Asia? Of Africa? Of the slave trade? Of Christian mistresses? Of the Indians? (22.) Of Japan? Of China? Of Persia? Of Turkey? Of Saracenic chiefs in Hindostan? Of Clive and the

East India Company? (23.) Of Catharine of Russia? Of Frederick of Prussia? (23.) Of Italy? (24.) Of Austria? Of the pontiff? Of the Kings of Spain and France? Of other European States? Of Choisseul at St. Cloud,* Rousseau, and Voltaire? Of subjects, kings, and literati? (24.) Of the colonies? (25.) What prevented war? What happy results of peace? (25.) What was King George's policy in March, 1766? (26.) . Who was made Prime Minister? What is said of Pitt's administration? (26.) How was this prevented? (27.) What did King George trade in? (27.) How did the king's empire compare with Satan's? (27.) Who outwitted Chatham? (29.) What use did the king make of Chatham? What effect had the repeal of the Stamp act? What effect on the king had Chatham's illness? (29.) Who, in Chatham's absence, ruled the Cabinet? (30.) What did he propose to tax? (30.) What is said of the effect of this taxation? Of a gold coin? Of the king's pride? Of the old nobility? (30.) Of England's literati? (31.) Of music in Boston? Of the military tramp? Of peaceful citizens? Of the battle of Blenheim? Of the people? Of banded sticks? (32.) Of soldiers at New York? Of the indignant people? Of Samuel Adams? Of the tools of tyranny? Of Dalrymple? (32.) Of each soldier? (33.) Of bold bravado? Of fruits of folly? Of victims of superstitions? (33.) Of Europe's refusal to persecute religionists? (34.) Of Spanish executions of republicans at New Orleans? (34.) Of stupid weaklings ruling England? Of the wisest ruling the colonies? (34.) Virginia's Burgesses? (34, 35.) Of the king? Of the colonists? Of the troops? Of the people? Of Boston? Of British lead? Of bright moonbeams? (35.) Of flowing blood, March 5, 1770? (36.) Of the guilty? Of the thoughtful people? Of the rabble? Of those who shot? and those who fell? (36.) Of Warren and Otis? (37.) Of the king and queen when their reign began? Of old abuses? (37.) Of the royal children? (38.) Of virtue and decency? Of fine arts? Of music? Of painting? Of poetry? Of discord? Of foreign foes? (38.) Of Indians? (38, 39.) Of Asia's sons? Of distant lands and isles of every sea? Of the present time? Of unlawful taxes? (39.) Of Whitfield? (40.) Of Southern seacoasts? Of the hunters? Of death in a cabin? Of the backwoods funeral? (40.) Of an Irishman in 1760? Of his name? Of two families of Irish in New York? (41.) Of their names? (42.) Of Capt. Webb? (42.) Of Robert Williams? (43.) Of Francis Asbury? (43.)

BOOK THIRD.

What is said of Virginia's burgesses? (44.) Of a selfish world? Of possible ingratitude? Of her stalwart sons? (44.) Of the farmer's letters? (45.) Of the letters of "Junius" and their

---

* French Prime Minister.

authorship? (45, 46.) Of backwoods burgesses? (46.) Of tea? (46.) To what places was it sent? (47.) Of Hutchinson? Of fifty men arrayed as Indians? Of Griffin's wharf? (47.) Of the war whoop? (48.) What caused the privy council to meet January 11, 1874? (48.) What is said of the king's ministers? Of Franklin? Of these highborn dignitaries? Of Wedderburne? (48.) Of the king's command? (49.) Of rudest wrathfulness? Of insanity? Of peace? Of Gen. Gage? (49.) Of Lord Mansfield? (50.) Of Parliament and king? Of Virginia? Of the Boston Port bill? Of Boston's population? (50.) Of hanging? (50.) Of signs of mourning in Philadelphia, June 1, 1774? (51.) Of Virginia? Of the Southern colonies? (51.) Of New England's gratitude to the South? (52.) Of the Congress of October 25, 1774? (52, 53.) Of the British yoke? Why not cast off? (53, 54.) What is said of Boston's families? (54.) Of Gadsden of Carolina? (54.) What ought all time to witness? What ought to be household words in Boston? What is said of Gen. Gage? (54.) Of his pledge to the king? (55.) Of the wall that inclosed him? Of the escape by sea? Of the peaceful counsels? Of more troops? While helpless, what does he see brave Virginians do? To whom had the king given their territory northwest of the Ohio? (55.) What Congressmen are named? (56.) What is said of the dawn of independence? Of Franklin? Of royal governors? Of breezes from the North? (56.) Of Virginia's military plan? (56, 57.) Of Dunmore's threats? Of driving him to his ships? (57.) Of Georgia? (58.) Of South Carolina? Of North Carolina? Of a triumphal march? (58.) Of the braggart governor? (58, 59.) Of Norfolk? (59.) Of last official acts? Of Randolph and Bland? Of Paul Revere? Of Sullivan? Of Pitcairn? (59.) Of his order? (60.) Of Americans killed and wounded? Of boasting Britons? How did they take ammunition? What two patriots were they ordered to arrest? What is said of the Congress of June 15, 1775? (60.) What did Virginia tell King George when Harrison nominated Hancock for President of Congress? (60, 61.) What is said of John Adams? (61.) What is said of the battle of Bunker Hill, June 17, 1775? Of its effect on England? (61.) Of the fire in Charlestown? (62.) Of wealth and war? Of wealth in ancient nations? Of Warren? Ticonderoga? (62.) Of Crown Point? (63.) Of Ethan Allen? Of Prescott? Of Gridley? Of Putnam? Who reviewed the American army July 10, 1775? (63.) What is said of England? (64.) Of Lord North? Of Wesley? Of London? Of the crazed king? Of independence? Of a French agent? (64.) Of Carolinians? (65.) Of Fort Moultrie? Of Lord Campbell? Of Montgomery? Of Canadian hearts? (65.) Of Washington's army? (66.) Of what he lacked? Of Dorchester Heights? Of Boston set free? Of the army's hope? Of Washington's knowledge? (66.) Of the enemy's numbers? (67.) Of the French jealousy of Britain? Of Virginia and the South? Of New England? Of the Middle

States? (67.) Of the declaration worded to suit Georgia, the Carolinas, and New England on slavery? (68.) Who eloquently advocated independence? When was independence declared? (68.)

BOOK FOURTH.

To whom was December 25, 1776, a sad Christmas? Why? (69.) With how many did Washington escape across the Delaware? What is said of Charles Lee? Of Sullivan? Of Congress? (69.) Of the country? (70.) Of Cæsar and Monk? Of an ice bridge? Of Cornwallis? Of Howe? Of allies and helpers of Washington? (70, 71.) Of the noise of battle December 25, 1776? (71.) Of hated Hessians? Of Rahl? Of Trenton's garrison? What did Americans fight before they fought the Hessians? What was the effect of the victory? How many did the enemy lose? What is said of the great chief? Of Cornwallis? (71.) Of Princeton troops? (72.) Of Princeton's classic ground? Of January 4, 1777? Of the British army? (72.) Of thousands surprised in Princeton? Of raw recruits? Of Mercer and valiant veterans? Who fell? What voice rung out upon the air? (72.) What of the morning breeze? (73.) What is said of Saratoga, October 17, 1777? (73.) Of Burgoyne? Of John Stark? Of two recent battles? Who surrendered with Burgoyne? What was taken besides captives? What will be the effect? (73.) Why not peace? (74.) What of Trenton and Princeton? (75.) Of ships up the Chesapeake? Of Brandywine? Of Germantown? Of Howe? Of Valley Forge? What came with spring? What way did Howe seek safety? Who were victims of vice? (75, 76.) To supplant Washington what was done? (76.) Was it accomplished? What sound was heard near Monmouth, N. J., June 21, 1778? (76.) Who came retreating? (77.) Who met them? What did he say to Charles Lee? How did Lee reply? Who followed Washington? With what result? What is said of the falls of the Ohio? (77.) Who came from afar July 30, 1778? (78.) Why had Virginia sent them forth? What had she done when France intruded? What when King George gave her territory to the Canadians? What had those men taken from Great Britain? (78.) Who led these Kentucky Virginians? (79.) What five States occupy that ground? (79.) What is said of the French and English fleets? How many French were at Savannah October 8, 1779? How many Carolinians? What is said of the Butlers? Of the torch? Of the Parliament? Of Piggot? Of Wayne? Of Maj. Lee? Of Pickens? Of Prevost? Of Campbell? (80.) Of Pulaski? (81.) Of Lincoln? Of Jasper? Of D'Estaing? Of the fort? Of mammon and covetousness? (81, 82.) Of Arnold and Andre? Of the captors of Andre? Of Arnold and fire fiends? Of Tarleton? (82, 83.) Of William Washington? (83.) Of Cornwallis? Of Greene? Of Gen. Hayne? Of the fight at Eutaw Springs September 18,

QUESTIONS. 285

1781. (83.) Who and what were vanquished at Yorktown, Va., October 19, 1781? (84.) What is said of French help? Of Savannah and Newport? Of West Point? Of ragged troops? Of generous Philadelphians? (84, 85.) Of a French Loan? Of New York? Of Cornwallis? (85, 86.) Of Lafayette? (86.) Of Clinton? Of Americans and French? Of French fleets? Of Hamilton and Lafayette? What did Virginia see? (86.) What is said of prisoners? (87.) Of guns, etc.? Of O'Hara? Of Cornwallis? Of the victors? (87.) Of a messenger from Yorktown in Philadelphia October 23, 1781? (88.) What was the effect of his news? What is said of the Congress? (88.) Of our newborn nation, December 26, 1783? (89.) Of its freedom? Of peace? Of heroes of independence? Of Washington? Of what he gave? (89.)

BOOK FIFTH.

What is said of the Federal Convention August 15, 1787? (90.) Of a perfect union? Of a small tax? Of selfishness? Of small States? Of large? Of the rich South? Of the poor North? Of slaves? Of State sovereignty? (90.) Of Charles Pinckney? (90.) Of Mason and Lee? (91.) Of Ames? (91.) Of Rufus King? Of Hamilton? (91.) Of Franklin? (92.) Of Sherman and Ellsworth? (92.) Of slaves? Of New England, Georgia, and the Carolinas? (92.) Of strong government? Of friends of civil liberty? (92.) Of God? (93.) Do swindling statesmen cost less than honest soldiers? Was the Constitution to be ratified or rejected by the States? (93.) What States had not ratified June 24, 1788? (94.) What is said of Massachusetts? (94, 95.) Of South Carolina? (95, 96.) What did Virginia claim if she acceded? What is said of despots? Of majorities? Of force? Of a mighty tribunate to forbid selfishness and prevent war between States? (96, 97.) Of Henry's oratory? (98.) Of angels bemoaning Virginia's destiny? Of a storm to interfere with Henry's effort? (98.) To what is creation subject? (99.) What is said of the new government? (99, 100.) Of fiendish hatred? (100.) Of Western gales of liberty? Of the French? Of wars between Americans predicted? Of their effect? What is said of the States? (101.) Of the federal sovereignty? (101, 102.) What did the States put into its hands? What would result from clashing interests? Of upstart insolence? Of fanatic faction? (102.) Of Satan's boast? (102, 103.) Of Adam and Eve? Of Cain and Abel? Of antediluvians? Of heirs of Noah? Of ancient cities and nations? (103, 104.) Of this newest of the nations? (104.) Of the inauguration of the new administration? Of the Book of God? Of France? (104.) Of the savages? (105.) Of rum and whisky? Of political strife? Of Hamilton? Of Jefferson? (105.) Of strifes of Europe here? (106.) Of Boston common July 9, 1792? (106.) Who were those horsemen? What did they bring? Why had New England picked up cast-off heresies of other lands? (107.) What better way to obtain relief from Calvinism did these men of the South bring? (108.) How many converts had Lee gained in two years? What is said of reluctant Boston? What of ten thousand such? (108.) Of young Americans? Of Jefferson and Hamilton? Of the people? Of the sword of Washington? Of France? Of Britain? Of Genet, the French Minister? Of Jay? Of Jay's treaty? (109.) Of Eastern men favored by an Eastern man? Of Southern men robbed of slaves? Of the British lion? (110.) What news had arrived at Washington, D. C., June 1, 1803? (111.) What is said of the States? Of the frontier men? Of trade? Of the Indians? Of whisky fiends? Of France? Of Pinckney? Of the waves? Of the French change of rulers? (111.) Of fears of the people? Of how happily proved unfounded? What is said of Jefferson and Marshall? (113, 114.) Of growth in wealth? In population? Of new States? (114.)

BOOK SIXTH.

WHAT would follow the continued rule of sober, upright men? (115.) What is said of Lewis and Clark? Of Fulton? (115.) Of pirates? (116.) Of Indians? Of Burr? Of Hamilton? Of Harrison? Of Britain's lords of trade? Of Frenchmen? Of ships in their own ports? Of the embargo? Of New England? Of John Henry? Of Craig? (116.) Of ships of neutral nations? (117.) Of the English language? Of the six thousand Americans kidnapped? Of the "Leopard" and "Chesapeake?" Of nonintercourse? Of the "Little Belt" and "President?" What else was done to provoke war? Did John Henry prove to Madison that New England's factions had negotiated for annexations to Canada? What of idle throngs in seaports? What of the woodsmen of the West? What of the young statesmen? (117, 118.) In what did the Christian nations agree on December 25, 1812? (118.) What did they make the world? What is said of all soils? Of Protestants? Of angry millions here? Of bold statesmen? What nation did they strike? Had they prepared for war? What is said of Hull? Of the Northwest? (118.) Of Van Rensselaer? (118, 119.) Of New York's militia? Of one Smyth? Of naval heroes? Of Winchester? Of Proctor? (119.) Of Dudley? (120.) Of Chauncey? Of Dearborn? Of Pike? Of Winder and Chandler? Of Lawrence? Of naval warfare on shore? At the battle of the Thames (October 5, 1813) who fled? What is said of the British regulars? Of Kentucky horsemen? Of Tecumseh? Of the Indians? (120.) Of Isaac Shelby? (121.) Of Harrison? Of Croghan? Of Johnson? Of Perry? Of children of the West? (121.) What is said of Chippewa? (122.) Of Lundy's Lane? Of distinguished generals? Of the siege of Fort Erie? Of Prevost and Downie? Of Plattsburg and Lake Champlain? Of McDonough and Macomb? Of Ross at Washington? Of Smith at

North Point, near Baltimore? Of Fort McHenry? Of the star-spangled banner? (122.) What of the times when Adams ruled? What did New England know her sons to be? Why did she lose patience? What was too bad to endure? When Louisiana was bought, what did a faction say? When did the faction demand war? What did those she called imbeciles adopt? When the embargo ruined trade, to whom did they listen? (123.) What was proposed? (124.) Where? What is said of John Adams? Of the law? When war was declared according to their wish, how did they act? Did they hastily secede? Why? What would they do? What would they claim? What would they call what others call robbery. (124.) What is said of the Hartford conventionists? (125.) What of New England? What is said of Andrew Jackson at Fort Mims? (125.) At Fort Bowyer? In Spanish Florida? At New Orleans? Of Napoleon's conquerors? Of Pakenham, Gibbs, and Keen? Of Lambert? Of the loss of Americans? Of the loss of British? Of the truce? (126.) What was gained by the Americans? (127.) By the British? What is said of a court to prevent war? (127, 128.) Of Judge Hall, who fined Jackson for contempt of court in enforcing martial law? Of Jackson? Of his submission to a civil court? Of Decatur? Of the pirates? Of the exiles? (128.) Of the Greeks? (129.) Of Spain? Of France? Of Liberia? Of Jackson? Of Texas? Of sectional politics? Of Monroe? Of the next President? Of States added to the Union? Of Missouri? Of her right? (129.) Of sectional jealousy? (130.) Of supercilious piety? Of what the States gave the Congress? Of the wish of many? Of the compromise line? Of coequal citizens and States? Of French residents? Of King majority? (130.) Of purblind statesmanship? (131.) Of the slave trade? Of foreign tonnage? Of masters? Of slaves? Of flames of hatred? (131.) Of Bunker Hill, June 17, 1825? (132.) Of Daniel Webster? Of Lafayette? Of gratitude? Of the new republics? (132.) Of the "Monroe Doctrine?" Of the "Brandywine?" (133.)

BOOK SEVENTH.

WHAT is said of Jackson's inauguration, March 4, 1829? (134.) Of the factory lords? (134.) Of the wives of Jackson's cabinet? (135.) Of Van Buren, the widower of Kinderhook? (135.) Of J. C. Calhoun, the Vice-president? (136.) Of the President? Of sectional parties? (136.) Of Jefferson and Adams? (137.) Of railroad cars? (138.) Of the cabinet? Of Van Buren, March 4, 1833? Of the manufacturers? Of the fiery South? Of the Force bill? Of Hayne? Of Webster and Calhoun? Of Livingston? (138.) Of twenty years? (139.) Of Carolinians? Of Clay? Of Calhoun? Of Jackson? Of Austin? Of the Alamo, where Texans were butchered? Of the cholera? (139.) Of Black Hawk? Of France? Of Portugal? Of New York?

Of politicians? Of death? (140.) Of Monroe? Of the issue of the battle at San Jacinto, Tex., April, 1836? Of Sam Houston? Of Santa Ana? Of Slade of Vermont? Of threescore Congressmen? Of Southern Congressmen? Of British emissaries? Of poets? Of smartlings? (140, 141.) Of hireling lecturers? (141.) Of pulpit politicians? Of contracts of their sires? Of the British? Of the capital? Of fair bargains? (141.) Of one honest way? (141.) Of covenant breaking? Of brazen impudence? Of the great name of Christ? (142.) Of Clay? (143.) Of petitions less frequent. Why? Of self-love and self-conceit? Of change of rulers? Of Van Buren? Of Harrison? Of Tyler? (143.) Of Michigan? Of Arkansas? Of Seminoles? Of Cherokees? Of retribution? (145.) Of the magnetic telegraph, May 29, 1844? (145.) Of all nations neighbors? Of Morse, the benefactor? Of the manufacturer's pocket-nerve? (146.) Of what they plead? (147.) Of protected wealth when war shall hold millions by the throat? Of Taylor's troops at Palo Alto? Of Resaca de la Palma? Of Monterey? Of Buena Vista, February 23, 1847? Of Zachary Taylor? Of Jefferson Davis? (147.) Of Mississippians? (147, 148.) Of officers? Of Jacob Goodson? (148.) Of Clay, McKee, and hundreds of brave men? Of entering their foe's capital? Of Bibles? Of Fremont, Stockton, and Sloat? Of Kearney? (148.) Of Doniphan? (149.) Of Vera Cruz? Of Twiggs? Of Santa Ana? Of West Point officers? Name some of the generals. (149.) What is said of President Polk? (150.) Of Texas? Of war? Peace brought what? Of the British treaty? Of States admitted? Of Smithson? (150.) Of Jackson and Adams? (151.) Of Clay's compromise? Of honored names? Since Clay's compromise what has been threatened? (151.) What is said of sectional hatred? (152.) Of New England's clergy? Of self-government? Of Nebraska? What did the clergy want? What is said of the South? (152.) What is said of the ocean telegraph? (153.) Of Crystal Palace? Of Perry? Of Ingram? Of Field? Of John Brown at Harper's Ferry, 1859? Of Brown's guilt without his bravery? (153.) Of not one man in twenty thirsts for blood? (155.) Of halls of Congress? Of the multitudes? (155.) Of a thousand mad men? (156.) Of the ordinance of 1787 shutting slavery out of the States of Illinois, Indiana, Ohio, Michigan, and Wisconsin? Was it lawful? Of the Missouri compromise? Did the North abide by it? (156.) What did the faction want? (157.) Had the most guilty been caught when Brown was hung? (157.)

BOOK EIGHTH.

WHAT is said of a great State leaving the Union? (158.) Of twelve more? Was it wise to dissolve the Union? (158–160.) Who have thought disunion a State right? (160.) What is said of the West? Of the East? Of the North for sixty years? To a ruling faction of the North what did the Constitution seem? What did their statesmen say? (161.) What said the men who made the Constitution? For what has the Federal government troops? (162.) What would war on a State be? What did Morris and Hamilton say the Federal government would do? What would result from such base action? (163.) Can the States be held together without force? (163, 164.) What is said of the faction that claimed the right to rule? What of the wickedness of the Northern and Southern factions? (164.) If the Northern faction wished to free slaves, what was the honest way? (164.) If to fight to free slaves, how could they do it without violating plighted faith? (165.) What is said of the faction holding power? Of Virginia and Kentucky? Of the faction holding the purse and sword? Of the kindly heart of the new President? (165.) Of his fierce followers? Of the least furious of them? How did they regard Pinckney, Gadsden, or Washington? What was done by sober Southerners? What was necessary to preserve the ruling faction? (166, 167.) What fatal defect characterized the Federal government? (168.) How were citizens made traitors in spite of true fidelity to both State and Federal governments? (168.) What is said of the President? How would war begin? (168.) What had been the boasts of North and South? What would follow on firing on the flag? (169.) Who commanded in the attack on Fort Sumter, April 12, 1861? (171.) Who surrendered? What is said of Baltimore? Of Bethel? Of Philippi? Of Romney? Of Garnet? Of Rich Mountain? Of Cheat River? Of West Pointers? Of men in gray? (171.) Of troops from the West? Of the panic-stricken? Of Northern policy? Of Southern policy? (172.) Of folly's most absurd desire? (173.) Of one live yankee? Of the South's lost opportunity? (173.) Of Wilkes? (173.) Of Palmerston? (174.) Of the lion in his lair? Of Missouri? Of Jackson? Of Price? Of Harney? Of Lyon? Of Sigel? Of Boonville? Of Carthage? Of Wilson's Creek? Of Lyon slain? Of McCullough? (174.) Of Mulligan? (174, 175.) Of Fremont? (175.) Of Hunter? Of Halleck? Of Grant? Of Polk? Of Baker? Of cannons made of wood? Of McClellan? Of four hundred thousand men? Of Garfield? Of Marshall? Of Thomas? Of Zollicoffer? Of Crittenden? Of Fort Henry? Of Fort Donelson? Of Grant? Of Foote? (175.) Of Pillow and Floyd? (176.) Of Buckner? Of Kentucky? Of Tennessee? Of Shiloh, April 7, 1862? Of Grant? Of Albert Sidney Johnston? Of Buell? (176.) Of Porter and Farragut at New Orleans, April 26, 1862? (177.) Of Jackson's statue and Ben Butler? Of McCullough, McIntosh, and Pike at Pea Ridge? Of Curtis? Of the dead? Of Burnside and Goldsboro? Of Pope? (177.) Of bombardment of the forts? (178.) Of to capture? Of stealing? (178.) Of Farragut? Of Porter? Of the Shenandoah conflicts? Of Jackson? (178.) Of McClellan's strategy? (179.) Of his battles? Of Southern strategy? (179.) Of earth walls? Of Northern heroes? (180.) When was the ironclad, "Virginia," sent to

19

Hampton Roads? March 8, 1862. What did she destroy? What did Virginia suffer for the lack of? When and where did the first steamboat move against a current? When and where was natural gas first used? Where did McCormick invent the reaper? What caused the loss or inefficiency of Confederate ironclads? (180.)

BOOK NINTH.

WHAT is said of Fredericksburg, December 15, 1862? (181.) Of virtues become vices? Of West Point? Of courage? Of wealth? (181.) Of Cedar Mountain? (183.) Of Manassas? Of Centerville? Of Chantilly? Of Pope? Of trembling Washington? Of Frederick, Md.? Of Hagerstown? Of Harper's Ferry? Of Antietam? Of sharp steel pens? Of McClellan's head? Of Burnside? (183.) Of Murfreesboro, Tenn., January 3, 1863? (184.) Of Rosecrans? Of artillery? Of Kentucky? Of Kirby Smith? Of Manson? Of Kentucky towns? Of Perryville? Of Bragg? Of precious stores? Of Iuka? Of Van Dorn and Price? Of Sherman? (184.) Of Hooker? (184.) Of Lee? Of Jackson? (185.) What is said of July 4, 1776? (186.) Of July 4, 1863, at Gettysburg? (186.) Of Vicksburg? (186, 187.) What was claimed? (187.) What is said of prayers? (188.) Of with the Lord? Of going to Stonewall Jackson? Of going to John Brown? Of politicians? Of Lee, Meade, and other soldiers? (188.) Of desperate valor at Vicksburg? (189.) Of Arkansas Post? Of passing the forts? Of Port Gibson? Of Grand Gulf? Of Jackson, Raymond, Champion Hills, Black River bridge? Of Pemberton? Of Grant's assault? Of thirty thousand starving men? (189.) Of the commerce of the West? Of a wall of waters? Of flag of truce? (189.) Of Charleston, S. C.? (190.) Of Dupont? Of Dahlgren and Gilmore? Of swamp angels? Of Holmes at Helena? Of Steele at Little Rock? Of Lawrence, Kan.? Of Quantrell? (190.) Of Longstreet? (191.) Of Thomas? Of Virginia blood? Of Rosecrans? Of Hooker? Of Sherman? Of Grant? Of Southern heroes? Of Chickamauga, September 20, 1863? (191.) Of Bragg giving notice? What is said of the fight above the clouds? (191, 192.) Of the second fight on Mission Ridge? (193.) Of the loss of Tennessee by the South? (193.) Of John Morgan at Covington, Ky., November 20, 1863? (193.) Of his character? Of his bad treatment? Of his enemies disgracing themselves? Of his escape? (194.) Of three armies? Of Banks? Of "Rough and Ready's" son? Of Gen. Richard Taylor? (194.) Of "no generals to hurt?" (195.) Of the two B's.? of their native land? Of its poets? Of its pulpits? Of transcendentalists? Of its really great men? (195.) Of the lasting glory of that famous land? (196.) Of Grant's losses? (196.) Of brave men dying to defend cowards? Of Federal force making war on States? What was it? Striking Virginia was what? (196, 197.) What had she given the Union? (197.) How did her sons fight? How treat their enemies? (197.) Of her sons a living wall? (198.) While she fought a world in arms, whom did her enemies call on to save them? Of grand, brave men in Northern armies? Why in Virginia should they wear laurels soaked in blood? (198.) What is said of Lee? Of Johnston? (198.) Of the battles north of Richmond? (199.) Of the cadets and Sigel? Of Hunter and Early? Of Breckinridge and Lew Wallace? Of the fighting of Sherman and Johnston? (199.) Of Atlanta's importance? (200.) Of Johnston's Fabian policy? Of a desolated valley? (200.) Of the best of Adam's race? Of defense of native land? Of every craven heart? Of one so brave as Sheridan? (201.) Of war or felony? Of not thus that Grant and Sherman learned to fight? (201.) Of earthly retribution? Of Tecumseh S.? (202.) Of Johnston superseded by Hood? (203.) Of his move backward? (203.) Of Thomas distrusted? If removed, how may Hood win victories? What is said of fighting like crazy fiends at Petersburg? Of Early threatening Washington? Of Wright? Of Chambersburg? Of the barbarian torch? (203, 204.) Of Sheridan's ax and torch? (204.) Of Early's victory? Of Sheridan's greater victory? Of great barbarism? Of Union fleets? Of Cushing? Of Farragut? (204.) Of Winslow? (205.)

BOOK TENTH.

WHAT is said of Nashville, Tenn., December 16, 1864? (206.) Of Andrew Jackson? Of the generalship of Thomas? (206, 207.) Of Schofield? Of Hood's bravery? Of defeat? (207.) Of atrocious crimes? (208.) Of lawless villains? Of saintly Bachman? Of the hell hounds? (208.) Of the oft defeated army almost victorious at Bentonville, N. C., March 19, 1865? (209.) Why? What is said of Kirkpatrick's cavalry? Of Terry? Of Sabbath morning in Richmond, April 2, 1865? (209, 210.) Of afternoon? (211, 212.) Of McLean's Orchard, Appomattox C. H., Va.? Of the strife growing fiercer? Of the surrender of Lee? Of Grant's generous magnanimity? (212.) Of Lee in adversity? (212, 213.) Of Ford's Theater? Of Washington, April 14, 1865? (213.) Of a bloody tragedy? Of the President? Of Booth? Of Beall? (214.) Of under the flag 'neath which their fathers stood? Of Sherman, Johnston, Breckinridge? (215.) Of "one more social drink?" (216.) Of the right of a supreme commander over prisoners? Of the kindness of the President? Of his death? Of fanatic fury going to hanging? (216.) Of Johnston? (217.) Of Breckinridge? (217.) Of peace? (218.) Of God's goodness? Of secession and disunion? Of slaves free? Of Johnson's theory? Of Lincoln's theory? Was coercion, if they were not right, a most atrocious crime? (218, 219.) Did he love the Union? Was he the poor man's friend? What is said of a vicarious sufferer? (219, 220.) Did God give a law to make slaves of freemen? (220.) What is said of the guilt of slavery in the South? (220.) Of predictions of Haytian horrors? (221.) What prevented it? (221.) What is said of Africa Christianized? Of the guilt of Southern men? (221, 222.) Of the domestic slave trade? (222.) Of retribution? (223.) Is the white man's lot like what the slaves have been? What is worse than plantation government? (224.) What is said of the vile treatment of Jefferson Davis? (225.) Of stern retribution following fast? (226.) Of rulers of this continent? Of Davis, Lincoln, Maximilian, Johnson? (226.) Of Alaska? Of a costly party? (227, 228.) Of a miscreated, monstrous government in the South? (228.) Of Johnson acquitted? Of fires in Boston? (228.) Of Chicago and the North-west? (228.) Of reminders of Virginia and other Southern fires? (229.) Do fraudful States raise fraudful citizens? Of "Black Friday?" Of Tweed? Of the "Credit Mobilier?" (229.) Of the country's growth? (230.) Of the boomerang? (230.) Of fifteen and a half millions of dollars? Of Sumner and Grant? (231.) Who sleep in quiet graves? (232.)

BOOK ELEVENTH.

Who took places in the Centennial building at Philadelphia? Who prayed? Whose hymn was sung? (232.) What is said of the Pittsburg fire? (233.) Of Sherman's tactics? Of Hamilton's finance? Whose loss? To whom does less wealth mean less comfort? What had war taught Northern workmen? (233.) What is said of strife between labor and capital? Of a just court? Of men and machinery working on? Of a just bounty? Of a general tax? Of corporations and syndicates? (234.) What else will save the millions from the millionaires? (235.) Why not divide all wealth in equal parts? What could not wealthy rulers buy? (236.) How did an aristocracy of wealth rob? How corrupt? (237.) What is said of that Scotchman? (238.) How was silver demonetized? Why? Was paper currency paid for in gold? (238.) What is said of trade dollars? (239.) Do banks expand currency when it is plenty, contract when it is scarce? What is said of a stable, well-secured currency? (239.) Of President Garfield? (240.) Of the Czar of Russia? Of John Brown as a model saint? (240.) What noted men have died? What is said of Ralph Waldo Emerson? (241.) Of the iron creed? (242.) Of the truth of God? (242.) What had prayerful people come to celebrate? What reply do they make to those who say there is no God? (243–145.) What is said of only God filling immensity? (245, 246.) Of the period when he was the All? Of his now existing in all? Of God the Father? Of his ubiquity? Of his invisibility? Of God the Son manifested? Of his incarnation? Of his crucifixion? (247.) Of his rising? Of his reigning? Of God the Holy Ghost manifested? (247.) Of his making human bodies his temples? Of his giving men access to the Father through the Son? Of a unitarian God? (248.) Of the sovereignty of God? (249.) Of God's unchangeableness? Of his knowledge? (249–251.)

What is said of unfettered finite freedom's loftiest flight? (252.) Of God's all-encircling infinite freedom?

BOOK TWELFTH.

WHAT is said of Washington's example? (253.) Of shortsighted men? Of parties? (256.) Of the telephone? (256.) Of the phonograph? (257.) Of electric lights? Of electric motors? Of natural gas? Of Gen. Grant's obsequies? Of his life? (257, 258.) Of Hancock? Of Johnston and Buckner? (258.) What can a nation need that this has not? (259.) What does Satan claim? (259.) What would he do if he could? (259.) With what does he threaten our country? (260.) What will the decent people of this land do? (260.) What is said of filthy liquors? (261.) Of the hatreds of strong parties? Of an election force bill? (262.) What would the people do in five weeks? (263.) Of Northern capital? (263.) Of noble Northern men? (263, 264.) Of wealthy Northern men? (265.) Of Northern working-men? What would election day see? (265.) What took place in the capital at that hour? (266.) What does one million for the treasury take from the people for the capitalists? (267.) What is said of Cleveland and Harrison? (268.) What will the people do with the robber tariff? (268.) What of rich men's greediness of gain? (269.) What system of finance is proposed? (270.) What is said of lifting the burden from the poor? What should wealth pay? (271.) What will this great nation not permit? What will this nation find? (272.)

VIRGINIA VISITED.

SELECTED POEMS.

VIRGINIA VISITED.
RICHMOND, VA., MAY, 1886.

HERE, loveliest of mothers,
　At home, from sorrows free,
I leave all else to others;
　And in my childish glee,
Entranced by charms that grace thee
　I stand beside thy knee;
Thy loving arms embrace me,
　While thrilling ecstasy
Bids care and gloom and sadness
　With quick'ning speed depart,
As in this hour of gladness
　I nestle near thy heart;
And lay my flushed cheek lightly
　Upon thy tender breast,
Where in my childhood nightly,
　I dreamed of heav'nly rest.

Through years of weary wand'ring,
　I've languished for thy smile,
My spirit fondly pond'ring,
　On ev'ry winning wile
That won my love, and bound me
　With fascinating pow'r,
And twined my heartstrings round thee,
　In childhood's guileless hour.
That sacred tie, unbroken,
　Still draws me to thy side,
With many a wish unspoken,
　That here I might abide.

A dreary road, and lonely,
   I'll tread when we must part,
Though I have brought thee only
   A loving, homesick heart.

O best beloved of mothers!
   The "Iliad of thy woes"
Wrings from my noble brothers,
   And even from thy foes,
The bitter tears of sorrow
   And sympathetic grief,
That seek from God to borrow,
   For virtue, sweet relief.
'Twas when thy homes were blazing,
   By vandal fires consumed,
Th' indignant world stood gazing,
   And saw thy face illumed
With more than earthly glory;
   And thy majestic form,
Though battle-scarred and gory,
   Rose grandly through the storm.

Thermopylæs a hundred,
   And Marathons by scores,
Still tell where cannons thundered
   To guard thy sacred shores.
Yet not from puny Persians,
   Thy bloody fields were won,
Nor troops whose brief incursions
   End with the rising sun;
But men thou wouldst have cherished
   Were fiercest of thy foes,
And when they bravely perished,
   In agonizing throes,
Thou laidst their countless numbers
   Beside thy boldest braves,
To peaceful, quiet slumbers,
   In "hospitable graves."

O mother of the mighty!
   Thy matchless, gallant sons

Take precedence, and rightly,
  Of all earth's valiant ones;
Not Cæsar, nor Napoleon,
  Nor he of Macedon,
Nor German, Frank, nor Briton
  Could do what they have done.
The fabled hosts that Homer
  Made high Olympus tread
Were dwarfed beside each roamer
  That "Stonewall" Jackson led;
No gods of Grecian story
  Could bear comparison,
On fields of martial glory,
  With Lee or Washington.

By old Britannia's charter,
  A continent was thine;
Hills, plains, and sparkling water,
  Each forest and each mine.
The silv'ry voice of science
  Still pleads thy rightful claim,
And boldly bids defiance
  To all who scorn thy name,
"Virginiensis," brightly
  Her jeweled hand engraves
On birds that carol lightly,
  On tenants of the waves;
Fair flow'rets breathe it sweetly,
  It flashes on the tide,
The wild deer bears it fleetly
  Far up the mountain side.

Thy name, beloved, immortal
  Shall live when others die,
And to thy glowing portal
  Thy children ever hie.
When Time his course is ending,
  When all his works shall cease,
All eyes shall see, descending,
  The glorious Prince of Peace;
Then coming down from heaven,
  Christ's Virgin Bride shall shine,

Fair, sinless, pure, forgiven,
Illustrious, divine!
And thou and thine shall with them
Be blessed and satisfied,
As in the New Jerusalem,
Virginia's glorified.

I'LL THINK OF THE SAND BANKS.*

LEXINGTON, KY., APRIL, 1839.

I'LL think of the sand banks when morn's early beam
Illumines the meadow and brightens the stream,
When noon's sultry sunshine invites to repose,
When night spreads oblivion o'er pleasures and woes;
E'en my dreams shall be peopled with forms that were there,
And their voices shall echo in fancy's rapt ear.

I'll think of the sand banks when spring paints her flow'rs
And calls her winged minstrels to gladden her bow'rs,
When summer's warm smile glows above the parched soil,
When autumn's rich stores bless the husbandman's toil,
And the chill winds of winter shall bring to my mind
The mem'ry of friends whom I there left behind.

I'll think of the sand banks while youth's eager eye
Still rests on hope's bow in futurity's sky;
When manhood with cares shall encircle my feet,
Or leave me, unfriended, life's troubles to meet;
And when age bids me gaze in the mirror of truth,
I'll think of the sand banks, the home of my youth.

TO MY MOTHER.†

I LOVE the land that gave me birth,
The fires that warm my native hearth,

---

* Accomac, Va.
† Written at John Prather's, six miles East of Lexington, Ky., in the spring of 1842, and published in the *Ladies' Repository*, Cincinnati, O.

I'll think of the sand banks when spring paints her flowers
And calls her winged minstrels to gladden her bowers.

The fields where childhood's sunny hours
Mid rip'ning fruits and op'ning flowers
Breathed pleasure in the floating air,
Nor thought of pain nor dreamed of care.

I love the home of infancy,
Virginia's charming scenery,
The sand banks of my native shore,
The whistling winds, the ocean's roar,
The storm careering fearfully,
The snow-capped surges wild and free.

I love the friends of early years,
Who kindly wiped my infant tears,
The humble church without a spire,
Where blazed devotion's hallowed fire,
The ministers of sacred truth
Who chid the wand'rings of my youth:

I love them all—God bless my home—
And shall where'er my steps may roam.
But, mother, when compared with thee,
To me they're less than vanity;
Next to the God she loves so well,
My mother in my heart shall dwell.

To guard my unprotected hours,
To strew my ev'ry path with flow'rs,
To make my childhood's sky grow bright,
To quell my fears was thy delight;
And with a love almost divine
Thine eyes grew dim in watching mine.

Dear mother, in my boyish dreams,
When fancy ruled her magic realms,
I gathered wealth that thy free hand
Might scatter blessings through the land,
I climbed Parnassian hills for fame,
To give thy house a deathless name.

I sought for honor's thorny road,
To mingle with the giddy crowd;
And when the rosy wreath was gained,

Though toil and blood its leaves had stained,
Delighted, at thy feet I'd bow,
And with it deck thy honored brow.

Those dreams have passed, and hopes of heav'n
To nobler themes my thoughts have giv'n;
Wealth's golden stores may ne'er be mine,
Nor fame my humble name enshrine.
The pathway of humility
Must lead my footsteps to the sky.

But, mother, when my wand'rings end
Where tall archangels lowly bend,
Joyful, their sovereign Lord to own,
And worship him who fills the throne;
Should Jesus deign to smile on me,
My thoughts shall fondly turn to thee.

And should a heav'nly harp be mine,
A crown of righteousness divine,
A mansion in the land of love,
A home in that bright world above,
'Twill sweeten all the joys of heaven
To know they're to my mother given.

A WIFE'S FIFTIETH BIRTHDAY.

JEFFERSONVILLE, IND., APRIL 20, 1878.

SINCE first I saw thee, thou hast ever been
My bright ideal of the beautiful,
The type and pattern of all loveliness.

Whether in gleeful gambolings, tripping
O'er flow'ry paths, where pleasure led the way,
In youth's bright morn; or at the noon of life,
Attending on love's myriad ministries
With steady step; or trudging cheerfully,
In later hours, o'er rough and rugged roads,
Where stern domestic drudg'ry drives her slaves—
Love's partial eye has seen in all thy steps
The poetry of motion and of grace.

Or at the noon of life
Attending on love's myriad ministries.

Through all these happy hours thy gentle voice
Has seemed to pour upon my ravished ear
The music of that heav'n to which we go.
No weight of years has bent thy graceful form;
No sorrow dimmed the love light of thine eye;
The rose of beauty blooms upon thy cheek,
Still fadeless through the frosts of fifty years.
The hearts that long have gladdened in thy smile
Now gather round to hail thy natal hour.
So in the time to come this joyous day,
The brightest in the calendar, shall find
Thy throne of love, amid thy family,
In home's delightful summer land of bliss.

A TRUTHFUL IDYL OF REST AND RAPTURE.
ORLANDO, FLA., SEPTEMBER 4, 1888.

LET the bright needle rest to-day;
Books, pens, and work are laid away;
No toilsome thought shall hither stray;
The sportive sunbeams idly play
On the full ears of perfect corn,
That fertile, restful fields adorn.
They gayly dance and brightly smile
On many a lonely tropic isle;
Their languor-laden glory shines
Where ocean lazily reclines
In his broad bed at perfect ease,
And bids his slow-paced wavelets tease
The shy and modest slumb'rous shore
With their unceasing, sullen roar.
This sluggish air is not inclined
The paths of busy trade to find;
The soft-winged angels of repose
Float lightly on each breeze that blows.
Those grand old trees that, tow'ring high,
Rest their tall heads against the sky
Have done their work—borne buds and flow'rs
And rich, ripe fruit—in former hours.
The birds sit silent on the spray;

Their tender fledgelings, flown away,
Have left no chirping nursling brood,
With hungry cries demanding food.
In patriarchal grace and pride,
They're quiet, grave, and dignified.

Our tuneful offspring, loved and blest,
Have long since left the parent nest;
The children's children blithely play
Through all this fair September day.

Give me the hand that holds the thread,
The hand I long have gently led.
In loving clasp it still must stay;
Let the bright needle rest to-day.

Hold there! With speed old cares depart;
The warm pulsations of the heart
Rejuvenate the blood of age,
And all the faculties engage
To quicken life's slow, latent springs,
And give to fancy youthful wings.
Th' ecstatic, dear, delightful dream
Turns time's old turbid tide upstream:
Threescore and ten goes hobbling off;
See twenty-five his chapeau doff,
And gently bow his gallant form,
In heartfelt homage, high and warm,
Where graceful sixty-six resumes
The beauty that at twenty blooms.

Come to the parlor; take the arm
That still protects and shields from harm.
Tread lightly on the hopes and fears
Of four and forty wedded years,
Whose blissful hours come smiling here,
To fill our hearts with lofty cheer.
Sing softly songs of former times:
There's rapture in their simple rhymes.
Let the old tunes that charm the soul
Sublimely swell and sweetly roll.

In this piano-prison bound
There's many a captive thrilling sound.
In harmony they all agree,
And wait your touch to set them free.
Though now their vocal chords are mute,
You'll find a remedy to suit;
The life of music lingers still
In fingers that, with magic skill,
Can draw from each obedient key
Sweet, soul-entrancing melody.

That heav'nly strain repeat, prolong:
An angel well might hush his song,
To pour upon his ravished ear
The rich, mellifluous sounds I hear.

We're young again, my precious bride;
And I, enraptured by thy side,
Recall the loveliness and grace
Of faultless form and matchless face
That won the heart that still is thine
And still delights to call thee mine.

THE FASTING, PRAYING CHURCH.

Written in Louisville, May, 1844, on the day set apart for prayer by the General Conference on motion of Dr. John P. Durbin. Published in the *Ladies' Repository*, Cincinnati, O.; copied by Dr. Thomas E. Bond, Sr., in *New York Advocate*.

CHURCH of my early choice, thy sons
　Are bathed in sorrow and in tears,
A company of sighing ones,
　A band of weeping worshipers;
Youth lays its joyousness aside;
　Age bends beneath its weight of care;
Beauty and strength forget their pride—
　All bow submissively in prayer.
And shall the suppliants depart
　In sadness from a throne of grace?
Shall quiv'ring lip and throbbing heart,
　Despairing, leave the sacred place?
O can the bruisèd, bending reed
　Be broken by the God of love?

No, Jesus lives to intercede;
   Thy living Head still reigns above.

Church of the living God, to thee
   A nation turns with anxious eye;
Gloom gathers o'er thy destiny,
   And darkness spreads along thy sky;
Yet shall the storm cloud pass away,
   The lurid lightning cease to blaze;
The sunshine of a brighter day
   Shall gild thee with its gladd'ning rays.
E'en though thy legions should divide,
   One standard of the cross would wave,
One leader in thy front would ride,
   Mighty to conquer, strong to save.
Th' eternal God thy refuge is,
   The everlasting arms are thrown
Around the subjects of his grace,
   And he will safely keep his own.

Church of the poor, no creed of thine
   Has taught thy sons exclusiveness;
They never claimed a right divine
   To curse the souls they could not bless;
To fetter thought or chain the mind;
   They ne'er have moved the civil pow'r.
Nor with the foes of man combined
   To lengthen out oppression's hour;
No widow's tear, no orphan's sigh,
   No ashes of the martyred dead,
No cries of sainted souls on high
   Have called for vengeance on thy head.
But glad for thee the wilderness
   Now echoes to thy cheerful voice;
Cursed by the world, 'tis thine to bless
   Earth's erring sons with heav'nly joys.

Church of our fathers, 'tis thy hand
   Shall guide their offspring to the skies;
While through thy courts, from ev'ry land,
   The hosts of the redeemed shall rise.

While wand'ring o'er his native sands,
  Or through the world in slav'ry driv'n,
The Ethiop, with outstretched hands,
  Shall seek through thee for rest in heav'n.
The Indian shall forget to roam,
  The war songs of the West shall cease,
And tenants of each wigwam home
  Be subjects of the Prince of Peace.
Through thee the Lord of hosts shall claim
  The distant nations for his own,
Till tribes of ev'ry tongue and name
  Fall worshiping before his throne.

THE APOSTLES' CREED IN VERSE
ORLANDO, FLA., 1888.

I BELIEVE in God the Father,
  The almighty, the divine,
Father of my Lord and Saviour,
  And, O blessed thought! he's mine.
I believe in God the Father;
  Not in chance nor gloomy fate:
That 'twas he with wond'rous wisdom
  Did the universe create:
That he made the earth and heav'ns
  For the children of his love,
And intends that they shall ever
  Dwell in bliss with him above.
He is my own loving Father,
  No poor orphan waif am I;
I'm an heir of endless glory,
  I'm a child of the Most High.

I believe in our Lord Jesus,
  The divine, anointed One;
He alone is the Begotten,
  He is the Eternal Son.
Born of blessed Virgin Mary,
  By the Holy Ghost conceived.
He was love divine incarnate,
  Yet by men was not received.

That he, under Pontius Pilate,
    Suffered, bled, was crucified,
Bearing all our sins upon him,
    When in agony he died.

I believe his body buried
    Lay in Joseph's marble tomb
Till the third auspicious morning
    When he left it's dismal gloom:
Then o'er death and hell triumphant
    He ascended into heav'n,
At the right hand of the Father,
    Where to him all pow'r is giv'n.

On his great white throne descending,
    He will judge the quick and dead,
When the awe-struck earth and heavens
    From before his face have fled.

I adore thee, Lord and Saviour,
    For thou wast and art divine,
On the throne of Triune Godhead,
    Or in this poor heart of mine.
I adore thee in the myst'ry
    That incarnates deity,
In the judgment hall of Pilate,
    In expiring agony;
In thy vict'ry over Satan,
    Over death, hell, and the grave,
Giving perfect demonstration
    Of omnipotence to save.
I adore my Mediator
    In the heav'nly heights above,
On his awful throne of judgment,
    Which to me's a throne of love.
He will vindicate his people,
    Be thou jubilant, my soul!
Thou shalt reign in joyous rapture,
    While eternal ages roll.

In the Holy Ghost eternal,
    I with all my heart believe;

In his offices and person,
  His divinity receive.
I rely on him for comfort,
  And for freedom from all sin:
He will cleanse his human temple,
  And enshrine himself within.
'Tis by him that we have access
  To the Father, through the Son,
He will guide and help and strengthen,
  Till our work on earth is done.

In the Church of God believing,
  I would seek no hermit's cell;
Church on earth, and in the heavens
  Let me with your members dwell.

I believe in sweet communion
  With the saints of the Most High,
In their fellowship I'm living,
  And among them I shall die.
I believe in the remission
  And the blotting out of sins;
When, with faith in the Redeemer,
  Everlasting life begins;
Not to end when this poor body
  Heaves it's last expiring breath,
But exist in conscious glory,
  Endless ages after death.

In the body's resurrection
  I implicitly believe,
As the Lord descends from heaven,
  All his people to receive;
They, arising in his likeness,
  Shall be glorious like their Lord,
Incorruptible! immortal!
  And, according to his word,
Shall in joyous exultation
  And ecstatic rapture sing:
"Where, O grave, is now thy vict'ry?
  Where, O death, thy pointless sting?"

THE WORLD LOST, THE UNIVERSE GAINED.

FEBRUARY 10, 1888.

When wakened by the voice of truth,
From daydreams that entranced my youth,
Earth's fleeting vanities no more
Put on the glowing charms they wore:
In stern reality's own light,
The realms of romance passed from sight,
Each dear delusion, fancy held,
Was instantaneously dispelled.

My herds, that fed on boundless plains,
All fatt'ning to increase my gains;
My flocks, that sipped from countless rills
Or nipped the herbage of the hills;
My bounding steeds, that seemed designed
To leave the swiftest winds behind—
All, with the lands they trod upon,
Were in a moment lost and gone:
No acre in the wid'ning West
By any hoof of mine was pressed.

Unmeasured fields, where growing grain
Drank the refreshing summer rain,
Shrunk into nothingness, and left
Their owner saddened and bereft.

Beneath a sky without a frown
My ev'ry home-bound ship went down.
My fleets that safe at anchor lay,
In harbor, river, lake, and bay,
Stretched their white wings and soared away,
Nor have I seen them since that day.

The cities that my enterprise
With magic touch had caused to rise—
Each London, Rome, and Babylon—
Sunk into dust without a groan.

Insane ambition doffed his crown,
Laid his enchanting scepter down,
Fled from the ruins of his throne
And all he claimed or called his own;

Hushed his demands for high renown,
And at the feet of Christ fell down.
Then penitential faith was blessed,
With pardon, peace, and joyous rest;
No selfish thought or wish remained:
The world was lost, it's Lord was gained,
And by the gift of love divine,
The whole broad universe was mine.

THE WIFE OF THE DRUNKARD.
LEXINGTON, KY., WINTER OF 1838-39.

'Twas midnight; in sadness the drunkard's wife gazed
On her hovel's dark hearth where the last fagot blazed,
Nor knew whence the fuel it soon would require
Could come when the flames which now waned should
  expire.
She thought of the time when in childhood's glad hours
The hand of content strewed her pathway with flowers,
When the smile of a father a sunbeam would prove
To dispel every cloud from the heaven of love,
When a mother life's cup filled with joy ever bright,
And a sister's affection enhanced the delight.
She thought of a brother, the pride of her heart,
And a lover—what thrilling emotions now start!
Love's Eden has faded, no pleasures are there,
And the buddings of hope yield the fruits of despair.
Hark! what is that noise which now falls on her ears?
Can it be the harsh tones of the storm king she hears?
Does the blast of his trump call his troops from the
  north,
And bid them to deeds of destruction ride forth?
Ah no; 'tis a sound which more terrors impart:
'Tis her husband's rude voice sends a pang to her heart.
A moment has passed; now before her he stands,
With his eyes flashing wildly, and death in his hands.
She falls on her knees, with her eyes turned above,
Then points to her infant, the pledge of his love;
But alas! all is vain, for his reason is gone:
The man has departed, the fiend takes his throne.

He turns to his victim, as lowly she bends,
And deep to its hilt the keen dagger descends.
Ah! never again shall affection's fond smile,
Or endearing caresses his sorrows beguile;
No more shall she hasten his coming to greet,
For the wife of his bosom lies low at his feet.
Ye guardians of freedom who fearlessly stand,
The bulwarks of justice, the pride of our land,
How long will your laws give such potent control
To the demon of death, the dark fiend of the bowl?
Stop now, and no longer grant license to kill,
But crush that vile monster, the "worm of the still."

THE TRIUMPHS OF INTEMPERANCE.

PHILADELPHIA, FALL OF 1837.

He breathed upon the loveliest flowers
Of beauty, and they withered. At his touch
The patriot's arm raised in his country's cause
Was palsied. Where proud genius read the stars,
Or called on fancy for a fairer world,
He came, darkened his once bright intellect,
And placed him on a level with the brute.
He entered where pure inspiration's flame
Blazed on religion's altars, and snatched down
With sacrilegious hand the sacred desk's
Most splendid ornaments. The orator
Whose voice had charmed the soul, and captive led
The passions at his will, is heard no more:
He too has owned this mighty tyrant's power.
An infant hung upon its mother's breast,
And claimed that care which brutes do not withhold;
Yet, tasting of intoxication's cup,
The mother from her bosom spurned the child,
And left it in its helplessness to die.
A mother leaned upon her son's strong arm
In conscious safety; and she fondly hoped
That he in riper years would ever be
Her guardian and defender—but vainly:
The tempter placed the goblet to his lips,
And lured him to an ignominious grave.

A father with emotions of delight
Gazed on each smiling face and lovely form
That crowded round his fireside, and he felt
A sacred joy, which none but parents feel;
Nor dreamed that aught might ever mar his bliss.
But he became a victim of the bowl,
And, fiend-like, drove his wife and children forth
To try the mercy of the midnight storm.
'Tis thus intemperance treats its devotees,
Nor age nor sex nor rank nor beauty spares;
Monarch and slave, peasant and lord alike
Have felt its evils and endured its sting.

LIBERIA, THE COLORED MAN'S REFUGE.*
PHILADELPHIA, JUNE, 1838.

On the gales of the South comes the cry of the slave,
From the horrors of bondage he asks us to save.
But alas! 'tis in vain, for the law's stern decree
Assures us: "The negro can never be free!"
On the skies of the North, like the light'ning's red glare,
Shoot the flames from his house mid the shrieks of despair,
While the mob stands exulting, the scene to survey.
No law can protect him, the negro's their prey.
From the land of his forefathers, far o'er the sea,
Comes a voice which invites him from bondage to flee
And dwell in contentment on Africa's shore,
Where oppression and insult shall reach him no more.

BEST OF THY KIND.
PHILADELPHIA, FALL OF 1837.

Best of thy kind, I fain would keep thee longer,
  At least till specie circulates again;

---

*Offered to the *Philadelphia Saturday Courier*, June, 1838, but declined on account of the subject being too inflammatory. The editor said he discovered great merit in the writer, and asked for an interview. The writer was too bashful to grant that interview, but continued to slip articles into the contribution box.

But then, alas! necessities grow stronger,
    And thou must go, my credit to sustain.
Go on, and, like a minister of mercy,
    Still clothe the naked, and the hungry feed;
Though men abuse and slander while they use thee,
    Mind not their rudeness, nor their insults heed.
I send thee forth as Noah sent the raven,
    Return not if hard money may be found;
But thou shalt ever have a welcome given
    While the "shin plaster" deluge rages round.

"IT IS NOT THE DAYDREAM."
1837.

It is not the daydream of fancy so bright
Can give to the heart a true sense of delight:
Nor is it the wealth of the Indies can say
To sorrow, Depart; or to care, Flee away.
The soft voice of music which floats on the air
Is often disturbed by the shrieks of despair;
And the glitt'ring tear, called by memory, will start,
Where pleasure and glee strive to gladden the heart.
While fame twines her wreaths for the conq'ror's brow,
And the slaves of his caprice in suppliance bow,
How often does conscience remind him again
Of the cries of the dying and shrieks of the slain!
The high road to honor, so charming and fair,
Is often impressed with the footsteps of care;
And royalty's diadem has not the power
To banish distress, e'en for one short-lived hour.
Then where shall we seek for this dearest, best prize?
Is it found 'neath the sunshine of Italy's skies?
Does it dwell 'mid the Russian's drear regions of snow?
Or sport where the clear purling rivulets flow?
Or gaze on the ruins of classical lands?
Or rest in the shade where the pyramid stands?
Or does it select as its fav'rite abode
The valleys and plains where the prophets once trod?
Or gladden that hill where with wondering eyes
The apostles beheld their Redeemer arise?

Confined to no station, no country can claim;
A plant of Elysium, from heaven it came.
Below in earth's gardens it blooms for awhile,
If warmed by the sun of contentment's bright smile;
And, enjoying its sweets, to the virtuous is giv'n
A foretaste of that which awaits them in heav'n.

DAUGHTER OF AFFLUENCE.
SPRING OF 1842.

Daughter of affluence, fav'rite of heav'n,
Much is required where much has been giv'n.
Wealth brings her treasures to lay at thy feet;
Pleasure attends thee in each loved retreat;
Nature has lent to thy form ev'ry grace;
Rose tints of loveliness bloom on thy face;
Genius has kindled her fires in thine eye;
Hope's brightest bow gild's futurity's sky;
Jesus has warmed thy young heart with his love;
Piety points thee to blessings above;
Honored and envied, loved, flattered, caressed,
God smiles upon thee, and men call thee blessed.
Daughter of affluence, blessed as thou art,
Think of the poor and the broken in heart;
Mercy's fair minister, onward still go,
Haste to the wretched, the children of woe;
Comfort the mourner, relieve the distressed;
Point them to mansions of heavenly rest;
Think of thy sisters in heathenish night;
Scatter their darkness with heavens own light;
Send them the gospel, to tell of a home
Where tears are all wiped, where sorrows ne'er come.
Trust in the Lord, and the light of his smile
Thy cares shall all banish, thy sorrows beguile.

BIOGRAPHICAL SKETCH.

PARTIAL friends have demanded a history of THE AMERICAN EPIC and of the author's earlier poetry. The epic was inspired by an ardent love of native land and an intense desire for human happiness. Its seed thought was found in 1861, while reading "Elliott's Debates and Proceedings of the Federal Convention." The storm that disturbed Patrick Henry's speech in the Virginia Ratifying Convention seemed to be supernatural. Since 1861 the hope has been indulged that one of our distinguished poets would make that storm the central thought of a great American epic poem. It was deeply regretted that Mr. Bryant did not, instead of writing a new translation of "Homer's Iliad," give us a grand epic superior to anything written by Homer, Virgil, Dante, or even Milton. A letter to a distinguished poet, editor, and publisher was closed with the question: "Why do you not write the American epic?" The reply, written on the first of February, 1889, was as follows: "Your private note was most interesting. I thank you very much for it. If you are ever in New York, I hope you will find it convenient to call at my office. It gives me the deepest pleasure to meet any one who knew my father." But this gifted correspondent wrote not one word about an American epic. On his way from the post office the author stopped at the office of Mr. Palmer, now Mayor of Orlando, Fla. There, as he turned over a few pages of Bancroft's "United States," the entire scheme of the American epic flashed through his mind. The afternoon of February 5, 1889, produced several pages. The next day certain sermons were versified, to make nine pages now printed between pages 243 and 252. The third day completed what is now the first scene of the second book, from page 21 to page 25. Then followed Patrick Henry and the Storm, from page 96 to page 99. Before leaving Florida, early in April, 1889, he had written to the 68th page, besides the reference to Henry and the Storm, and the nine pages of theology beginning on page 243. In Nashville, Tenn., between April, 1889, and September, 1890, the book was continued as far as page 240, except pages 215-217. The Death of President Garfield, the Burial of Emerson, and the last book were written at Bucyrus, O, between September 15 and October 15, 1890

The earlier poems, some of which are printed here with their dates, will probably give all the information desired about an obscure man except his parentage and education. His parents were Drummond and Mary Henderson Welburn. He bears his father's name, and was born ten weeks after his father's death,

in Horntown, Accomac County, Va., near the Atlantic shore, on the 22d of October, 1818. His mother's mother was a Marshall. his father's mother a Corbin, his grandmother being a Drummond. The first American Welburn was from Wales. He landed on the 10th of May, 1610, with Sir Thomas Gates and other officers of the colony of Virginia, after having been shipwrecked on Bermuda nine months before. The second of America's gospel ministers, Rev. Mr. Bucke, arrived on the same ship, the "Sea Venture." The Welburns have been hereditary merchants and planters. Our author was from his eighth year, when not at school, a merchant's clerk. The village post office was kept at the store. This gave the boy access to the Richmond, Washington, and Philadelphia papers. Ritchie, Pleasants, Gales and Seaton, Duff Green, Atkinson, Poulson, and Walsh introduced him to Irving, Bryant, Drake, Halleck, Lofland, and other rising American writers, as well as to more distinguished British authors. He also became familiar with the names of our most noted statesmen, and had a rich enjoyment of their oratory as reported. When eleven and a half years old, he ceased to attend the very commonest of common schools from one to three months out of every twelve. His post office and newspaper instruction was no longer enjoyed, but the Holy Scriptures and the hymns of the Methodists still cultivated his literary taste. The skill of his schoolmasters had been exhausted in teaching him reading and arithmetic, and in unsuccessful efforts to teach him penmanship. From his pious mother he learned religious truth, morals, and manners.

In April, 1830, Philadelphia became his home. There sixteen hours out of every twenty-four had to be devoted to the dry goods business. During the greatest activity of the spring and fall trade merchants and clerks were often up nearly all night. The store-house at the north-west corner of Second and Pine Streets was to him "the house of bondage," and to him threatened to become the grave of learning. He, however, continued to read much, between 10 and 12 o'clock at night and on Sundays. During his last two years in the great city he was released from business every other night, and attended the meetings of a literary lyceum * once a week. He also joined the Pennsylvania Literary Institute,† which had more than three hundred members, an extensive library, and a large hall on Chestnut Street. He was elected to deliver one of its anniversary addresses to a large congregation in August, 1838. With an almost insane desire for literary distinction, he frequently scribbled the crude thoughts of one who had not been taught a rule of grammar, nor a line of geography or history. In the fall of 1837 he wrote on the back

---

* Among the forty or fifty members of the lyceum were Graham and Peterson, afterward noted publishers of literary and fashion magazines.
† W. L. Lane, one of the founders of the now famous *Public Ledger*, was also elected to speak at the Institute's anniversary.

of a note of the Southern Loan Company the lines beginning, "Best of thy kind." They were printed in the *Saturday Courier*, and complimented as "an exquisite *morceau*." The same paper printed "It Is Not the Daydream" and "The Triumphs of Intemperance." "Liberia, the Colored Man's Refuge," was declined in June, 1838. The editor wrote: "We shall be happy to welcome more poetical favors from this pen to our columns. We discover great merit in this writer, and regret that his last production is of a kind we cannot give. Will the writer favor us with a personal call?" The writer was too bashful to call on the editor of a great literary paper. The burning of the Abolition Hall had created intense excitement, and led to the exclusion of a reference to slavery.

In October, 1838, Lexington, Ky., became our author's home. There he continued to write, but as his friend, George R. Graham, had become editor of the *Casket* and the *Saturday Evening Post*, his contributions appeared in the *Post*, or in the Lexington papers. The Union Philosophical Society of Transylvania University* accepted him as a member, and in 1839 elected him to deliver one of its anniversary addresses. On the 10th of May, of that year, he was

"Wakened by the voice of truth
 From daydreams that entranced his youth."

"Those dreams had passed, and hopes of heaven
 To nobler themes his thoughts had given."

The salvation of his own soul and the souls of others seemed to him to require the renunciation of earthly ambition. He turned from oratory and poetry and everything that could take attention or time from the work of the Christian ministry. As a favor to himself, his associates of the Society kindly relieved him from the task of honor they had imposed. After this he wrote little poetry and published less. From 1844 to 1880 he had nothing printed. He has been a Kentucky Methodist preacher fifty-two years; is now a superannuate, connected with the Kentucky Annual Conference of the Methodist Episcopal Church, South. He lived in Virginia until April, 1830; in Philadelphia until October, 1838; in Kentucky until September, 1857; in Jeffersonville, Ind., until April, 1887; in Orlando, Fla., until April, 1889. Since April, 1889, he has resided in Nashville, Tenn. In all his wanderings, having never ceased to be a Virginian, he has continued to

"Drag at each remove a lengthening chain."

---

*B. Gratz Brown and Edward Marshall were members of the Society.

COLUMBUS AT THE HELM.

CAPITOL OF THE UNITED STATES, WASHINGTON, D. C.

TENNESSEE STATE CAPITOL, NASHVILLE.

THE EPICS OF THE AGES.

THE epics of the ages must ever be intensely interesting to admirers of classic poetry. A busy generation of newspaper and magazine readers will not fail to appreciate brief notices of their illustrious authors. Even the illiterate will be pleased with pictures illustrating the homes and haunts of the most gifted sons of song. It is hoped that these imperfect references to departed genius may awake in some "mute, inglorious Milton," of our land, a lofty ambition to write earth's grandest poem. Patriotism may be pardoned for asserting that our country presents sublimer scenery, a more interesting history, a nobler ancestry, and happier environments than belonged to any of the other classic nations, ancient or modern. Our countrymen ought, therefore, in grand, intellectual achievements, to surpass all the noted writers of other lands. The unequaled sons and daughters of our glorious Southland should be the brilliant leaders of the gifted American poets.

THE PYRAMIDS AS SEEN BY MOSES IN HIS YOUTH.

MOSES FOUND BY PHARAOH'S DAUGHTER.

(324)

MOSES.

MOSES RECEIVING THE TABLES OF THE LAW.

MOSES.

MOSES, the first and grandest of historic poets, has held so high a rank as saint, prophet, lawgiver, and ruler that his merits as a son of song have attracted little attention. A descendant of Abraham, through Isaac, Jacob, Levi, Kohath, and Amram, this child of illustrious ancestors was born a slave, and doomed to death. Found among the rushes by the Nile, he was adopted by Pharaoh's daughter, and is supposed to have been in the line of succession to the Egyptian throne. When forty years old he fled from Egypt and taking refuge with Jethro, priest of Midian, became the husband of his daughter Zipporah. At eighty he was sent with a message of deliverance to his people. After witnessing the fearful sufferings of the enslavers of Israel and their overthrow in the Red Sea, he became teacher, prophet, leader, deliverer, and ruler. As lawgiver of Israel and of mankind he was honored with a divine burial. Centuries afterward he appeared with Elijah in glory at the transfiguration of his Lord. In the vision of St. John on Patmos the saints were heard singing the song of Moses, the servant of God, and the song of the Lamb. No other mere man ever received equal honors. Space cannot be spared for a notice of the sublime beauty of Hebrew poetry, but in our English translations it can be happily understood, admired, and enjoyed by the least scholarly of English readers.

MOSES WITH THE TABLES HE HAD PREPARED.

MOSES SMITING THE ROCK.

HOMER.

ACHILLES, THE HERO OF HOMER'S ILIAD.

SMYRNA, WHERE HOMER WAS EDUCATED.

HOMER

WAS unquestionably the first and greatest of uninspired epic poets. Smyrna, Rhodes, Colophon, Salamis, Chios, Argos, and Athens all claimed the honor of being his native place. It is probable that he was born on the bank of the Meles, a river near Smyrna. The name of his father is not known. His mother, Critheis, became the wife of a schoolmaster in Smyrna, who gave her son a liberal education. Homer himself became a teacher. Invited by Mentis, the master of a trading vessel, he traveled by sea to distant places, among them Italy and Spain, and some say Egypt. Returning with Mentes to Colophon, he became entirely blind. He recited his verses at Cumea, and afterward at Chios, where he established a school of poetry, acquired property, married, and became the father of two daughters.

Intending to visit Athens, the ship landed at Ios, where Homer died. These particulars of his remarkable life were generally believed by the most intelligent of the ancient Greek and Latin literary men. But because Pisistratus of Athens collected and edited the great poems five hundred and forty years before Christ, some have asserted that prior to that time they were unwritten fragmentary verses, recited by unknown rhapsodists. The consistency and regular connection of the different parts of the grandest uninspired poems ever written have failed to convince these hypercritics that these books proceeded from the pen of one unequaled genius.

It was originally proposed to give lengthy extracts from the "Iliad" and the "Odyssey," but lack of space forbids. Six lines from Pope's translation of "Agamemnon's Defiance of Achilles" must suffice.

> Haste, launch thy vessel, fly with speed away!
> Rule thy own realms with arbitrary sway;
> I heed thee not, but prize at equal rate
> Thy short-lived friendship and thy groundless hate.
> Go, threat thy earthborn Myrmidons, but here
> 'Tis mine to threaten prince, and thine to hear.

ATHENS, WHERE HOMER'S WORKS WERE EDITED AND PUBLISHED.

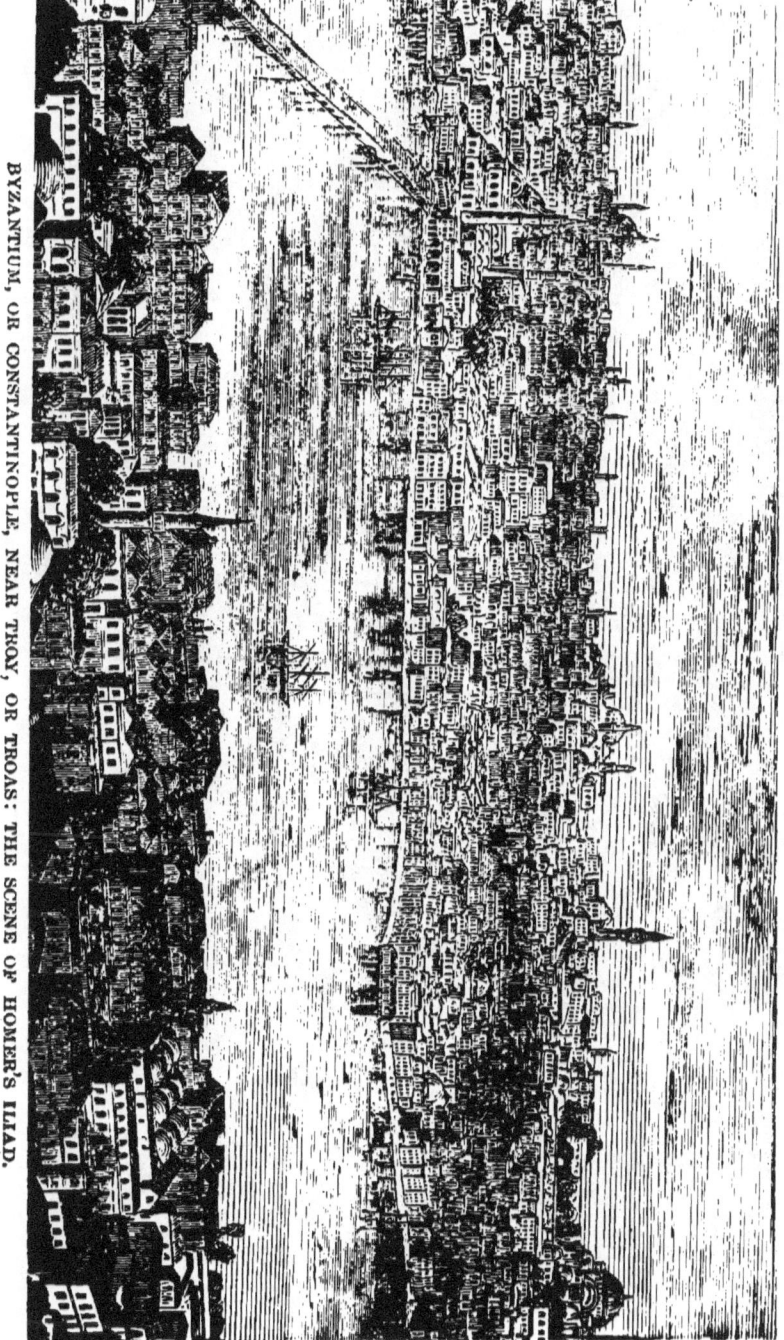

BYZANTIUM, OR CONSTANTINOPLE, NEAR TROY, OR TROAS: THE SCENE OF HOMER'S ILIAD.

(335)

CORINTH, VISITED BY HOMER IN HIS YOUTH.

VIRGIL.

VESUVIUS, NEAR VIRGIL'S FAVORITE RESIDENCE.

THE COLISEUM.

VIRGIL.

PUBLIUS VIRGILUS (or Vergilius) MARO was born at Andes, a village near Mantua, October 15, 70 B.C.; and died in Brundusium September 22, 19 B.C. It is said that the modern village of Pietola now occupies his birthplace. His early education was received at Cremona and at Mediolanum (now Milan). He studied Greek at Naples under Parthenins, who was a pupil of Syron the Epicurean. He was ever a close student. His land inherited from his father was taken from him to reward the victorious soldiers of Augustus. But he regained it through the influence of Asinius Pollio, who admired his poetry. Mæcenas became his friend, and Augustus enriched him. At the imperial court he was a favorite, but preferred to reside at Tarentum and Naples. In the year 19 B.C., he went to reside in Athens, that he might properly finish and polish the "Æneid." Meeting the emperor in Athens, he set out with him for Italy, and died on his way home. He was buried on the road leading from Naples to Puteoli.

The fourth Eclogue of his "Bucolics" was addressed to his friend Pollio. The "Georgics,' a didactic poem in four books, is considered the most highly finished production of his pen. It was addressed to Mæcenas.

The "Æneid," or the adventures of Æneas after the fall of Troy, is by critics said to be an almost slavish imitation of Homer's "Odyssey" and "Iliad." This great work was at his death not completed. It fell so far below his model and his ideal in his own estimation that he instructed his literary executors to destroy it. The emperor's authority saved it from destruction. He directed the author's literary friends to edit and finish it with the utmost care. The productions of the friend of Augustus became the text-books of the youth of the empire. For nineteen centuries they have been studied in academies and colleges. They still hold their places as text-books in the grandest universities of the most enlightened nations.

Here we insert Virgil's description of Camilla:

> Last from the Volscians fair Camilla came,
> And led her warlike troops, a warrior dame
> Unbred to spinning, in the loom unskilled.
> She chose the nobler Pallas of the field,
> Mixed with the first the fierce virago fought;
> Sustained the toils of arms, the danger sought,
> Outstripped the winds in speed upon the plain,
> Flew o'er the field, nor hurt the bearded grain.
> She swept the seas, and as she skimmed along
> Her flying feet unbathed on billows hung.

NAPLES, THE BAY, AND VESUVIUS.

THE EPICS OF THE AGES. 341

LUCAN.

CHRISTIANS GIVEN TO WILD BEASTS TO AMUSE THE
ROMANS IN LUCAN'S TIME.

POMPEY'S PILLAR.

LUCAN.

MARCUS ANNÆUS LUCANUS was born in Corduba (Cordova), Spain, about A.D. 39; and died A.D. 65.
He was a nephew of the philosopher Seneca. At an early age his father placed him under competent instructors in Rome, where his talents were noticed and his recitations admired. His great heroic poem "Pharsalia,' contains fierce invectives against tyranny and sublime praises of liberty. His admiration of Pompey the Great and his love for republican Rome must have been very offensive to Nero, the tyrant emperor. It cannot now be ascertained whether his flattery of Nero was written in ignorance of the despot's character, or after his own arrest with a hope of saving his life. It is known that by an offer of pardon he was induced to turn informer and involve his best friends in serious trouble. His execution was ordered for complicity in the conspiracy of Piso. When he lost all hope of life he opened his veins and died repeating his own verses describing death by bleeding. For more than eighteen hundred years his poem has been highly prized by friends of human liberty.

ADDRESS OF LENTULUS TO THE BANISHED SENATE AT EPIRUS.

When the Tarpeian Seat was consumed by the torches of the Gauls, and when Camillus was dwelling at Veii, there was Rome. Never by change of place has our order lost its rights. Sorrowing abodes does Cæsar possess, and deserted houses, and silenced laws, and judgment seats shut up in sad cessation from the law. That Senate house beholds those Senators alone whom from the full city it banished. Whoever is not expelled by us from an order so mighty is here.

Unacquainted with crimes, and at rest during a lengthened peace, the first fury of warfare dispersed us: once again do all the members of the state return to their place. Behold, with all the might of the world do the gods above recompense us for Hesperia lost.

INTERIOR OF THE PANTHEON OF THE GODS AND GODDESSES, REFERRED TO BY HOMER, VIRGIL, AND LUCAN.

(314)

DANTE.

LEANING TOWER AT PISA AS KNOWN TO DANTE.

MILAN CATHEDRAL AS SEEN BY DANTE.

DANTE.

DANTE (contracted from Durante) DEGLI ALIGHIERI was born in Florence May 14, 1265; and died in Ravenna September 14, 1321. His father, supposed to be of noble blood, died when his son was but nine years old, and the same year the poetic boy fell in love with Beatrice Portinari, who died in 1290. In 1289 he fought at Campaldino on the side of the papal party. After this experience of a soldier's life he tried matrimony with Gemma dei Donati, of noble blood. She, by an ungovernable temper, made the poet miserable, but during his banishment raised his daughter and his five sons respectably. After matrimony he tried statesmanship, and became for a short time chief ruler of Florence. While on an embassy to Rome in January, 1302, sentence of exile was pronounced against him and others of his party. During nineteen years he was a wandering politician, vainly endeavoring to secure the happiness which could only be found in his beloved Florence. The poet is avenged on bad Pisans and Florentines by the fearful horrors which his "Inferno" represents two of them as enduring:

I saw two frozen in one hole so closely that the one head was a cap to the other. And as bread is chewed for hunger, so the uppermost put his teeth into the other where the brain joins with the nape.

From the fell repast that sinner raised his mouth, wiping it upon the hair of the head he had laid waste behind.

The sons of Dante and their descendants were highly honored citizens of Florence. His daughter Beatrice recalls the undying love of her father for Beatrice Portinari, immortalized in the impassioned lines of his "Vita Nuova" and his "Convito."

Immediately after his death Italy rang with his praises. With the invention of printing, translations of his works began to be multiplied. They continue to grow in popularity among all the enlightened nations. New translations have recently been made by Carlyle and Longfellow, while the great publishers vie with each other in efforts to produce the most ornamental and costly editions.

348   THE AMERICAN EPIC.

VENICE, ONE OF THE PLACES VISITED BY DANTE A SHORT TIME BEFORE HIS DEATH.

CAMOËNS.

PORTUGESE NAVIGATION ON THE COAST OF GOA, WHERE CAMOËNS WAS WRECKED.

BUDDHIST TEMPLE IN INDIA IN CAMOENS'S TIME.

CAMOËNS.

LUIZ DE CAMOËNS (in Portuguese Camõez) was born in Lisbon in 1524; and died in that city in 1579. His father, a sea captain, was wrecked on the coast of Goa, India, in 1552.

The poet acquired a very high literary reputation at the University of Coimbra, where he became a student in 1538. Catarina de Atayde won his affections, but King John the Third, his rival, banished the poet, and saw the affectionate young lady die of a broken heart. Camoëns survived his lady love thirty years, but never married. Disappointment and despair led him to join the Portuguese expedition against Morocco, in which he lost one of his eyes, which disfigured him for life. In 1553 he went to Goa, where he wrote: "Honor and self-interest are never found in the same sack." This offended the Portuguese rulers, who banished him to Macao, where he was appointed "Provedor des Defunctos" (Administrator of the effects of the deceased). Here the poet determined to do for the Portuguese what Homer had done for the Greeks. At that time his country richly deserved such a distinction. She had whipped the Moors, had sailed around the Cape of Good Hope, and found a way to India; was founding colonies, extending commerce, converting heathen, and leading the nations in the grandest of enterprises.

Camoëns called his great epic poem "Os Lusiadas" (the "Lusiad"), after the mythological hero, Lusus, who, in company with Ulysses, is said to have visited Portugal and founded the city of Lisbon, under the name of Ulyssipolis. The "Lusiad" was completed during the author's enforced residence at Macao, where a grotto is still shown as the place where much of the immortal poem was written. In 1561, when permitted to return to Goa, he was shipwrecked and lost all his property. He was then imprisoned for debt until 1569, when he returned to Lisbon. King Sebastian granted him a pension of about $21, but soon withheld it. Helpless and friendless, he lived on alms collected by a servant who was his only nurse, until removed to a hospital, wherein abject poverty he died.

After death medals were struck in his honor, a monument was erected to his memory, and he was called the "Apollo Portuguez, Camões a Grande." There have been many translations of his poems into foreign languages. Odes, elegies, comedies, and sonnets illustrate the poet's talents, while the name of Catarina proves the constancy of his love.

Gama's Return to Portugal.

O'er India's sea, winged on by balmy gales
That whispered peace, soft swelled the steady sails;
Smooth, as on wing unmoved the eagle flies,
When to his eyrie cliff he sails the skies,
Swift o'er the gentle billows of the tide,
So smooth, so soft, the prows of Gama glide;
And now their native fields forever dear
In all their wild transporting charms appear,
And Tago's bosom while his banks repeat
The sounding peals of joy, receive the fleet.
With Orient titles and immortal fame
The hero's band adorn their monarch's name.
Scepter and crown beneath his feet they lay,
And the wide East is doomed to Lusian sway.

Camoën's Appeal to King Sebastian.

Yet thou, Sebastian, thou my king attend,
Behold what glories on thy throne descend!
Shall haughty Gaul, or sterner Albion, boast
That all the Lusian fame in thee is lost?

PAGODA IN BOMBAY, INDIA, WHICH BELONGED TO PORTUGAL
WHEN CAMOENS WROTE.

A WEDDING PROCESSION AS SEEN IN INDIA WHEN THE LUSIAD WAS WRITTEN.

PORTUGESE NAVIGATION AROUND THE CAPE OF GOOD HOPE IN CAMOËNS'S TIME.

A STATE PROCESSION IN INDIA, WHICH BELONGED TO PORTUGAL WHEN THE LUSIAD WAS WRITTEN AT MACAO.

356   THE AMERICAN EPIC.

A MOUNTED WARRIOR.

TASSO.

CRUSADERS ON THEIR WAY TO JERUSALEM.

BATTLE BETWEEN CRUSADERS AND SARACENS AS DESCRIBED BY TASSO.

TORQUATO TASSO

WAS born in Sorrento March 11, 1554; and died in Rome April 25, 1595. His distinguished parents were favorites in the courts of princes. His father, a noted literary character, was at his death Governor of Ostiglia. His mother, Ne Porzia de Rossi, entered a monastery when her son was ten years old, but her gifted boy was proficient in Greek and Latin, and had recited admirable original verses. At sixteen he went to the University of Padua, where at eighteen he wrote and published "Rinaldo," a charming romantic poem. At Padua he planned the "Jerusalem Delivered," quit the study of law, and went to the University of Bologna. At twenty-one the honored poet went to Ferrara, in the suite of Cardinal de Este, whose brother, Duke Alfonso II., received Tasso with great distinction, and attached him to his court, with a salary of fifteen crowns a month, but without duties. The duke's sisters, Lucrezia and Eleonora, were very partial to the poet, who indulged a singularly romantic passion for Eleonora. He spent about a year with Cardinal de Este in Paris, where Charles IX., Catharine de' Medici, and the French poets showed him marked attentions. This was in 1570. In 1573 his celebrated pastoral drama was performed with great splendor at the court. His great epic poem, "Il Goffredo," afterward called "Gerusalemme Liberata," was completed in his thirty-first year.

He was the most distinguished of living poets, and Europe rang with his praises, but in the prime of life his health failed and his mind became unbalanced. He was cheated by publishers, dreaded the Inquisition, feared assassination, and was shunned as a maniac. Escaping from a convent in the guise of a shepherd, he fled to the house of his sister in Sorrento. His bodily health improved, but forsaken by his early friends, he was for seven years surrounded by maniacs and treated with cruel harshness. In 1586 he was released, but continually traveled from city to city, vainly hoping to improve his condition. Princes, literary men, the common people, and even the brigands, heaped honors on the wanderer. Having remodeled his great epic poem, he dedicated it to Cardinal Cinzo Aldobrandini, who induced Pope Clement VIII. to propose the crowning of Tasso in the capitol. The poet reached the Vatican November 10, 1594, but died in a monastery before the time set for his coronation.

JERUSALEM FIRST SEEN.

Winged is each heart, and wingéd every heel;
  They fly, yet notice not how fast they fly;
But by the time the dewless meads reveal
    The fervent sun's ascension in the sky.
    Lo, toward Jerusalem salutes the eye!
A thousand pointing fingers tell the tale;
"Jerusalem!" a thousand voices cry.
All hail, Jerusalem! hill, down, and dale
Catch the glad sounds, and shout "Jerusalem, all hail!"

JERUSALEM ENTERED.

Thus conquered Godfrey; and as yet there glowed
  A flash of glory in the 'fulgent West,
To the freed city, the once-loved abode
    Of Christ, the pious chief and armies pressed.
    Armed as he was, and in his sanguine vest,
With all his knights, in solemn cavalcade
  He reached the temple; there supremely blessed,
Hung up his arms, his bannered spoils displayed,
And at the sacred tomb his vowed devotions paid.

JERUSALEM AS SEEN BY GODFREY AND HIS ARMY.

362 THE AMERICAN EPIC.

THE MOUNT OF OLIVES NEAR JERUSALEM.

THE FORD OF THE JORDAN IN THE TIME OF THE CRUSADERS.

ST. PETER'S AT ROME AS SEEN BY TASSO.

INTERIOR OF ST. PETER'S, WHERE TASSO WORSHIPPED.

VOLTAIRE.

NOTRE DAME AS SEEN BY VOLTAIRE.

THE FRENCH GRAPE HARVEST IN VOLTAIRE'S NATIVE LAND.

VOLTAIRE.

FRANÇOIS MARIE AROUET DE VOLTAIRE was born in Paris November 21, 1694; and died there May 30, 1778. His godfather, Abbe Château neuf, and Ninon, his mistress, taught him to ridicule all established institutions —religious, political, and social. In his twelfth year brilliant literary talents secured for him 2,000 francs to purchase books. The gifted boy was connected with the French embassy at the Hague, but was compelled to retire on account of a scandal. Then, though only twenty years old, he was accused of writing lampoons against Louis XIV. and confined in the bastile. During his confinement he undertook to write the "Henriade." He also completed the tragedy of "Œdipe," which was received with great favor and has ever since held possession of the French stage. Pleased with the play, the Regent ordered his release and gave him a considerable donation. He continued to write for the stage, and was an honored guest at the tables of the nobility. His ready wit offended a cowardly noble, who had him seized and whipped, imprisoned six months, and then banished. He went to England and remained three years—from 1726 to 1729. The infidels of England found in him a most gifted and active follower. They introduced him at court and secured for him the favor of George II. The king and his ministers headed the subscription for a most splendid edition of the "Henriade." The gay, gifted Frenchman was lifted to the summit of renown, and returned to France as the idol of his own people. Successful speculations and popular literary ventures made him quite rich in early life. He was for more than sixty years Europe's most successful writer. Though he wrote against despotism, Catharine of Russia highly honored him, and Frederick of Prussia received him with transports of joy. The king and the poet were both witty, imperious, and irritable, and of course had many lovers' quarrels. He was opposed to all religions—Romanist, Protestant, and Jewish. Letters of certain Jews gave him a well-deserved castigation, which he deeply felt, in spite of the adulations of multitudes and the patronage of monarchs. In his eighty-fourth year he took to Paris his new tragedy, "Irene." His carriage was drawn by the people. His rooms were crowded with grandees. At the theater he was crowned with roses and laurels, and death overtook him while intoxicated with applause. We add nine lines descriptive of Henry IV. in battle:

> Henry appeared that moment in their midst;
> Brilliant as lightning in the tempest depths,
> He flies before the ranks, moves at their head;
> He fights, they follow; and their fate is changed:
> Lightning is in his eyes, death in his hands.
> Round him the chiefs reanimated press;
> Victory returns, the leaguers disappear
> As at the rays of day, that dawns and shines,
> Night's starry lusters dissipate are dimmed.

PLACE VENDOME, PARIS.

CITY OF LYONS, FRANCE.

CATHEDRAL OF ST. DENIS.

MILTON.

OLD LONDON BRIDGE, IN MILTON'S NATIVE CITY.

LIGHTHOUSE ON THE COAST OF ENGLAND.

JOHN MILTON.

JOHN MILTON was born in London December 9, 1608; and died in that city November 8, 1674. He was the handsomest and most learned of poets. His father secured for him the very best educational advantages. The poet was a hard student. In early life he read till midnight. In blind old age his studies continued from four in the morning until six at night, interrupted only by time to eat, an hour devoted to exercise, and another hour to music. From six to eight at night he conversed with visitors, and at nine slept. At sixteen he composed Latin prose and verse with ease and elegance, was familiar with Greek and Hebrew, and had no mean apprehension of the sweets of philosophy. He was in religion a Puritan, in politics a republican, and for twenty years was the foremost literary champion of English liberty. Cromwell made use of his unequaled abilities in the preparation of state papers and the defense of his administration. Of all our great writers, he has most extensively influenced the language, the literature, and the social and political character of Englishmen and their descendants. Considered as mere literary productions, his earliest poems, written after he left the University, are regarded as his best; but it is upon "Paradise Lost" that his abiding fame will rest. Milton was thirty-seven years old before the first small edition of his poems appeared. The second edition did not appear until he was an old man. "Paradise Lost" was sold to Samuel Simmons for five pounds, and the promise of the same sum on the sale of the first 1,300 copies of each edition, no one of which was to exceed 1,500 copies. The entire sum paid for the greatest of poems was twenty-three pounds. What a contrast between this and the princely incomes of Scott, Moore, Tennyson, and less distinguished later writers!

The unhappy marriage of the poet may account for his mischievous writings in favor of divorces. We give six lines descriptive of Eve:

> On she came
> Led by her heavenly Maker, though unseen,
> And guided by his voice; nor uninformed
> Of nuptual sanctity and marriage rites;
> Grace was in all her steps, heaven in her eye,
> In every gesture dignity and love.

BRITISH MUSEUM.

OLIVER CROMWELL.

THE CLIFFS OF ALBION (ENGLAND), MILTON'S NATIVE ISLAND.

RICHARD GLOVER.

RICHARD GLOVER was one of fortune's favorites. He was born in London in the year 1712, and died in 1785. His father, John Glover, was a Hamburg merchant, and was delighted to see the studious habits of his son. At the age of sixteen the gifted young man wrote a poem to the memory of Sir Isaac Newton. "Leonidas" was first printed in 1737. It was received with such enthusiasm that three editions were demanded in a few months. Our author was a successful merchant, but found time to write poetry and to associate with distinguished scholars and great statesmen through a long and very active life. Among his intimate associates were the great William Pitt, Earl of Chatham; Frederick, Prince of Wales; Earl Temple, Lord Cobham, and Lord Littleton. His friends, charmed with the liberal sentiments of his epic and the love of liberty which it expressed, thought no praise was too high for its author. Lord Littleton classed him as a poet with Milton and Pope.

If posterity has not concurred in the judgment of his lordship, Mr. Glover while living enjoyed the benefit of it richly.

In 1761 Mr. Glover was elected to Parliament. His son Richard afterward enjoyed the same honor. Besides "Leonidas," our poet wrote "London, or the Progress of Commerce;" "The Athenia," a sequel to "Leonidas;" "Boadicea," a tragedy; "Medea," a tragedy; and "A Sequel to Medea." We add the reply of Leonidas:

> Return to Xerxes. Tell him on this rock
> The Grecians, faithful to their trust, await
> His chosen myriads. Tell him thou hast seen
> How far the lust of empire is below
> A freeborn spirit; that my death, which seals
> My country's safety, is indeed a boon
> His folly gives; a precious boon, which Greece
> Will by perdition to his throne repay.

ROCK OF GIBRALTAR.

(381)

THE AMERICAN EPIC:
A CONCISE SCENIC HISTORY OF THE UNITED STATES,
AND OTHER SELECTED POEMS.
WITH REFERENCES TO THE EPICS OF THE AGES, AND BRIEF BIOGRAPHIES OF THEIR AUTHORS.

Revised and Enlarged Edition, for Schools, the Family Circle, and the Leisure Moments of the Busy Millions.

This revised edition of the "Epic" has thirteen pages of questions, adapting it for use in the schools of the country, in which it is rapidly becoming a favorite.

Of the manuscript, the *Nashville American* said: "We hope to see it in print soon, and bespeak for it a permanent place in the literature of our language."

Mr. Thomas Nelson Page, of Virginia, writes: "I found much entertainment in reading it. I carried it up to my old home, in the country, and left it for my people to read, who will enjoy it as I did."

Of the "American Epic" the Hon. W. R. Garrett, Tennessee's Superintendent of Public Instruction, writes: " I have read it with much interest, and am gratified to see a work of such literary merit produced by a citizen of our State."

An intelligent Scotch gentleman was reading to his family from the pages of Tennyson, the most distinguished of living poets, when his literary wife said: "The effort to understand it wearies me." He then read the unpretending lines of the "American Epic," to the delight of his entire family circle.

The *Louisville Courier-Journal* said of the manuscript: " Who shall say that the war of intellects that has been going on for the last hundred years is not as full of poetic inspiration as Homer's interminable siege? The statesmanship of Pitt, and sociological questions of absorbing interest are discussed."

Rev. W. G. E. Cunnyngham, D.D., in the *Sunday School Magazine*, writes: " We regard it, under the circumstances, as an extraordinary book. His imagination clothes the sober events of history with the drapery of poetic imagery. The shadowy outlines of the past glow again with light and life."

Mr. J. L. Kirby, of the *Sunday School Visitor* and *Magazine* says: " We enjoyed the unusual pleasure of a private reading of the manuscript of the poem, ... and since its publication we have reread it with even greater zest. . . . That portion of the ' Epic ' reciting the causes which led up to our civil war, the incidents of the gigantic struggle, the strange doings of the reconstruction days following, and the mutations of the political world since will be found especially interesting. It is not only true to the facts of history, but it abounds in passages of decided literary value. . . . Another edition of this work has already been called for, and its lasting popularity seems to be assured."

The *Western Christian Advocate*, Cincinnati, O., says of the "American Epic:" " The fact that such a poem as this appears without the name of its author is indicative of additional merit. It is a performance far above the mediocre. In fact, it has high merit. Its conception is splendid. The plot is well maintained, the periods are well chosen, and the true poetic genius is poured forth in such moderation or in such force as the occasion and the eloquence of the moment seem to require. The time from March 10, 1764, to October 1, 1890, is the platform of the story. Celestial characters and demons are used for the speakers, and the theology of the 'Epic' is all against hatred, and in favor of truth, justice, love, and Federal unity. We predict the 'American Epic' will take high rank, and that the author a hundred years hence will be on the high road to immortality—of fame. It is a book that will endure, and not vanish with the hour."

Nashville American: "The 'American Epic,' the splendid history of the United States in poetic form by Mr. Drummond Welburn, has appeared in a new and enlarged edition. . . . The poem is known to many, and the growing appreciation in which it is held is shown by the early demand for a newer and larger edition. . . . The present edition contains questions which make it a useful text-book for schools.

Nashville Banner: "A revised and enlarged edition of the 'American Epic' has recently been published by the Methodist Publishing House of this city. . . . The 'Epic,' the author says, ' was inspired by an ardent love of native land, and an intense desire for human happiness.' It also gives some indication of the spirit of controversy, and a determination to vindicate the author's views by presenting history in their support. The following lines will indicate the kind of error it seeks to combat:

'I knew that earth and hell had long proclaimed
That Plymouth Rock was freedom's native home,
And pure religion's earliest cradle bed;
But marvel much if heaven has been deceived.'

The poem goes through all periods of American history to the present time. It is written in easy blank verse, and consists of dialogues between archangels and archdemons, who strive not with swords and cannon, as did Milton's creations, but with the suasive powers of good and evil, to obtain mastery over the destinies of this great western world. Aside from the tone of historic and political argument that characterizes the 'Epic,' much space is given to religious thought. If the author were not known, it would be easy to guess that he is an ardent Southerner, a stanch Democrat, and a devout Methodist."

FROM MRS. AMELIE RIVES CHANLER.

Dear Sir: Mrs. Chanler has been very ill for a long time, or she would have acknowledged your very kind courtesy in sending her your two volumes some time ago. They came safely, and she wishes me to say that she had looked over them with a great deal of interest, and is very much obliged to you for sending them to her. She appreciates them very highly. . . .
Very truly, MEHETABEL STRABRIDGE, *Secretary.*

FROM THE PRESIDENT OF TULANE UNIVERSITY, OF LOUISIANA.

Dear Sir: Your "American Epic," embodying the history of our country in verse, is a quaint and interesting book. I am glad to see that your angels are always on the right side, and as patriotic as they are poetic. Your book contains a vast amount of information.
Very truly yours, WILLIAM PRESTON JOHNSON.

FROM HON. W. E. GLADSTONE, NO. 10 DOWNING STREET, WHITEHALL.

Sir: Mr. Gladstone desires me to thank you for the copy of the "American Epic," which you have kindly sent him.
Your obedient servant, SPENCER I. MELLEN.

FROM A NASHVILLE DAILY PAPER.

The "American Epic" and "Tales of Early Love" are two well-illustrated books of the month by a citizen of Nashville. The "American Epic" is a concise history of the United States, written in the dignified and lofty style which every epic requires. The originality of the poem, its didactic nature, and the pure vein of patriotism which pervades it throughout, render the book well worth perusal. In the latter part of the poem the politics of the day are introduced, upon which the opinions of the author are expressed. "Tales of Early Love" is a small volume consisting of one long poem which bears the title name, and several shorter poems of a religious and patriotic nature. The theme of one of the poems is the ever sweet and pathetic story of an old man recalling the days of his youth. The style, while befitting the thought, is bright and sparkling, with now and then a merry ripple of humor which, while pleasing in its own sense, brings into relief the beautiful pathos of the story. . . . The author of the "Epic" is now preparing a much larger edition, which will contain extracts from the great epic poets with brief biographical sketches, making this edition more valuable than the others. The author is a citizen of Nashville, and the book is highly complimented by competent critics.

The *Forum*, Bucyrus, O., says: "We confidently predict for it a most favorable reception by the American people."

The distinguished traveler and writer, Mr. J. B. Gorman, says: "The 'American Epic' is a wonderful book, and fills me with delight."

The *Richmond* (Ky.) *Climax* says: "As a history it is valuable; as a poem it has merit. Accuracy is a prominent feature of the book."

The *Leader*, Lexington, Ky., says of the "Epic:" "A new book rapidly becoming a famous one. It is pronounced by critics a creditable poem as well as faithful history."

Dr. J. H. Carlisle, in the *Southern Christian Advocate*, says: "This is a bold design, in which not to succeed may be to fail utterly. Let us rather say that not to fail entirely is to achieve a good degree of success. The author has not failed entirely."

Dr. Hoss, of the *Nashville Christian Advocate*, writes: "This is a poem to attract the attention on sight. . . . The contents are accurately described in the title. , . . Considered as history the book is a marvel of accuracy. The author is evidently a man of wide reading, of accurate memory, of discriminating judgment, and of very positive convictions."

Rev. R. H. Rivers, D.D., in the *Central Methodist*, writes: "He is the author of the 'American Epic,' a book of stirring facts, of extensive research, and of rare poetic beauty. It is evidence of lofty patriotism, of vivid imagination, of deep piety, and of a genius akin, and close akin, to that of the great Greek bard, the blind Homer. The 'American Epic' will place the old superannuate alongside of Milton, and will hand down his name to posterity as one of the greatest of Southern poets. I write these lines after spending days in reading this grand production of sanctified genius."

In the same paper another intelligent literary gentleman writes: "It is, as its name implies, an historic poem in heroic verse. It begins with Cæsar's invasion of Britain, and comes down to President Harrison's administration. There is no break in the line of historic events. The author shows himself possessed of a very full vocabulary of chaste and elevated language, well suited to the literary form of his story. The young reader may learn much from these pages; older readers will be entertained by the ingenious form of the story, and will have their memories refreshed by its facts; and all will have their attention called anew to the overruling hand of God in our history."

The great *Methodist Review*, New York City, says: "Here is an unique and in some respects splendid history of the United States in poetic form. The author has carefully studied American history from the period of the Stamp act to the present hour, and has traced the nation's development through its vicissitudes of partisanship, slavery, rebellion, reconstruction, and general political changes, both in the North and the South, weighing the same in the scales of a judgment quite as much biased as if he had been a Northern investigator of our country's history. Laying aside the drapery, and forgetting the spirit in which it is written, we are attracted by the unity and coherence of its order of thought, and are led to believe that it is necessary to study the war-period of the nation from both viewpoints to accurately determine its meaning and the relative value of its results. This author is frank, sincere, political, and Southern; but knowing his characteristics, we may all the better appreciate his work. He carries the nation beyond the present period of political disturbance into the far future, when righteousness shall reign in every heart, and this view of progress and of the indestructibility of the nation atone for those political peculiarities which one under Southern influence is quite likely to feel and assert."

---

384 Pages, 12mo. Paper Cover, 60 cents; Plain Cloth, $1; Gilt Cloth, $1.25; Morocco Gilt, $3. A very liberal discount to teachers and agents.

www.ingramcontent.com/pod-product-compliance
Lightning Source LLC
Chambersburg PA
CBHW032024220426
43664CB00006B/351